Gifted & Talented
Children with
Special Educational Needs

Gifted & Talented Children with Special Educational Needs

Double Exceptionality

Diane Montgomery

David Fulton Publishers
London

David Fulton Publishers Ltd
The Chiswick Centre, 414 Chiswick High Road, London W4 5TF
www.fultonpublishers.co.uk

David Fulton Publishers is a division of Granada Learning Limited, part of the
Granada Media group.

First published 2003

British Library Cataloguing in Publication Data
A catalogue record for this book is available from the British Library.

ISBN 1 85346 954 8

Typeset by Servis Filmsetting Ltd, Manchester
Printed and bound in Great Britain by Ashford Colour Press Limited,
Gosport, Hants

Contents

Contributors

Sandy Alton is Advisory Teacher for pupils with Down's Syndrome and Complex Medical Needs in Oxfordshire and also Teacher Advisor for the National Down's Society. She has published articles and information sheets on DS and as part of a multiprofessional Consortium provides training across the country and runs an accredited course on supporting children with DS in mainstream schools.

Philip A. Baker has been a class and resource teacher, principal, school psychologist, enrichment consultant, and coordinator of special services. He is now an Instructor/Academic Advisor of an access programme at Winnipeg University and has authored books and articles on 'at risk', creativity and gifted education.

Mike Bergsgaard has been a teacher in several States in Canada, an administrator for Aboriginal Education in Nebraska and Director of programming for the Gifted and Talented in an inner-city school in Winnipeg. He has published extensively on teacher evaluation and the effectiveness of violence prevention in the public schools.

Shirley Kokot teaches Educational Psychology at the University of South Africa, is a practising psychologist and the founder/Educational Director of a school for gifted children in Johannesburg. She is affiliated to the HANDLE Institute in the USA. Her two main fields of interest are giftedness and learning problems caused by neurodevelopmental issues. mailto:kokot@icon.co.za

Ken W. McCluskey is a Professor of Education at the University of Winnipeg having spent 25 years as a school psychologist, special educator and administrator. He is a recipient of many awards for his work with 'at risk' students and has authored and co-authored over 100 books and articles.

Andrea A. McCluskey is an Aboriginal Student Advisor at the University of Winnipeg and has worked as a consultant in more than 40 Native communities. She is coordinator of a number of internationally acclaimed projects and co-author of articles and chapters including, with Ken, the bestseller *Understanding ADHD: Our Personal Journey.*

Diane Montgomery is a qualified teacher, chartered psychologist and consultant in teaching method, SEN and Gifted Education. She is Emeritus Professor of Education at Middlesex University, London. She is the author of 15 books, many articles and MA distance learning programmes and is editor of the NACE journal *Educating Able Children*.

Dorothy Sisk is a world-renowned expert in gifted education. She holds the endowed Conn chair as Professor of Education at Lamar University, Texas. She has served as President of the World Council for GTC, and the Association for the Gifted, and was founder and President of the American Creativity Association. She has edited journals and is author and co-author of many books and articles on a wide range of subjects.

Rosemary Starr is an educational and developmental psychologist with teaching qualifications in special education. One of her areas of interest is exceptional children – gifted and those with other special needs. She works in schools and in private practice.

Wendy Stewart has an MA in Gifted Education and has worked as an Adaptive Education teacher since 1999 at St Ignatius College in South Adelaide. She was formerly editor of the Gifted and Talented Children's Association magazine in South Australia and she designs and runs study and organisational skills programmes for gifted students with learning disabilities.

Carrie Winstanley is Senior Lecturer at the University of Surrey Roehampton, working with Education students interested in SEN. She taught in schools for ten years and has higher degrees in Psychology and History of Education. She runs workshops for GIFT and others and her PhD studies consider the notion of high ability from a philosophical viewpoint.

Introduction: Giftedness and talent

There are three children in a million who are 'profoundly gifted'. Conventionally this means they have measured IQs of 180+. It is likely they will have spoken in sentences at 6–9 months, learned to read and spell by the age of 2½, self taught, and are ready for formal learning by the age of three. Placed in kindergarten or preschool they quickly settle and will perhaps read to the 'little ones'. Within a week, however, they can begin to become upset and difficult to manage. They learn very rapidly, grasp complex and even abstract ideas easily and are in an environment where everything is taking place, in their terms, in very slow motion. They are bored and, unfortunately, almost no classroom will be suitable – even ones for gifted children.

These tiny tots require intellectual challenge and to be talked to as adults. They question what teachers say and do and will want to follow their own ideas and interests whatever the classroom routines might require. They ask if they can learn things such as algebra rather than fiddle about with sand and dough or prance about to a tune. However, the child is physically still three to five years old and when constraints are imposed any underlying tendencies to hyperactivity may be provoked as well as the full range of tantrums, trances, screaming, biting and kicking.

For these special children an accelerated programme of learning is necessary – probably home–school linked. By the age of 10, if allowed, they will have learned the whole of the National Curriculum and passed GCSEs and be ready for A levels. By this stage they will need the support of mentor–tutors and distance learning materials. Within a year or so they will have passed A levels and be ready for university and hopefully a useful career thereafter.

Having prodigious memories means that such children cannot abide the repetition of the usual schooling process and few children of this kind can be maintained happily in mainstream education (Hollingworth 1942; Pickard 1976). In Kay's (2000) case studies parents had to withdraw such children from mainstream education because the rigidity of the system and the inflexibility, even of 'gifted educators', was damaging their children. They found answers in home schooling, here called 'Education Otherwise' (www.education-otherwise. org.uk). Fortunately, the development of computers and the Internet has made a huge range of new learning opportunities available to children educated at home.

Unfortunately, gifted children from disadvantaged backgrounds are unlikely to get this level of support and have to bear two 'ill fitting' environments, one at home and the other at school. These two aspects of dyssynchronicity can have profoundly disturbing effects upon learners. Gross (1993) found in her Australian studies that the difficulties in socialisation with peers were also profound because of the discrepancies between them and the gifted child's reading interests, hobbies and play preferences. From their earliest days in school they had difficulties in establishing positive relationships.

If children with high abilities also have a learning disability, such as reading and writing difficulties, we refer to them as doubly exceptional but perhaps cannot imagine the conflicts set up when a whole area of opportunity for learning is closed off for years. The highly active brain can turn its attention to all things manipulable, including human beings, and the dyssynchronicity may turn the child into an overactive troublesome toddler and result in early exclusion from school for tantrums and behaviour problems – a career in disruption begins.

Fortunately, perhaps, for parents and teachers such exceptionally gifted children are very few. However, there are far more gifted, talented and highly able children both in and out of school, than might be supposed and for whom an IQ score is no good indicator – as authors in this book will show.

Hollingworth (1942) and Pickard (1976) found that with an IQ above 155 very few children were happy or could be maintained in ordinary classrooms but it was possible with the right sorts of provision for others with IQs up to this level to lead happy and fulfilling lives there. The difficulty is of course in identifying and making the 'right sort' of provision. In earlier publications I have suggested that the either/or of acceleration or enrichment is inappropriate to meet the needs of the gifted and that every school should have available seven levels of provision; ranging from 'developmental provision' in the classroom to which every pupil has access; through acceleration and fast tracking to enrichment, mentoring and distance learning (Montgomery 2000).

Over the last decade there has been an increasing level of official interest in the UK both in the needs of gifted and talented children and in the needs of underachievers across the ability range. Curriculum managers and coordinators for the gifted and talented have been appointed and there is now a wide range of materials and training courses available to help them.

The opening up of the field of giftedness and talent to research and experiment in the UK began with the House of Commons Inquiry (1998–9) and the setting up of the Government's Giftedness and Talent Advisory Group (1998–2001), which prompted a special strand for provision to be trialled in the *Excellence in Cities* (DfEE 1999) initiative. Prior to this it had been assumed that grammar schools, streaming and setting within comprehensive schools and grant maintained schools or public schools (private education) could cope with the need.

Teachers tended to regard the gifted as having enough advantage already, and that they should be in a position to help themselves rather than be given special help and extra resources. Nevertheless a gifted education 'underground' operated, mainly without funding, pursuing and developing initiatives set up in the 1970s and 1980s. The 'underground's' main strength was to develop ways in which gifted children's needs could be provided for within mainstream education and without extra resourcing. It was so successful that HMI (1992) found that where this provision existed all the learners in the school benefited.

Logically, it might be supposed that a new government with an understanding of the issues came to a benign decision to open up the area to research and resourcing, however, all may not be as it seems. Tannenbaum (1993) explained that educators in the 1970s in the USA fought to keep order in classrooms, especially in the big city schools. Scholastic achievements were three to five levels below average and there was vandalism, violence, truancy and drug-taking. Many middle-class families had fled the inner cities and were opting for private education for their children.

Administrators decided that one way to encourage these families back was to provide gifted education programmes in the cities. They opened the 'magnet schools' that offered 'enrichment' activities in particular subjects to attract sufficient numbers who might have been studying elsewhere. They found that the presence of the ablest began to make a difference to the total school atmosphere. The 'gifted' were rescuing public education. 'Again special education for the gifted was initiated for the sake of solving social problems rather than solely for the sake of those who need, or could benefit from it' (Tannenbaum 1993: 21). No need to labour the point.

The *Excellence in Cities Project* (DfEE 1999) required schools to select their top 5 to 10 per cent for the able strand provision and this approach has been 'rolled out' countrywide. It seemed to be their preference to regard 1 to 3 per cent as their 'gifted group' but this was disputed by members of the Advisory Group. The smaller the percentage the less costly the provision of course. In schools we have to refer to the 'potentially gifted and talented', as most high achievers do not demonstrate early or prodigious talent.

When Tannenbaum (1993) reviewed the position across western societies he found that in order to include the gifted it was usual to identify the top 15–20 per cent in general ability terms (by IQ for example) and then also identify the top 15–20 per cent in separate subject areas to pick up those with specific talents. The begrudging 5–10 per cent of UK administrators will miss out large numbers of our most gifted children. What, in addition, will be the feelings of those not selected? Selecting 3 per cent to attend the National Centre for Gifted and Talented Youth at Warwick University tells 97 per cent of our school population they are not special or talented.

It is a far better provision – which is integral to every classroom with opportunities for all – to self select for broader and deeper studies according to need. This mode requires updating inservice programmes for all teachers on a regular basis and would provide a reservoir of resources to enrich all forms of learning.

At the same time as all this is happening in the realms of the gifted and talented, or the 'highly able', schools must work to become more inclusive. Thus curriculum managers have a difficult brief. How can selection for gifted education programmes and master classes be consistent with inclusion? Well of course in its present incarnation it cannot.

The best form of provision is inclusive, challenging and interesting to all the learners. It is dependent not on subject teaching but subject learning both cooperatively and independently where appropriate. This requires some radical changes in teaching method from the 'excitable teacher talk' currently promoted to 'the teacher as learner and explorer' with the pupils. Good teachers teach mixed ability classes and still gain the highest standards. We need research to identify how they do this.

There are more than a million potentially gifted and talented pupils in the country but the National Curriculum was only designed to meet the needs of the average learner so it does not reach the hard to teach, the gifted or the able underachiever. Providing summer schools and master classes is not going to reach them either.

Having announced the presence of so many gifted among us, it is perhaps a duty of this introduction to define the terms and explain what 'gifted' and 'talented' and 'high ability' refer to in this book. Each chapter author will also make statements about these terms but will focus more on the special need and the provision and how these interact with high ability. In an analysis of the terms Gagné (1993) assigned giftedness to those abilities naturally or non systematically developed, whereas talent applied to those areas of human endeavour in which skills and abilities were systematically developed (p. 72). Thus giftedness refers to general abilities, some of which can be captured on IQ tests purported to be measures of 'general problem solving abilities', and talent which is perhaps latent and needs acquisition and practice time such as playing a musical instrument, running a business, leading a group, painting and so on. Just occasionally we meet an infant prodigy such as Peggy Somerville, who painted extraordinarily mature paintings at three years of age. Most other painters now more famous than her only began to show promise in adolescence. Some had to die before their achievements were recognised. The talent in some children may only be discovered by accident when they experience something new. Hence the broadest base of experiences and opportunities is essential for all children and yet so many live such narrow lives.

Gagne's definition of terms is merely another version of Spearman's (1927) two factor theory of intelligence with 'g', a general problem solving ability, and 's' denoting specific capabilities. There is perhaps less evidence for the existence of the 'multiple intelligences' (Gardner 1983) although he did suggest that they might be better termed 'talents'. The notion of multiple talents permeated by a core of general problem solving ability seems to me to be more consistent with the evidence and the pupils' behaviour.

The term 'high ability' is frequently used in UK literature before the new initiatives as it is a term that does not imply something perfectly formed and immutable such as a 'gift', rather it encompasses a wider range of capabilities.

Intelligence itself is now known to be capable of increasing over time with the right sorts of education and environment and an IQ, that part measured by an intelligence test, only needs to be about the level of 120 for the highest achievement to be attained (Torrance 1963). In research studies of the gifted it is usual to confine the 'gifted' sample to those who have at least one IQ score at 130 or above. In terms of educational provision it has been characteristic to include those with IQs at or above 115, or one standard deviation above the mean, so that all possible potentially gifted might be included, though even then some would be missed and so any with an above average potential should be included (Montgomery 1996, 2000). To overcome some of these difficulties Silverman (1989) suggested that the level for inclusion into Gifted Ed programmes should be dropped by 10 points in the case of those with a learning disability. In addition, of course, the standard error of the tests which is usually plus or minus three points suggests that any fixed score can only be an arbitrary one.

The area of special educational needs has a longer history and an even greater resource than gifted education in the UK but only recently has a concern for 'Double Exceptionality' developed. Nevertheless gifted pupils with special needs exist and are more widely found than perhaps had been expected. Silverman (1989) for example found that one third of the gifted in her large sample had learning disabilities and Whitmore (1980) maintained that 70 per cent of children showed a deficit of one standard deviation between IQ and school attainments.

Those who have tried to bridge the gifted/special gap over the years have had difficulty obtaining resources or research funding because the topic falls between two stools and could be regarded as too small a population to merit concern. Equally, from the intervention point of view, the most obvious sign of difficulty is the special need; the other, the giftedness, is regarded as a bonus but they can cancel each other out.

Although in the UK the term 'difficulty' is used in preference to 'disability', on a world stage the notion of disability is more readily understood and so the parts in this book have been labelled as 'disabilities'. It also emphasises the dys-synchrony and powerful effect they can have on an otherwise potentially gifted individual. 'Extremely high intelligence often comes with quirks that require great tolerance from the teacher, these tend to diminish as the child gets older' (Thomson and Wallace 1998).

References

DfEE (1999) *Excellence in Cities*. London: the Stationery Office.

Gagné, F. (1993) 'Constructs and models pertaining to exceptional human abilities', in K.A. Heller, F.J. Monks and A.H. Passow *International Handbook of Research and Development of Giftedness and Talent*. Oxford: Pergamon Press, pp. 69–88.

Gardner, H. (1983) *Frames of Mind: The Theory of Multiple Intelligences*. New York: Basic Books.

Gross, M. (1993) *Exceptionally Gifted Children*. London: Routledge.

HMI (1992) *The Education of Highly Able Children in Maintained Schools*. London: HMSO.

Hollingworth, L. (1942) *Children Above 180 IQ*. New York: World Books.

Kay, K. (ed.) (2000) *Uniquely Gifted: Identifying and Meeting the Needs of Twice Exceptional Children*. Gilsum, NH: Avocus Publishing Inc.

Montgomery, D. (1996) *Educating the Able*. London: Cassell.

Montgomery, D. (2000) *Able Underachievers*. London: Whurr.

Pickard, P. (1976) *If You Think Your Child is Gifted?* London: Allen and Unwin.

Silverman, L.K. (1989) 'Invisible gifts, invisible handicaps', *Roeper Review*, **22**(1), 37–42.

Spearman, C. (1927) *The Abilities of Man*. New York: Macmillan.

Tannenbaum, A J. (1993) 'History of giftedness and "gifted education" in world perspective', in K.A. Heller, F.J. Monks and A.H. Passow *International Handbook of Research and Development of Giftedness and Talent*. Oxford: Pergamon Press, pp. 3–27.

Thomson, M. and Wallace, B. (1998) 'The total teacher for the total child', *U. O. Gifted*, **11**(1).

Torrance, E.P. (1963) *Education and the Creative Potential*. Minneapolis: University of Minnesota.

Whitmore, J.R. (1980) *Giftedness, Conflict and Underachievement*. Boston: Allyn and Bacon.

PART ONE:
LEARNING DISABILITIES

Learning disabilities is the term used worldwide to indicate that there is a discrepancy between pupils' school attainments and what they might be expected to achieve given their level of ability. In the UK this group of conditions is referred to as Specific Learning Difficulties. This term carries with it the assumption that if the difficulties can be remedied or circumvented by appropriate education or therapy then normal achievements will be attained. General learning difficulties refers to the profile of the slower learner who may also have specific learning difficulties. In some individuals the learning difficulties are overt and can easily be identified but in many other cases they are covert or silent and are frequently not identified. When giftedness and learning difficulties co-occur then they can cancel each other out and to all intents and purposes the pupil appears average in ability and attainment. There is evidence to suggest that some 50 per cent of pupils are affected by these silent difficulties.

Three children in 100 statistically have IQs above 130 so there is likely to be one in every class but in reality there are at least 5 or 6 potentially gifted children in every mixed ability class and many more with specific talents, and 50 per cent who are 'more able'. The discrepancy diagnosis using an IQ test such as WISC-lll is a popular means of identifying specific learning difficulties such as nonverbal learning difficulties and dyslexia but there are questions about its sensitivity and relevance. Alm *et al.* (2002) concluded that even the ACID profile (difficulties with Arithmetic, Coding, Information and Digit span on WISC) was a group phenomenon but did not refer to any individual dyslexic.

Three different groups of underachievers are known to exist:

Group 1 (usually identifiable)
- those who have been identified by discrepancies between high scores on ability tests and low achievement in school subjects, attainment tests, or SATs
- those who show discrepant scores on IQ tests between verbal and performance items (for example, CAT scores) but may be performing in class at an average level
- those who show an uneven pattern of high and low achievements across school subjects with only average ability test scores
- those whose only high achievements seem to be in out of school or non-school activities

Group 2 (usually the disability masks their abilities)
- those who have a specific learning difficulty – dyslexic type difficulties in the presence of average reading test scores and school attainments
- those with spelling or handwriting difficulties and average or below attainments
- those with gross motor coordination problems, or sensory impairment and average or below school attainments

Group 3 (usually not identified)
- pupils with social and behavioural difficulties
- daydreamers, uninterested in school, or 'lazy' pupils
- linguistically disadvantaged background but average ability and functioning – showing a great deal of compensation going on.

All three groups have learning difficulties, many of which have not been identified. Group 1 pupils, although they have some high scores on ability tests, will have underlying learning difficulties which can be uncovered and given support and will need curriculum modifications and changes in teaching strategies in order to profit. Group 2, because of their overt double exceptionalities, have patterns of depressed scores on abilities tests that mask their potential, or their difficulties are focused upon and their giftedness is not attended to. They will need a 'talking curriculum' while being given specialist support for their specific learning difficulties. Group 3 underfunction for a variety of reasons such as the need for the 'cool' image in boys so they fear to try in case they fail, or their 'culture' is that school is not 'cool'. Others fear the label 'boff' and the bullying that can ensue. Girls may develop similar images about what is 'cool' and 'uncool' but also become vulnerable, especially in co-educational schools, to seeking not to do well or pursue such 'non feminine' subjects as maths or be seen to work hard. For them it even becomes 'childish' to do what the rest of the class is doing; they prefer to sit out and chat. Some pupils come from a linguistically disadvantaged background that hampers their ability to express themselves adequately in 'academic' subjects or in school life as a whole and practice in talking and listening is essential.

Underlying all of these underachievements a low sense of self esteem is to be found with a range of strategies being used to defend the sense of self or to prop it up. Characteristic also is the need in these pupils to have something interesting and challenging intellectually to engage with. But because in many classrooms the lessons are teacher led and information is imparted verbally, has to be recorded in writing and then learned, these pupils lose motivation as their involvement in making meaning for themselves diminishes. Most commonly they find school 'very boring', and if they cannot achieve top levels in SATs they feel undermined and grow disaffected as their failures and perceived failures multiply.

The curriculum manager needs to encourage all departments to identify the top 20 per cent of pupils in their subject area in each class or year. This will enable the building of patterns on a grid which shows, for example, subjects, CATs test scores, SEN and behaviour problems. Particularly significant will be the identification of pupils who are good orally but 'cannot write it down' or only very good when there is some kind of problem to solve, or have a lot of common sense but only 'good average attainment'; excellent at art or PE but 'no good' at so called academic subjects; a leader in every bit of mischief but not school work. The Special Educational Needs Coordinator will have an important contribution to make as do parents and the pupils themselves.

We know that boredom and lack of cognitive challenge in the daily curriculum is playing a major role in causing more pupils across the ability range to become more disaffected and underfunctioning than was formerly the case. Gifted and underachieving pupils are particularly vulnerable. An inservice training strategy for key staff such as learning mentors, 'G and T' coordinators, and SEN staff should begin with shadowing one pupil for a day to see exactly what pupils are subjected to.

The four chapters in this Part discuss a range of approaches and strategies which are typical of the field. The first two illustrate the complexities of cases in remediation and curriculum provision. The second two deal with verbal and non-verbal learning difficulties. In Chapter one Kokot details the methods she uses based upon 'HANDLE' (Holistic Approach to Neurodevelopment and Learning Efficiency) to overcome the complex and deep learning disabilities of her students. This approach, in which underlying mechanisms and pathways are addressed, is reinforced and further exemplified in Chapter four in relation to non-verbal learning disabilities. In Chapter two, Stewart gives details of how the curriculum for students with a range of learning disabilities can be modified and differentiated to meet individual patterns of needs based upon her case work with the gifted. Chapter three looks specifically at dyslexic type difficulties in gifted undergraduates and how their needs can be met in curriculum and remedial terms and then traces these difficulties back to school and kindergarten age showing what should have been done to help them. A hidden population of gifted dyslexics with residual spelling problems masking their abilities is identified as well as methods for overcoming their difficulties. Chapter four deals with the more neglected areas of non-verbal learning difficulties in handwriting and coordination difficulties as well as Attention Deficit Hyperactivity Disorder. Each non-verbal learning disability can mask high ability and talent but some unfortunate pupils have both non-verbal learning disability and dyslexia.

Reference

Alm, J. and Kaufman, A. S. (2002) 'The Swedish WAIS-R factor structure and cognitive profiles for adults with dyslexia', *Journal of Learning Disabilities*, **35**(4), pp. 321–33.

1 A neurodevelopmental approach to learning disabilities: diagnosis and treatment

Shirley Kokot

The question of why some gifted children fail to thrive in school is a tantalising one that has occupied researchers for many years. Underachievement is usually considered to be the result of individual, family and/or school-related factors (Baker, Bridger and Evans 1998) but many gifted children are recognised as having neurobiological problems that interfere with academic and social/emotional functioning. It is common practice to label these according to the symptoms they manifest. Labels frequently used include ADD, ADHD (Leroux and Levitt-Perlman 2000), Visual or Auditory Perceptual problems, Tourette's Syndrome, Dyslexia (Winner 2000), Dyspraxia, Asperger's Syndrome (Neihart 2000), Autism (Cash 1999), and so on. These conditions may be accompanied by learning disabilities that persist in spite of diverse therapies being tried by often desperate parents.

Therapeutic approaches to learning disabilities

Many different therapies exist that claim to successfully treat particular learning disabilities. It is not within the scope of this chapter to discuss each one but suffice to say that too few have had significant success and so the search continues for real understanding of what causes the behaviours that impede learning.

Most gifted children with learning disabilities show a scatter of high and low abilities across different tasks. Early theorists and specialists in the field of learning disabilities believed that composites of traits or faculties (called 'processes') were activated when a child performed a task. Weakness in one or more of the processes would account for the child's failure on the task. Following this, it seemed logical that strengthening the faulty process would lead to improvement of the child's performance (Farnham-Diggory 1992). Among these specialists were Ayres, who focused on sensory integration; Kephart, on perceptuomotor matching; Frostig, on visual–perceptual training; Delacato, on neurological organisation, and many developmental optometrists, who believed that aberrant visual systems have an impact on reading and subsequent learning. However, during the 1970s and 1980s these theories and related practices were evaluated and found to be scientifically invalid and ineffectual. Despite such criticism and coupled with the fact that later practitioners using those approaches did not effectuate the predicted successes, these therapies are still utilised in many countries around the world.

The late 1980s and 1990s saw an explosion of brain research that clarified some issues and, indeed, led to support for the basis of many of the earlier theories. It seems to be accepted now that movement is responsible for the structure of the brain (Changeux and Conic 1987; Ito 1984; Lisberger 1988) and that the brain's proven plasticity means that through movement it becomes possible to restructure the brain (Le Poncin 1990). These findings mean, in effect, that the body organises the brain rather than the other way around. Given this understanding of how the brain functions, it is likely that individuals struggling to cope with the demands of life and learning may be doing so not because of brain damage in a specific area of the brain, but rather due to inefficient functioning of several interactive sensory and motor sub-systems. Take the example of dyslexia. Previous thinking attributed the problem to an impairment within the language centre of the cerebral cortex. Evidence now suggests that the person with dyslexia may be manifesting deficits of visual memory, directionality, visual tracking, concentration and delayed processing of auditory and/or visual stimuli.

In his studies of Chronic Fatigue Syndrome, Lewis (2001) found that more sub-systems and more energy may be required by some individuals to function, giving rise to myriad difficulties. This concurred with the theories of Bluestone, who has been successful over the past 35 years in treating individuals of all ages with a wide range of problems. She has integrated recent and more long-standing knowledge and arrived at new insights as to the origins and treatment of learning difficulties. These she has evolved into the HANDLE approach, the acronym standing for Holistic Approach to NeuroDevelopment and Learning Efficiency.

A hierarchy of integrated systems

Figure 1.1 shows the chart that Bluestone developed to represent diagrammatically the integrated and interdependent sub-systems responsible for our efficient functioning. The relative position of each sub-system on the chart is indicative of the hierarchical nature of the neurological system, and illustrates how higher level functions depend on those at a lower level. For example, problems with reading or maths may be traced all the way back to a dysfunctional vestibular system. In this way, HANDLE attempts to identify the roots of a learning problem. Practitioners drafting a therapy plan would sequence and prioritise exercise activities according to where an individual's weaknesses would show up on the hierarchy.

Lowest level systems would be addressed first so that, strengthened, they may support the functions of higher level systems, which could then benefit optimally from corrective therapeutic activities. To address 'higher level' functions – which, in this paradigm, amount to splinter skills – before strengthening the weakened foundational systems is an exercise in futility: frustrating to the child and the teacher because such an approach achieves at best minimal gain, and serves only a stop-gap purpose. While such an approach may possibly improve a particular splinter skill at the time, it would not resolve the causal issue. This

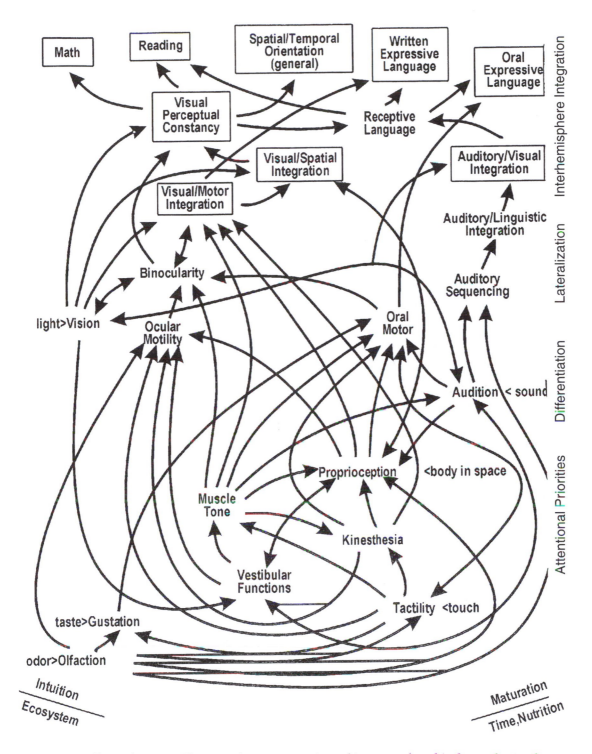

Figure 1.1 Chart showing Bluestone's representation of integrated and independent sub-systems. *Source:* Bluestone (2001b)

results in the weakness remaining to affect other skills – possibly simultaneous in time, such as interpersonal and emotional skills, but assuredly skills that show up later – needing those same weak foundations. In addition, even if the higher level function is relatively intact, energies from these higher levels may be used to compensate for a weakness in a more foundational system, emphasising the need to address inefficient functioning of lower level systems. For example, if a child's visual system is well developed, but the tactile system is hypersensitive, s/he may use vision to remain hypervigilant of the surroundings rather than to use it freely for tasks of visual discrimination (Bluestone 2001a).

Diagnosing the root causes of learning difficulties

The HANDLE perspective defines neurodevelopment not as a given sequence of accrued skills but as an interactive hierarchy of brain functions, with a vestibular foundation for skills (such as speech, maths, visual tracking and so forth) presumed by other perspectives to be isolated in particular sites in the brain. When neurodevelopment is understood as interactive, no time frame limits brain function. Learning is thus the lifelong process of using sensory, motor, social and emotional input to realign output into effective behaviour (Suliteanu 2001). The holistic nature of the approach also requires recognition of internal and external influences. This means acknowledging possible causal roles of chemicals, allergens, nutritional deficits (especially the absence of essential fatty acids), dehydration and toxins of any kind. In addition, it includes the individual's social environment, such as the increasing cocooning lifestyle that keeps children indoors and inactive and the decreased demand on their creativity as a result of graphic media (Suliteanu 2001).

Each learning disability and each individual has unique aspects, but the trained observer can determine patterns of dysfunction in the neurological subsystems required to support learning. Those patterns then suggest how to resolve the disability with gently progressive strengthening of the weak areas. Crucial observation during assessment of the individual learner includes:

1. what distracts attention from the task at hand
2. what requires energy needed for comprehension
3. what physical/environmental changes affect the learning, and
4. what learning modalities are most successful.

An interactive, non-standardised evaluation protocol identifies such factors as:

1. distractions due to tactile or auditory hypersensitivity
2. vestibular inadequacy to support muscle tone, visual tracking and linguistic/phonetic awareness simultaneously
3. irregular interhemispheric integration interfering with auditory-visual integration, parts-to-whole configuration as well as problems with central auditory processing due to an inability to integrate the word/language component with the picture/meaning of the word
4. light sensitivity and visual-motor dysfunctions that cause irregular visual/visual-motor feedback, etc.

Once information concerning these important issues has been gleaned from the individual's behaviour during assessment, an appropriate programme composed of activities and exercises is designed to strengthen the weak functions and resolve learning difficulties at their roots.

The HANDLE treatment programme – key elements

The hierarchical and interactive nature of the neurodevelopmental sub-systems is crucial to the success of this approach. To reiterate, it is futile to try and improve the efficiency of higher level systems before systems at a lower level are regulated and integrated. Lower level systems include the senses of touch, taste and smell as well as the vestibular and proprioceptive systems. The visual and auditory systems are at a higher level, and at the highest level would be systems relying on integrated interhemispheric functioning, such as visual–spatial, auditory–linguistic processes, and so forth. For example, visual problems such as difficulty focusing both eyes together on a target or tracking – following a moving object, or moving the eyes across a line of words – would not be addressed until the vestibular system can support the visual system.

A second key element to this approach is what Bluestone has coined Gentle Enhancement. This means the process of introducing therapeutic activities on a regular, consistent basis strictly according to how much the individual tolerates before that activity induces stress. For contrast, observation of patients treated with Doman-Delacato techniques suggested that the lengthy periods of re-patterning were causing stress to already stressed systems. For therapeutic benefit – that is, for the weakened system to accept and incorporate the input – clients must be carefully monitored for signs of stress, and treatment limited to as much input as their systems can use. Accordingly, rather than offering therapy once or twice a week at a therapist's venue, as well as possibly supplementing this with fixed periods of time devoted to rigorous activities at home each day, a home-based programme is designed that takes only a few minutes to complete each day – with careful monitoring of the client for signs of stress. Such signs include change of facial colour, reddening of the ears, change in visual focus, change in breathing or muscle tone, feelings of nausea or dizziness, or a general discomfort while performing an activity. In addition, self protection mechanisms, such as reflexive posturing in order to prevent a body position, would also be regarded as a definite sign of stress. This is a reason why HANDLE practitioners do not rely on therapeutic equipment. Rolling a child over a ball may be a vestibular specific exercise but will obscure the child's unwillingness to move beyond a certain point because of experiencing stress.

From theory to practice: case studies

The following case studies illustrate the HANDLE approach with two gifted children whose problems adversely affected their school performance. In the first the problem was considered 'dyslexia,' in the second 'Attention Deficit Disorder with Hyperactivity (ADHD).' As will be shown, in each case the label did not correspond to the deficits that actually impaired learning.

'Dyslexia': The case of Mary

Mary was seven years old when she was referred for help. She was a very bright, articulate, compassionate and fun-loving little person. She was also experiencing great difficulties in her first grade classroom.

Emotional reactivity and difficulty managing transitions were longstanding issues for Mary. However, these became especially problematic when she started formal schooling. Her school days were punctuated with tears and occasional show-stopping tantrums, as she could become overwhelmed by the sights and sounds of the classroom. The fast pace of the school day proved especially distressing for her and she would sometimes retreat into an imaginary world of her own. Stress was evident as she tore papers into tiny bits or chewed her hair at her desk.

Mary's thinking was, at times, inflexible. She could get 'stuck' on certain ideas, seemingly stubborn to those trying to help her. Once stuck, she found it difficult to devise solutions to her problems until she was able to distance herself from them with time. Attempts to control her environment to reduce her anxiety were construed as oppositional by her teacher.

As if tantrums were not enough to isolate Mary socially, her driving desire to touch things and others caused problems with her peers. Her ever-moving hands during instruction made her appear as if she was not listening, and fleeting eye contact made reading social cues difficult for her.

Despite her intelligence, Mary was beginning to fall behind her peers academically. Of primary concern was her writing ability. Verbally gifted and with an active imagination, she took pleasure in creating stories and songs. However, committing them to paper was excruciatingly slow and physically painful due to the death grip with which she held her pencil. Even rotating the pencil in her hand to shift from the graphite to the eraser was a task for Mary. She would typically drop the pencil and pick it up again to gain access to the eraser.

She often simply refused to write. When she did write, legibility was impaired by her letter reversals, uneven spacing and poor letter formation. As the rest of the class began incorporating accurate spelling into their writing, Mary did not seem able to break away from the phonetic 'invented' spelling techniques that were taught to her in kindergarten.

Reading and mathematics were not as problematic, but she often distracted herself during work time as she could not read or work at near point tasks for very long. Weak motor skills and disorganisation led to additional frustration. Although her teacher appreciated her exuberance and cheery smile, Mary was described as a highly distractible and sometimes difficult child with learning problems related to dyslexia/dysgraphia.

Background information

Mary's birth was normal and she was an easy baby. She became independent at an early age, and her curiosity was evident. She met her developmental milestones early, walking and speaking in multi-syllabic words by nine months. She appeared to be developing beautifully. As she progressed through toddler years, hints of a developmental derailing began to appear, only to be recognised by her parents in retrospect. Since Mary was their first child, they did not realise that her inability to dress herself, inconsistent success with toilet training, inability to pedal her tricycle, indifference to books and puzzles, and formidable tantrums regarding her car seat were signs of anything more than Mary's temperament.

Although her general disposition was enthusiastic and happy, Mary could reach emotional extremes. 'Terrible twos' lingered into three, four and five. Mary's mother recalls her pre-school teacher commenting that, at any given moment, Mary was either the happiest or unhappiest child in the school. 'Marching to her own drummer' was the theme of her kindergarten year, and it was recommended that Mary repeat kindergarten to be given some extra time to mature socially and emotionally. Although her second year of kindergarten was much smoother, the academic demands of first grade set off a downward spiral of poor conduct and poor scholastic achievement.

Observations

Mary was evaluated in late March. She performed well on many of the tasks included in the HANDLE assessment protocol and demonstrated deficiencies in others. Vestibular irregularities surfaced quickly, including the need to move frequently in a rotating pattern, and nystagmus – a jerky movement of the eyes – coupled with a sense of dizziness when using her eyes to track. When asked to wear a pair of glasses with one red lens and one blue lens, Mary's view was red in one area, blue in another. In rapid succession, Mary saw the white objects in the room as alternating from red to blue, indicating a visual irregularity known as alternating suppression. Additional tests revealed that the visual functions of tracking and binocularity were not operating optimally for Mary. Her eyes tended to move in a jerky fashion throughout the tracking challenges, and they tired easily when focusing at near point.

An auditory sequencing task indicated a decrease in processing upon hearing specific sounds, and it was noted that she retained last segments best. Overflow movements of her fingers, head and mouth were detected and a whole body reflexive response, which should have been integrated several years earlier, were observed. Mary lost track of her writing when her eyes were closed and she was unable to internalise, through muscle memory, a simple repetitive movement pattern. Additionally, the assessment revealed a weakness in the integration of the two hemispheres of the brain.

Conclusions

A complete profile of Mary's neurodevelopmental strengths and weaknesses was developed using her reported history and the practitioner's reflections on her general behaviour and performance of the assessment tasks. Areas of concern were identified. Several factors were identified as contributors to Mary's difficulties. Central were multiple ear infections and associated high fevers causing weakness in the vestibular system. The vestibular system supports and regulates audition, balance, dynamic use of the eyes, feeling at ease with where the body is in space (proprioception), and having an appropriate state of readiness in resting muscles (muscle tone). Mary's history of motion sickness, as well as problems with balance, proprioception and visual functioning, reinforced the conclusion that the vestibular system was faulty. For Mary, this translated to physical awkwardness and she displayed timidity in the performance of motor activities. Consequently, she avoided many typical childhood games, retreating instead to the safety of solo fantasy play. In this, she missed important opportunities for social learning and did not stretch herself to enhance vestibular functioning as most children do naturally through play.

Mary did not spend a significant amount of time in the crawling stage, which is a crucial period for the development of strong integration between the two hemispheres of the brain. This underdeveloped area could well have accounted for the many emotional shifts that Mary experienced, and was holding her back from reaching her full learning potential. Mary also had unresolved tactile hypersensitivities, many of which interfered with normal grooming. Her parents reported an aversion to tickling, and roughhouse play almost always ended with her physically striking out in a manner inconsistent with the intensity of the game. It was not uncommon for Mary to hit or act aggressively toward other children as a pre-schooler. She was particular about what she wore, seeking out comfortable clothing rather than fashionable clothes. Socks often came home in her backpack rather than on her feet. Tactile, kinaesthetic and proprioceptive irregularities were also found to impair Mary's abilities to express her thoughts in writing. She had difficulty sensing where her hand was and what movement it had made unless she monitored each movement visually. If she paid close attention to her hand, then she became frustrated about losing the ideas she had wanted to capture.

A weak suck reflex as an infant, coupled again with vestibular weakness, interfered with the healthy development of her visual functions. Mary sometimes lost her place while reading, her eyes tired quickly, and she had a vexing practice of reversing letters and numbers. The systems supporting vision and her sense of position in space were not strong enough to support reading, mathematics and general organisation in an efficient way. Visual inefficiencies also caused Mary to be somewhat oblivious to her surroundings. This, coupled with reduced muscle tone, diminished her ability to interpret facial expression and body language, an ability that is so integral to social interaction.

No wonder Mary was struggling, and was frustrated by her difficulty to prove herself despite all the wonderful qualities she possessed. How could her learning and behaviour improve before these root problems were identified and treated?

Recommendations

Mary and her parents were taught a programme specifically designed to address each deficiency in her neurodevelopmental profile. The programme was dynamic, changing over time to accommodate Mary's progress, and incorporating many HANDLE treatment activities. Each recommendation was carefully chosen to treat lower levels of neurological sub-systems first, to ensure that higher level systems did not become stressed by having to function without sufficiently strong supporting systems. So exercises to first strengthen the vestibular system, such as rolling slowly backwards from a sitting position to the floor and then up again and from one side to the other, were among the first on her programme. Simple activities such as drinking water with closed eyes through a straw manufactured with three loops along its length were recommended to promote sucking in order to help her gently and naturally practise eye convergence, as well as helping to integrate her two brain hemispheres. Specific massage techniques related to neurodevelopment were taught to her parents to help her tactile sensitivity and improve her proprioception.

Follow-up

For Mary, the downward spiral that began in first grade slowed, then stopped, and then gradually shifted direction. Tears and temper tantrums began to diminish. By the end of first grade, she could read for longer periods of time and, consequently, her reading skills began to flourish. By summer, the child who previously cried at the prospect of getting her face wet was jumping off the diving board and swimming. She learned to ride a bicycle without training wheels, and an 800 mile car trip was noticeably devoid of stops for car sickness. With the foundation set, she and her parents decided to give the local public school another try in the upcoming autumn.

Starting second grade has been a new beginning for Mary. She claims that 'second grade is a lot calmer', but clearly it is she who is calmer. Well integrated into the rhythm and routines of her day, school is a much less stressful place for Mary. Hair chewing and paper tearing are no longer recreational pastimes. Instead she is listening, reading, writing and computing. Writing is still her biggest challenge, and so she continues with specific HANDLE activities to strengthen this skill.

'Attention Deficit Disorder' renamed: The case of Alexis

The HANDLE approach holds a view that differs from the one implied by this 'diagnosis' of having a 'lack' of attention. It contends that no one has an attention deficit. Rather, everyone is always attending to something, and individuals who show difficulties in sustaining attention may be blocking certain types of stimulation and seeking others; they may have difficulties adjusting attention flexibly to meet varying demands from the environment. Therefore, a more accurate name for this set of behaviours is Attentional Priority Disorder (APD), and the condition is neither hereditary nor irreversible. HANDLE clinicians incorporate information gleaned from the evaluation session to discover where a specific individual's attentional priorities lie. Usually the answer is found in one or more of the interactive neurological sub-systems and APD can thus be treated at its origin, yielding permanent changes in the nervous system. That is, by resolving issues that focus the child's attention to more basic and pressing needs, such that those needs are met, HANDLE frees the child to attend to social, academic, and other demands from the environment.

While there may be genetic predispositions to neurodevelopmental disorders, such disorders arise not through heredity but rather through interactions with the environment. Drugs are not used as part of the HANDLE programme so symptoms are not masked and problems are treated at their root causes.

Common patterns of APD

Most people who have difficulty sustaining their attention and/or adjusting easily to the demands of changing situations show irregularities in specific neurodevelopmental functions on both input and output levels.

On an input level, there are frequently signs of:

- hypersensitivity to at least one modality such as touch, vision and/or sound;
- weakness in the vestibular system which supports and regulates such functions as listening, eye functions, balance, knowledge of where our bodies are in space, muscle tone and so on.

On an output level, individuals with APD may demonstrate:

- insufficient integration between the two sides of the body and brain;
- immature reflex integration and irregularity in differentiation of movement/ response.

The case of Alexis: a gifted child with diagnosed ADHD

Alexis was 7 years and 10 months old when she was referred for help. She was in Grade 2 and had been diagnosed with ADHD, as well as auditory and visual–motor perceptual dysfunctioning by a psychologist, neurologist and occupational therapist. She had also received vision therapy. In spite of some scatter among the scores of an IQ test, she still managed to fall within the superior range of intelligence. The school described her as a strong-willed child who struggled with a very short concentration span, and who was unable to sit still and listen or focus on her work due to distractibility. They considered her to be a very clever girl who was not reaching her potential.

On a modified Conner's Rating Scale, her teacher gave her the highest rating of 3 ('Very much') for restlessness/overactive; excitable/impulsive; disturbing other children; failing to finish things/daydreaming; constant fidgeting; temper outbursts/unpredictable behaviour; and a rating of 2 ('Substantial') for quick and drastic mood swings and frustration if demands are not instantly met. The neurologist had prescribed Ritalin and her teacher was very supportive of this.

During the HANDLE assessment, Alexis' mother expressed the wish that Alexis could get along better with her friends and be less selfish and jealous. Alexis wanted to be able to concentrate better and complete tasks before going on to the next one, but showed a developing low self-esteem with doubts that she would ever be able to do this or please everyone.

Background information

After a normal, easy pregnancy, Alexis' birth had some complications. She was a big baby, weighing 4.21 kg. After three hours of labour, she showed signs of distress so was delivered with the help of forceps. She had passed and inhaled some meconium *in utero*, which was suctioned from her lungs. However, her APGAR scores were eight and subsequent development was incident free, except that she did not have much movement stimulation as a baby. Her mother was content to leave her in her cot or carry her around in a baby chair for most of the early months. As long as there was something to look at, Alexis seemed to be happy to be mainly immobile. She achieved normal motor milestones (crawling and walking) and early language development. After experiencing colic during the first three months, she was a healthy child with no ear infections or other significant illnesses.

From toddler days, she showed an ever-increasing liking for movement and constant activity. She enjoyed wild roundabout rides as well as running and jumping, and spent long periods walking on her hands, which she mastered at 5 years. She also liked rocking on her school chair – backwards, forwards and sideways and did occasionally fall over. She went through phases of being clumsy, and got numerous bruises on her legs from bumping into chairs, walls, doors and even people. However, she was a slow starter in the mornings, showing little urgency to begin the day, and often spent a long time just gazing at herself in the bathroom mirror.

She was not an extremely restless sleeper but liked company in bed. She covered her head with her blankets when she slept. She was very sensitive to light and disliked sunlight, torchlight or waking up in the morning with her bedroom light burning. She had a very sensitive scalp and thought that her fingertips were also very sensitive to touch – hating having her fingernails trimmed. She was extremely ticklish and disliked having anyone pretend to tickle her. Her favourite foods were salads and french fries or fish. She was not very fond of meat and particularly disliked the texture of chicken and some vegetables. She was very conscious of smells and seemed to be more sensitive to odours than most of her friends and family members.

Observations

Alexis did not move very much during the evaluation but soon expressed a liking for eyes closed activities because she said that her eyes got tired very quickly. She showed some uneven saccadic movements when asked to follow a moving object with her eyes and also said that it made her dizzy. Her eyes could not converge easily at close distances either. Low muscle tone was suspected when she displayed an untidy handwriting and also showed a preference for having her body supported by the chair or the desk. Her mother further supported the conclusion of low tone by commenting that Alexis was often rebuked for 'slouching'. She showed a dominant right hand and right eye and it seemed that her left brain hemisphere processed information more rapidly than the right. She used a technique known as 'cognitive override' to cope with demanding tasks. For example, she quickly used counting to help her master a finger tapping task.

When given a series of nonsense syllables to repeat, Alexis had some difficulty accurately recalling syllables with the plosive 'K' sound, and she also forgot some details from a sentence read out to her.

Conclusions

Alexis' sensitivity on her scalp and fingers and her ticklishness are indications that her sense of touch is irregular. This, coupled with a hypersensitivity to smell and light, can be very distracting to a child in a classroom. Her need to move, difficulty processing the 'K' sound, issues with visual tracking as well as her lowered muscle tone showed that her vestibular system was weak and unable to support the many functions for which it is responsible. Her slow adjustment to the morning and her tendency to bump into things pointed to a weak sense of proprioception. Alexis' vision was still compromised, in spite of vision therapy. Her light sensitivity and problems with tracking and convergence caused her to experience dizziness and headaches, and she preferred eyes closed activities because they gave her eyes a chance to rest. Because of poor proprioception, however, she found it necessary to depend on her eyes, which became increasingly strained. Alexis needed a great amount of energy to sustain her weakened systems during the day and her short temper and frustrations were making it hard for her to maintain interpersonal relationships. One reason why she found it difficult to attend to language and directions from others is that their words interfered with her own thoughts through which she was directing her movement.

In spite of the problems Alexis was experiencing with so many irregular systems, she had been compensating well. She was thus using her superior intellect to her advantage, but she did not have the underlying support systems for focusing and sustaining her attention flexibly and for completing tasks. These were leading to distress in her relationships with schoolwork as well as with friends and adults and ultimately to her failure to realise her potential.

Recommendations

The programme designed for Alexis concentrated on activities to strengthen weak underlying functions and to enhance the connections among the various functions. Her programme included several activities to strengthen her vestibular system. These, as well as the special massage that was recommended to reduce Alexis' hypersensitivity to touch, were also targeting her muscle tone issues, to help strengthen this crucial function.

Other simple, non-taxing activities were suggested to strengthen her visual functions and reduce her light sensitivity, without stressing her weak vestibular system or relying on muscle tone and differentiation of eye movements from head movements. One of these was drinking through the 'crazy straw' with its many loops and small diameter. Alexis was also encouraged to supplement her diet with omega-3 fatty acids, to ensure myelination of those neural pathways that the exercises were creating and strengthening.

Follow-up

Alexis' initial assessment took place in September. By late November, her mother reported much progress. Alexis was beginning to make friends with girls with similar intellectual interests to her own and was coping better socially, with less aggression. She also showed an improvement in her manners and behaviour at school and home. According to reports from the school, she was sitting still and finishing her work, and this improvement was substantiated by the school awarding her certificates of excellence. They no longer thought Ritalin was necessary.

Alexis is continuing her HANDLE programme. It is gratifying that the improved ability to focus and sustain tasks has already helped to reverse her lowered self-esteem. She now feels proud of who she is and is rapidly forgetting that she was ever labelled as having ADHD and related learning problems.

Summary and conclusions

It is significant that labels, so commonly used to indicate a supposedly life-long condition, do not always correctly define a problem. Too frequently those people labelled with ADHD or dyslexia and so on are considered to be in for a life-long struggle against an irreversible condition. Management of the condition is most often in the form of medication and/or behaviour modification techniques that, while being empirically 'proven' to bring about changes in some individuals, are seldom, if ever, able to cure the condition or be effective enough to warrant the removal of the label. The label is merely a short-hand way of communicating the forms of behaviour the person may be displaying in an attempt to deal with underlying problems. Once the cause of the behaviour has been identified, much can be done to help individuals restore efficient functioning of their neurological systems. In this way, labels become redundant and fall away.

Following much anecdotal success over the past decades, empirical research is now underway to clarify the effect of movement on the brain, with particular reference to the exercises used by practitioners of the HANDLE approach. The results should serve as a basis for future developments.

By applying neuroscience in order to understand the problems experienced by many individuals with a variety of neurodevelopmental concerns, it is possible for them to gain or restore more efficient functioning. The fact that this approach successfully identifies the causes of manifested behaviour and learning problems and treats them at their roots through simple, inexpensive activities and exercises has important implications for the well-being of many children in education. This includes those gifted children who struggle to actualise their potential because of inefficient neurobiological systems.

References

Baker, J.A., Bridger, R. and Evans, K. (1998) 'Models of underachievement among gifted preadolescents: The role of personal, family and school factors'. *Gifted Child Quarterly*, **42**(1), pp. 5–15.

Bluestone, J. (2001a) 'Sucking and neurodevelopment: The most critical human function, with relationships to autism, bipolarity and other disorders'. Unpublished article.

Bluestone, J. (2001b) Personal communication.

Cash, A.B. (1999) 'A profile of gifted individuals with autism: The twice-exceptional learner'. *Roeper Review,* **22**(1), pp. 22–7.

Changeux, J.-P. and Conic, M. (eds) (1987) *The Neural and Molecular Bases of Learning.* Report on the Dahlem Workshop. Berlin, 1985. Chichester: John Wiley & Sons.

Farnham-Diggory, S. (1992) *The Learning Disabled Child.* Cambridge, MA: Harvard University Press.

Ito, M. (1984) *The Cerebellum and Neural Control.* New York: Raven Press.

Le Poncin, M. (1990) *Brain Fitness.* American Edition, New York: Fawcett.

Leroux, J.A. and Levitt-Perlman, M. (2000) 'The gifted child with Attention Deficit Disorder: An identification and intervention challenge'. *Roeper Review,* **22**(3), pp. 171–6.

Lewis, D. (2001) Personal communication with Judith Bluestone, Seattle.

Lisberger, S.G. (1988) 'Neural bases for learning simple motor skills'. *Science,* Nov. 4(242), pp. 728–35.

Neihart, M. (2000) 'Gifted children with Asperger's Syndrome'. *Gifted Child Quarterly,* **44**(4), pp. 222–30.

Suliteanu, M. (2001) 'Outcomes are in the eye of the beholder'. *ADVANCE Newsmagazine,* August 6, pp. 33–4.

Winner, E. (2000) 'The origins and ends of giftedness'. *American Psychologist,* **55**(1), pp. 159–69.

2 The gifted and learning disabled student: teaching methodology that works

Wendy Stewart

The characteristics of Gifted and Learning Disabled (GLD) students generally mean that they will display subject-specific weaknesses, subject-specific strengths and often have poor organisational skills. Some GLD students may display academic weakness across the curriculum and demonstrate their ability with higher order thinking skills in a purely oral way. Teaching that supplies success and builds upon strengths is essential as lack of success in school subjects links directly and negatively to motivation, perceptions of self-efficacy and self-image.

If you don't get a chance to come to bat, you don't get a chance to hit, according to Gallagher (1983). GLD students create their own challenges in a sterile educational environment that does not recognise their abilities. If their challenge is towards society, they are labelled a rebel or misfit. Those who can't cope challenge the system and/or drop out. In general it is true to say that if you do not look for giftedness, you might not find it.

The characteristics of the gifted and learning disabled student

General statistics indicate that more boys than girls are identified as having a learning disability and Bees (1998) discusses an educational programme where of 50 students, 46 were male. This of course does not mean that there are more gifted boys than girls, but that more boys than girls are found to have a learning disability. Ratios vary around about 4:1 boys to girls for dyslexic difficulties although even this has been challenged by Shaywitz (1995), who suggested the ratios are more equal and that boys are more frequently identified because they exhibit more problem behaviour.

Some common characteristics about the GLD learner that have emerged from the literature show that about 80 per cent of GLD students are visual spatial learners. This may of course be a function of their poorer verbal skills and part of a compensatory strategy. It has implications for both the 80 per cent and the 20 per cent who require different teaching strategies or different learning systems.

Psychometric assessments show a 'zig zag' or 'scatter' pattern on the Wechsler Intelligence Scales for Children (WISC) indicating weaknesses in the sequential skills such as arithmetic, coding, information and digit span, the

'ACID profile' (Thomson 1984) characteristic of many dyslexics. This also indicates limited working memory capacity, which is also affected to some extent by anxiety, so students who are anxious about their performance in a test may perform poorly.

Cognitive weaknesses

Students who are gifted with learning disabilities generally have difficulties in cognitive processing in just one, but sometimes more, cognitive areas, rather than affecting overall intellectual ability (Beckley 1999). Difficulties with spelling are very common, including reversals in reading and writing letters of the alphabet (Pendarvis *et al.* 1990); poor reading, writing and spelling skills (Mendaglio 1993); possibly problems with phonics and therefore spelling (Willard-Holt 1999; Silverman 1997b); language deficits (Elliston 1993); and difficulty in memorising spelling (Dix and Schafer 1996). One side of the argument would say that this indicates problems with auditory sequential processing impairments (Silverman 1994a; van Tassell-Baska 1992).

However, research done by Vellutino (1979) and Vellutino and Scanlon (1987) and followed up by Montgomery (1997) does not support this premise. These authors state that the problem is a phonological processing difficulty which then makes all verbal tasks difficult to code, and we see deficits in digit span, coding, arithmetic, naming tasks in general and learning of the alphabet. Thus when students have difficulty with segmenting and encoding in spelling, they appear to have auditory sequencing difficulties, however, the underlying cause is actually the phonological processing problem.

Another problem is the quantity of writing that these students produce. They may have untidy handwriting (Fall and Nolan 1993; Silverman 1997b) and they find it difficult to actually get thoughts down on paper (Hishinuma 1996a). In addition, the use of sentence structure, punctuation and grammar is more basic (Dix and Schafer 1996).

Reading is an area of frustration to both the GLD student and the teacher because the student displays obvious inconsistencies when reading aloud, such as good comprehension but poor reading skills, or good reading skills but poor comprehension (Dix and Schafer 1996).

Mathematics is another area of difficulty where GLD students may have problems such as with numeric transpositions, and often, problems with basic computations which require ability with coding and rote learning (Willard-Holt 1999).

Metacognitive weaknesses

Organisational skills are an area of concern and GLD students often stand out because of their obvious lack of organisation. An inability to organise themselves results in lower school marks, few successes and low motivation. On a practical level this is demonstrated by the inability to locate the appropriate materials or implements, failing to complete or hand in assignments, lack of time management skills, and poor concentration skills (Willard-Holt 1999; Toll

1993). An inability to organise time management skills, goal setting skills and study skills leaves these students feeling frustrated and negative about their schooling experiences (Westwood 1995; Rimm 1997).

While most people display some anxiety in a test situation, the GLD student is particularly disadvantaged. Memory and sequencing ability are vital skills in any test situation, so anxiety produced under test conditions would contribute to an increase in short-term memory problems, particularly rote learning problems and sequencing ability (Willard-Holt 1999; Lerner 1993; Elliston 1993). GLD students may also have long-term memory problems involved in processing, storage and retrieval of information. These difficulties with rote memorisation, sequential learning and performance are particularly obvious under timed conditions (Willard-Holt 1999; van Tassell-Baska 1992). Finally, the GLD student often has difficulties remembering more than three directions at once because of poor short-term aural memory (Vaidya 1993; Silverman 1997a). There are implications for the teacher when a student learns more easily from visual presentation and has trouble with tasks which are auditory in nature (Dix and Schafer 1996).

Negative affective impact

Often the GLD student has a poor self-concept, with low self-esteem. These students, lacking appropriate goal setting skills, set extremely high goals for themselves and are very critical of themselves when they fail to reach these goals (Lupart 1989; Baum 1990; Conover 1996). Poor skills in goal setting also lead to unrealistic expectations, an overly optimistic view of their progress and failure to complete assignments (Willard-Holt 1999; Davis and Rimm 1994). This of course contributes to a sense of low personal control over their lives, with an external rather than an internal locus of control. An external locus of control means that the student accepts responsibility for failures, but not for successes. A history of lack of success with schooling means that the GLD student is also often reluctant to take educational risks (Dix and Schafer 1996). GLD students may also suffer from an over developed sense of perfectionism, the type of perfectionism which paralyses rather than produces good work (Conover 1996).

GLD students have some personal characteristics in common. Impulsivity, where emotions can overpower reasoning, often a case of 'think it/do it' before reason steps in, is a real problem (Silverman 1994b, 1997b; van Tassell-Baska 1992). The GLD student also often displays characteristics associated with ADD, such as risk-taking, speaking out of turn, rough behaviour and an inability to relate consequences to actions (Vaidya 1993; Beckley 1999). Aggression, carelessness, low frustration levels and disruptive behaviours are all common, particularly in upper primary and middle school levels (Baum *et al.* 1989; Elliston 1993). No-one likes to admit to a perceived failing, so again, the GLD student attempts to hide the learning disability and acts out frustration in rough behaviour (Dix and Schafer 1996).

Negativity towards their educational experience is an on-going problem. These students use their undoubted intelligence in negative ways as defence mechanisms. These include voluble expressions of boredom; criticisms of

27

school or teachers; diversion of topics to those they feel comfortable discussing; creative avoidance of difficult tasks; absolute refusal to perform in areas of weakness; or becoming the class clown (Baum 1990; Korinek 1992; Scott 1993). On the other hand, sometimes there is the passive, withdrawn GLD student. These students are chronically inattentive, and daydream the day away (Scott 1993; Silverman 1994b). They find it difficult to settle down and pay attention, and are often unable to follow directions (Willard-Holt 1999; Pendarvis *et al.* 1990). Whichever way the GLD student responds to the situation, either by acting out or passively withdrawing, the large majority will also be supersensitive, possibly over-reacting to even the mildest criticism.

Socialisation difficulties

Socialisation problems, in school and within the family, contribute to the lack of self-esteem. These students do not seem easily to read body language and so make mistakes in their assessment of a situation (Mendaglio 1993; Piirto 1994). This means that many GLD students find it more difficult to relate to their peers, preferring adult company (Bees 1998; Hishinuma 1993). Most teachers will have encountered the student who prefers to walk with the teacher on yard duty and discuss a topic at an adult level because the student has had trouble making friends.

Perceptuomotor difficulties

One last problem affecting the self-image of the GLD student is that some have poor visual motor integration. Often, physical problems such as a tendency towards clumsiness mean that these are the students who inevitably kick the teacher's chair each time they squeeze past it! Outside the classroom, problems with motor skills, for example, poor ball handling skills, ensure that these students are among the last to be chosen on a team, or difficulties copying neatly from the blackboard all contribute to low self-esteem (Fall and Nolan 1993; Dix and Schafer 1996).

The strengths of the gifted and learning disabled student

High scores on the WISC in vocabulary, similarities, block design, abstract reasoning and spatial reasoning indicate a wide vocabulary which is used well, and generally, good visual spatial skills (Baum *et al.* 1989; Hishinuma 1996).

Cognitive strengths

The GLD student, as would be expected from high WISC scores in this area, has a high level of oral expression, with excellent communication skills and verbal adeptness, an above average vocabulary, and good creative, expressive ability. All of these skills allow the student to demonstrate superior abilities in class discussions, however, these skills are not easily transposed into written work (Willard-Holt 1999; Clark 1994).

As would be expected from a gifted student, students with GLD often have a wide variety of interests and intellectual curiosity (Baum 1990; Elliston 1993). On the other hand, some prefer to become an 'expert' in a specific subject, displaying great knowledge of and passion for a topic. Of course, this topic may not necessarily be related to school subjects (Toll 1993; Korinek 1992).

The complex nature of students with GLD means that where their giftedness is not compromised by aspects of their specific learning disability, these students have the chance to show their exceptional abilities. Providing the learning disability does not affect mathematical skills, they will often display exceptional skills in mathematical reasoning, geometry and science (Willard-Holt 1999; Piirto 1994). Also in mathematics, GLD students are often intuitive thinkers who arrive at the correct solution without writing down the basic steps taken (Silverman 1997b; Rivera *et al.* 1995). From an early age on they may demonstrate extraordinary capability with spatial tasks such as puzzles and mazes (Silverman 1994a).

Where the visual memory is not affected by the specific learning disability, they have a keen visual memory, and are quickly able to perceive spatial relationships (Silverman 1997b). The students are also often particularly skilled with computers, as the logic of computing suits them (Silverman 1994a; Piirto 1994). They often have great strengths in a creative or technological area, displaying strong artistic, musical or mechanical aptitude (Willard-Holt 1999). Often these students excel in one modality of learning such as aural or kinaesthetic channels (Dix and Schafer 1996). Despite having previously indicated that spelling is generally an area of weakness, some students with GLD are very successful spellers because of their strong visualisation skills, as they learn words in a visual fashion (Dix and Schafer 1996).

Metacognitive strengths

GLD students are very capable users of higher order thinking skills to develop their problem solving abilities. They use their superior reasoning abilities in complex concepts such as lateral thinking, abstract thinking and problem solving (Willard-Holt 1999; Fall and Nolan 1993). GLD students are often divergent thinkers and the teacher can expect the use of unusual, original, imaginative and creative thought processes, which are all difficult to judge, and often overlooked in the gifted student (Baum *et al.* 1989; Toll 1993). They also display flexibility and fluency in generating new ideas (Dix and Schafer 1996). These are the students who will ask astute questions and in general, they have very good comprehension skills (Silverman 1997a) and supply the teacher with penetrating insights about the topic being studied, however, these insights do tend to be verbal rather than written.

The ability to generate complex ideas and to be able to grasp complex relationships, together with a sophisticated sense of humour, means that the student is easily able to grasp satire, metaphors and analogies. This ability enables GLD students to understand and appreciate adult humour well before their chronological peers (Willard-Holt 1999; Scott 1993). These are the students who are systems thinkers, who are able to take a holistic overview, who are comfortable with complexity and pattern seeking (Willard-Holt 1999; Silverman 1997b). It is a source of confusion for the teacher when these students thrive on complexity and learn complex systems easily, but struggle with easy work.

Positive affective impact

It is possible for GLD students to display amazing productivity and motivation, especially when their personal interests are involved – unfortunately school work does not often fall into this category (Baum *et al.* 1993; Korinek 1992). In addition, GLD students also have a strong sense of fair play and justice which will become very evident in verbal discussions (Davis and Rimm 1994). It is most likely that GLD students will hand in their best work when they are encouraged to work on their own (Elliston 1993).

Teaching methodology

Academic practicalities

The successful teacher will show these students the big, holistic picture first, explaining why they are doing the work, what they will achieve by doing it and where they will be at the end of it (Silverman 1997b). Flexible teachers who are prepared to provide alternatives to the traditional styles of delivery and assessment of student work are essential. 'Chalk and talk' is one delivery style that teachers appear to feel very comfortable with, however, it is important to remember that there will be students who are seriously disadvantaged if this is the only delivery style. It is always a good idea to try to eliminate sources of distraction. A teacher could ask the student to sit in the front rows, could try to provide a quieter, less distracting environment in the classroom, perhaps provide earphones (or for adolescents who do not wish to stand out from the crowd, perhaps a Walkman) to help block out noise when concentration is needed, and lastly, touch the student's shoulder or establish eye contact before speaking (van Tassell-Baska 1992). Depending on the learning disability, the teacher could either provide tapes of lectures or photocopied notes of lectures from which the student can make notes. It is vital that the teacher ensures all assignments or directions are written down. The student is more likely to forget vital details unless they are written down where the student can easily access them (Silverman 1997b; Brody and Mills 1997). Rhythm and music can be used to help memorisation, ranging from singing the times tables to bouncing a basketball while essential rote learning occurs. The teacher could try giving two marks for assignments, with one (weighted more heavily) for content and one for the mechanics such as grammar and spelling (Silverman 1997b). It is also important to teach with empathy and understanding, and most of all, to make use of humour (Silverman 1997b; Bees 1998). Inclusive teaching methodology, where subject matter is presented in a variety of ways to students, and an emphasis on performance based assessment, allows students to demonstrate mastery using an array of products. Indeed the emphasis on assessment should be taken away from the traditional written essay (Nidiffer and Moon 1995; Fetzer 2000). Electronic assistive technology, both hardware and software programmes, has come a long way and can be particularly useful. When the teacher allows the use of word processors or lap-top computers to help with grammar, spelling and writing, anxiety about the mechanics of writing is lessened enabling the student to focus on producing creative work. The lap-top computer should be lightweight and robust and able to connect to a printer. It becomes possible for the student to produce their best work when the teacher also encourages the use of calculators, cameras, video recorders and cassette recorders (Baum 1990; Fetzer 2000).

Students with GLD often have poor time management skills, so it is recommended that they be given extra time in tests or examinations, which may help avoid anxiety and aid information retrieval (Bley and Thornton 1995). The teacher could even allow the student to take the test at home or give oral tests, or untimed tests (Silverman 1997b; Brody and Mills 1997). It is essential to make sure students know they are not in competition with others for marks, but competing against themselves.

Cognitive interventions

At all times it is important to remember that we are dealing with gifted students so it is necessary to provide instruction that appeals to the higher reasoning abilities which the gifted and learning disabled student excels in, rather than rote learning or drill-and-practice. For example, in spelling, concentrate on rule-based learning, or origins of words, rather than rote memorisation (Hishinuma 1993; Nidiffer and Moon 1995) and remember to use a sight recognition approach to reading, as well as phonics based instruction, because each methodology has its uses (van Tassell-Baska 1992). The teacher should encourage reading for fun and make use of fantasy (Silverman 1993, 1997b).

It is important to recognise prior mastery of a topic, and provide suitable curriculum modification because gifted students do not appreciate going over work that they have already mastered (Nidiffer and Moon 1995). The empathic teacher would encourage these students to discover their own methods for problem solving (Silverman 1997b) and aid motivation by teaching to their interests, providing meaningful topics or real world problems that are high interest, challenging and nurturing of the individual strengths of the GLD student. Where possible the teacher should use an interdisciplinary orientation, allowing transfer of techniques and information (Nidiffer and Moon 1995; Korinek 1992). On the other hand, it is equally important that the student is aware of areas of individual weakness. To support these areas where possible, teach gifted and learning disabled students strategies to compensate for their learning problems. Provide structured, explicit work sheets which are simply and clearly set out. Where possible, provide a graphic organiser (Swartz and Parks 1994) which forces the student to follow a certain way of completing an assignment. Give students direct instruction in basic skills, specifically teaching time management skills, self-management skills, and study skills such as note taking (try teaching note taking in pictorial form), sequencing, summarising, reviewing, memorising and test taking skills (Korinek 1992; van Tassell-Baska 1992). It would also be valuable to do some work on goal setting, where large goals are broken down into small, achievable and timetabled steps, so that the student has a plan of study to work towards, including due dates for assignments (Brody and Mills 1997). The GLD student finds being organised particularly difficult, so it is necessary to provide advance organisers to help in both receiving and communicating information such as syllabus notes, lecture notes, or study guides for each topic (Baum 1990). It would be useful to provide comprehension checklists to help with written materials (Dix and Schafer 1996). For those times when 'all the lights are on but no-one is home' get students to repeat instructions given to them. A strategy to prevent overloading of memory is to give instructions in chunks of less than three items together, to organise information given into related groups and to make it meaningful by linking it to something students already know about (Lerner 1993).

One very practical intervention is to simply reduce the amount of written work required and ask the student to devise some other means of proving mastery (Rivera *et al.* 1995). Other strategies to support a poor short term memory are to promote the use of visualisation and hands-on experiences, to teach the use of mnemonics for those facts that must be remembered, and to emphasise concepts, not dates or names (Baum 1990; Silverman 1993, 1997c). Always encourage students to make lists of things to be remembered (Silverman 1997b) and teach students to use mind maps or concept webs. This is beneficial as a strategy because it helps students to organise their thoughts in a logical fashion before beginning the written assignment, firstly by brainstorming, then by placing all useful information in an order of priority. Lastly, the use of loose-leaf folders should be promoted, where work can be inserted as necessary. The ring binder allows the students to carry all their work in the one folder, which in theory, is less likely to be misplaced (Silverman 1997b).

When teaching mathematics, new concepts need to be presented concretely, allowing for a 'hands-on' approach, which will help with the transfer of the concept to written symbols (Chinn and Ashcroft 1993; Nidiffer and Moon 1995). The empathic teacher would allow the student to use multiplication charts (Silverman 1997a), and to use calculators to avoid getting bogged down with basic computation or rote facts (Bley and Thornton 1995). It is also important to encourage the student to make an estimate before actual computation as a 'reality check' (Chinn and Ashcroft 1993).

Teachers should remember to use more over-learning than usual, to help overcome memory deficits (Korinek 1992). If possible, encourage the student to 'talk aloud' a problem, as this allows the teacher to find basic errors of understanding which may then be corrected (Korinek 1992; Bley and Thornton 1995). The teacher should also remember that full automaticity in number facts is more difficult for these students, so the process/discovery approach used on its own in mathematics lessons will disadvantage them and revision, re-teaching and over-learning are essential (Chinn and Ashcroft 1993). Again using music, rhythm or singing will help with rote learning facts (Munro 1996). The teacher could also try using daily speed and accuracy tests where students compete against themselves, and not each other (Westwood 1993). Particularly in the primary school, teachers could use a multisensory approach, especially a tactile/kinaesthetic one, to both teaching and learning, with as much variety as possible (Scott 1993; Dix and Schafer 1996).

Metacognitive interventions

It is very easy for teachers to notice the specific learning disability and to ignore the gifted aspect of the student. Therefore, it is important to try to focus attention on the development of the gift/talent in its own right and supply a programme which enriches rather than remediates, by paying attention to the areas of strength and not to the disability (Baum *et al.* 1989, 1993; Gentry and Neu 1998; Ingleheart 1998; Fetzer 2000). Teachers who enjoy working with GLD students will relish and reward divergent thinking and creativity (Baum 1990; Silverman 1997b). They will also supply a supportive environment that values and appreciates individual abilities. Often the use of mentors from outside the school, as role models, removes the potential for conflict and recognises that the student has talents to develop (Brody and Mills 1997).

As mentioned earlier, it is important to help gifted and learning disabled students become aware of their strengths and weaknesses by assisting them to cope with the wide discrepancies between the two (Baum *et al.* 1993; Reis *et al.* 2000). Interventions could include increasing self awareness, self esteem, and self management with appropriate activities, and building successes into the teaching programme. Students in general will find themselves more motivated to succeed when the teacher encourages them to take their part in active learning and decision making (Korinek 1992; Bees 1998).

Affective interventions

Poor self image and low self esteem need to be improved by teaching directly to the affective areas, by verbalising specific strengths, by giving training in social skills, by working to improve self esteem and self confidence, with the end result of developing responsibility and leadership (Hishinuma 1993). The teacher and the GLD student together could consider group counselling, one-on-one counselling and parental counselling (Silverman 1993; Brody and Mills 1997). It cannot be stated too often that teaching that addresses the gifted potential, rather than emphasising remediation, is an affirmation of ability, which the student needs to counteract the negative experiences of the specific learning disability (Bees 1998; Gentry and Neu 1998). The empathic teacher will also provide a meaningful connection with schooling for disenchanted students, helping them set goals that link schooling to their life after school. It is also important to encourage self advocacy and self knowledge in order to request appropriate accommodations (Reis *et al.* 2000). There is even a case for a 'personal coach' who advocates for the student where necessary and supplies encouragement, attention, support and positive feedback (Reis and McCoach

2000). Lastly, the teacher should carry a giant pencil case at all times! This pencil case should be filled with as many spare pens, pencils, rulers, erasers etc. as possible. These are made available in a non-judgemental and empathic way as the need arises. GLD students do not need to be reminded about their 'failings', this happens often enough.

Practicalities – a personal teaching programme

If students don't learn from the way you teach, you have to teach the way students do *learn.*

Until recently little has been published about the GLD student and secondary education; even less has been published about designing a curriculum for this type of student. The problem appears to be that this information is very general, for example, 'teach study skills' or 'teach time management skills'. This is of very little help to the classroom teacher 'at the chalkface' and the remainder of this chapter deals with a programme developed by the author, over the last five years, which attempts to address this issue. With two formally identified GLD children of her own, it became clear that when these children began school, they were going to be educationally disadvantaged because of a lack of knowledge at classroom level. This provided the impetus for the author to complete a Master of Gifted Education, specialising in the GLD student.

Burton and Halliwell (2001: 28) define curriculum as a 'dynamic and complex social process' which, of necessity, involves 'teachers, children, knowledge and milieu' but to this they add the importance of the social setting (wherever teaching of the particular curriculum takes place). Thus the subject matter of a particular curriculum should be expanded to take into account the complexity of interactions of the social setting – the people, the places, the educational ethos. Until now, with regard to the GLD student, very little has been done to change the educational ethos in secondary schooling. Reis *et al.* (2000) in their study of USA college students, advocate teaching specific compensatory strategies such as study skills, efficient learning skills, use of electronic assistive technology and practical (environmental) accommodations, all of which have been previously discussed. Remembering that a specific learning disability normally involves a processing deficit, and as this programme is firmly set in a secondary campus, it was decided to provide learning strategies that would enhance the way information was processed, that is, cognitive strategies. However, a multidisciplinary approach, across the curriculum, might be more possible in a primary educational setting.

The work done by these researchers provided support for the premise of concentrating on cognitive strategies. It discussed how a successful programme for high achieving university students with a learning disability commonly addressed the areas of study techniques, specific training which compensated for the learning disability and subject specific strategies. Sadly, this article stressed how many negative attitudes to secondary schooling could have been reversed if these coping strategies and skills had been taught then, rather than at college. Counselling was another vital component taking up much scheduled time with their students. However, they all stressed the value of counselling and remarked that one third of lesson time was taken up in counselling.

The author teaches in Adaptive Education at St Ignatius' College, a Jesuit school. One aspect of the Jesuit Charism is to encourage students to develop their abilities to become the best person that they possibly can. In this setting it was obvious that some clearly gifted students were underachieving and even educationally at risk. Personally and anecdotally, it appeared that Year 9 GLD students were at a crucial stage and this idea is supported by Bees (1998), who stated that this is an absolutely crucial year in student education. It will be no surprise then, to note that the majority of students who work with the author are in Year 9.

The ingredients for the development of the following programme were a cohort of underachieving but obviously gifted students in Years 7 to 10 (an area of greatest need initially); a teacher with an interest in GLD students and the qualifications to devise a programme; a programme based entirely around the needs of students; and a school prepared to pay for the luxury of a teacher working with small groups of students with GLD (who are after all, not really failing!). Students are invited to work with the author after the following steps have been taken: the first step is that initial problems in the student's organisation have been identified by a subject or home-group teacher; occasionally, parents may request the author's intervention because of concerns at home or problems at school that they are aware of; and the student fits the GLD profile (here an IQ test would be an obvious help). The next step is formally to contact the parents of the student to discuss school and parental concerns, and where possible, to answer any queries. Lastly, the student is offered the chance to complete an introductory session to gain a 'feel' for what it will be like.

Limitations of the programme include: time constraints; there are many more students requiring help than only one teacher can supply, thus there are a limited number of lessons available; space is limited because other Adaptive Education students share the same room and there is no home base for GLD students; the school has an academic reputation and some teachers are curriculum driven, they find it difficult to flex and teach inclusively; the emphasis of this programme is on organisational skills (time management, study and personal organisation) and there are other areas that should, but cannot, be included.

Our curriculum, the 'work smart' programme

In preference to a title that had connotations of remedial education, this programme was named 'Work Smart'. The emphasis is not on working any harder but on working smarter to achieve a better result. Realistically, it is impossible to develop an individual educational plan for each student. Thus the programme is based on common characteristics of GLD students in general. Individualisation of the programme is achieved to a limited degree by making the programme student-centred in two main ways. First, it is important to note that teaching of specific skills is not done in isolation but in conjunction with subject matter the student is having problems with and wishes to work upon. Students are given an overview of what will be taught and some time is spent discussing and understanding the individual components of the overview. They are then encouraged to ask to work on a skill that they think will be useful for their current assignment, giving them some ownership of what is being taught. Second, to keep student interest high and focused on content, we use many short quizzes or questionnaires to help students learn more about themselves and which are based on skills to be developed. For example, 'How well do I manage my time?' or 'What type of learner am I?' It is a very human characteristic to be interested in the results of a survey that has been completed.

Outline of the 'work smart' programme: a learning spiral to be revisited

1. Introduction, sharing of information. Find out what each student wants help with. Use of colour, highlighters, scheduling homework. Breaking work down into achievable goals.
2. Know yourself, an introduction to discovering personal strengths and weaknesses as a learner. Learning styles and modalities. Right brain, left brain. Multiple intelligences. Questionnaire.
3. Setting up an environment for active learning. Home and school.
4. Making dull subjects more interesting. Making effective use of technology to improve quality of work.
5. Homework – breaking work requirements into sections. Effective timetabling of sections of work to be done. Understanding own strengths and weaknesses as a learner. Using knowledge of these to improve quality of homework.
6. Motivation. Procrastination. How to combat. Self esteem, self efficacy. Bananas v. Oranges. Homework – setting up for effective homework. Knowing your preferred ways of learning efficiently. What can you change? Test to discover personality type for work at home.
7. Active reading skills, taking charge of your assigned reading. Reading skills revisited.
8. Tips for speed reading. Reading skills revisited.
9. Reading for different reasons – speed, enjoyment, challenge, study, and how to make the best use of your time.
10. Active reading skills, a selection of strategies. SQ3R, 3S etc.
11. Active reading skills, highlighting key words, topic sentences.
12. Review/revise – use it or lose it. Part 1.
13. Note-taking, continuing with topic sentences and key words. Practice session.
14. Note-taking, another practice session.
15. Research skills. Organising notes from research.
16. Mnemonics, chunking, silly sentences.
17. Brainstorming. Organising your thoughts. Prioritising ideas.
18. Graphic organisers.
19. Essay writing from notes. The topic sentence. Scaffolding. Practice session.
20. Essay writing, the paragraph. Scaffolding. Practice session.
21. Essay writing, linking ideas together. Practice session.
22. Habits of highly effective teenagers.

23. Habits of highly effective teenagers continued.
24. Review, revise. Use it or lose it. Part 2.
25. Learning for a test. Organising knowledge in preparation for a test – mnemonics, silly sentences, chunking. Sitting for tests, anxiety response, meditation (safe place). Having a wide knowledge of suitable techniques to aid learning for tests. Using selected techniques as required. What to do if 'you go blank' in a test.
26. Learning for exams. Organising knowledge in preparation for an exam. Trial questions. What exactly does the teacher ask? – decoding the question. Brainstorming. Writing an effective answer.

Below is a sample of a letter that students are expected to take home and complete with the help of their family. Most students genuinely wish to improve their skills but do not know how to go about it. It is a good starting point.

Dear .... (and family),
You have been invited to work with me and develop skills to help with your education and learning. I will certainly do my best to help you develop these skills. However, to improve *your* skills requires *your* input and dedication as well as mine. Please think carefully about the following questions, answer them, and discuss your answers with your family. Unless *you* have the desire to improve your skills and be more successful in your studies, I can be of little help.
Q: Are you hoping or planning to fail this year?
....
You are right of course, no one *plans* to fail. However, are you planning to succeed this year?
....
Q: How much do you want to succeed this year, next year and in the future?
....
Q: Are you prepared to do whatever is necessary to achieve this year's goals?
....
Q: Are you prepared to make sacrifices in order to achieve these goals?
....
Q: Are you prepared to make a commitment to your study?
....
Q: Do you understand that you will have to work harder than many other students to achieve a similar result to them?
....
Q: Are you prepared to work an extra thirty minutes each night to put in extra effort?
....
Q: Are you prepared to put in 'catch up time' on weekends if required?
....
'A journey of a thousand miles begins with the first step.'

Summary and conclusions

Gifted and Learning Disabled students not only have weaknesses, they also have strengths and it is these that teachers need to concentrate more upon in all areas of the curriculum. To help them there is a wide range of strategies that can be used to support the learning of rote items and conceptual aspects and these have been outlined in this chapter under the subheadings cognitive, metacognitive and affective aspects.

GLD students are intensely aware of their difficulties and shortcomings and need someone who will advocate for and support them especially if counselling is not available. In order to cope in their areas of difficulty they need time and someone to teach them strategies for overcoming or compensating for them. What they especially need is recognition and support for what they can do and are successful in and recognition also for their differentness. This is all too clearly expressed in the following poem by a doubly exceptional student.

'Square and Brown Inside'[1]

He always wanted to explain things but nobody cared, so he drew.
Sometimes he would just draw and it was anything.
He wanted to carve it on stone or write it in the sky,
And it would be the sky and things inside him that needed saying,
And it was a beautiful picture.
He kept it under his pillow and would let no one see it,
And he would look down at it every night and think about it,
And when it was dark and his eyes were closed he could see it still,
And it was all of him and he loved it . . .
When he started school he brought it with him,
Not to show anyone else.
Just to have it with him like a friend.
It was funny at school. He sat at a square brown desk,
Just like all the other square brown desks, and he had thought it would be red.
And his room was a square brown room like all the other rooms,
*   and it was tight and close and stiff.*
He hated to hold the pencil and chalk with his arms stiff and his feet flat on the
*   floor,*
stiff, with the teacher watching and watching.
The teacher came and spoke to him.
She told him to wear a tie like all the other boys.
He said he didn't like them and she said it didn't matter.
After that they drew . . . and he drew all yellow and it was the way he felt about
*   morning and it was beautiful.*
The teacher came along and smiled at him. 'What's this?' she said.
'Why don't you draw something like Ken's drawing? Isn't it lovely?'
After that his mother bought him a tie like everyone else and . . . he always drew
*   aeroplanes and rocket ships like everyone else.*
He threw his old picture away.

And then he lay alone looking at the sky and it was big and blue and all of
    everything but he wasn't *anymore.*
He was brown and square inside and his hands were still and he was like everyone
    else.
And the thing inside that needed saying didn't anymore.
It had stopped pushing and was crowded.
Crushed.
Stiff . . . like everything else.

Note

[1]*Gifted and Talented Children's Association of South Australia Magazine. Newsletter.* No. 31, October 1983. (Reprinted with kind permission of the editor, R. Stewart.) (This poem was handed to an English teacher shortly before its 14-year-old author committed suicide.)

References

Baum, S. (1990) 'Gifted but learning disabled: a puzzling paradox', *ERIC Digest,* #E479.

Baum, S.M., Owen, S.V. and Dixon, J. (1993) *To be Gifted and Learning Disabled*. Highett, Victoria: Hawker Brownlow.

Baum, S.M., Emerich, L.J., Herman, G.N. and Dixon, J. (1989) 'Identification programs and enrichment strategies for Gifted Learning Disabled Youth', *Roeper Review*, **XII**, (I), September, pp. 48–53.

Beckley, D. (1999) *Gifted and Learning Disabled: Twice Exceptional Students*. Storrs, C. T: University of Connecticut.

Bees, C. (1998) 'The GOLD Program: a program for gifted learning disabled adolescents', *Roeper Review*, December, pp. 155–61.

Bley, N.S. and Thornton, C.A. (1995) *Teaching Mathematics to Students with Learning Disabilities (3rd ed.)*. Austin, Texas: Pro-Ed.

Brody, L.E. and Mills, C.J. (1997) 'Gifted children with learning disabilities: a review of the issues', *Journal of Learning Disabilities*, **30**(3), May/June, pp. 282–96.

Burton, J. and Halliwell, G. (2001) 'Negotiating curriculum: discretion and collaboration in teaching teams: Curriculum Perspectives', *Journal of the Australian Curriculum Studies Association*, **21**(1), April, pp. 27–34.

Chinn, S.J. and Ashcroft, J.R. (1993) *Mathematics for Dyslexics: a Teaching Handbook*. London: Whurr.

Clark, B. (1994) *Growing up Gifted: Developing the Potential of Children at Home and at School (4th ed.)*. New York: Merrill.

Conover, L. (1996) 'Gifted and learning disabled: Is it possible?', *Virginia Association for the Education of the Gifted Newsletter*, **17**(3), Summer.

Davis, G.A. and Rimm, S. B. (1994) *Education of the Gifted and Talented (3rd ed.)*. Boston: Allyn and Bacon.

Dix, J. and Schafer, S. (1996) 'From paradox to performance; practical strategies for identifying and teaching GLD students', *Gifted Child Today*, January/February, pp. 22–31.

Elliston, T. (1993) 'Gifted and learning disabled . . . a paradox', *Gifted Child Today*, January/February

Fall, J. and Nolan, L. (1993) 'A paradox of exceptionalities', *Gifted Child Today*, January/February.

Fetzer, E.A. (2000) 'The gifted/learning disabled child: a guide for teachers and parents', *Gifted Child Today*, **23**(4), August, pp. 44–50.

Gallagher, J. J. (1983) 'The adaptation of gifted programming for learning disabled students' in L. Fox, L. Brody and D. Tobin (eds) *Learning Disabled/Gifted Children: Identification and Programming*. Baltimore MD: University Park Press.

Gallagher, J. J. (1985) *Teaching the Able*. New York: Allen and Bacon.

Gentry, M. and Neu, T.W. (1998) 'Project High Hopes Summer Institute: Curriculum for developing talent in students with special needs', *Roeper Review*, May/June, pp. 291–5.

Hishinuma, E.S. (1993) 'Counselling gifted/at risk and gifted/dyslexic youngsters', *Gifted Child Today*, January/February, pp. 30–3.

Hishinuma, E.S. (1996) 'Addressing diversity of the gifted/at risk, characteristics for identification', *Gifted Child Today*, September/October, pp. 20–45.

Ingleheart, J. (1998) 'How should districts serve twice exceptional students', *Gifted Child Today*, July/August, pp. 38–40.

Korinek, L. (1992) 'Gifted children with specific learning disabilities' in J. van Tassell-Baska (ed.) *Planning Effective Curriculum for Gifted Learners*. Denver, Colorado: Love.

Lerner, J. (1993) *Learning Disabilities: Theory, Diagnosis and Teaching Strategies (6th ed.)*. Boston: Houghton Mifflin.

Lupart, J.L. (1989) 'Beyond identification: assessing learning needs of gifted/learning disabled students' in S. Bailey, E. Braggett and M. Robinson (eds) *The Challenge of Excellence: A Vision Splendid*. Selected papers from the 8th world conference on gifted and talented children, Sydney, August 3rd to 7th Wagga Wagga: AAEGT.

Mendaglio, S. (1993) 'Counselling gifted learning disabled: individual and group counselling techniques' in Silverman, L. K. (ed.) *Counselling the Gifted and Talented*. Denver: Love.

Montgomery, D. (1997) *Spelling: Remedial Strategies*. London: Cassell/Continuum.

Munro, J. (1996) 'Cognitive style and mathematics learning', *Australian Journal of Remedial Education*, **27**(5), pp. 19–24.

Nidiffer, L.G. and Moon, S.M. (1995) 'Serving the gifted dyslexic and gifted at risk', *Our Gifted Children*, **2**(8), pp. 39–43.

Pendarvis, E.D., Howley, A.A. and Howley, C.B. (1990) *The Abilities of Gifted Children*. New Jersey: Prentice Hall.

Piirto, J. (1994) *Talented Children and Adults: Their Development and Education*. New York: Macmillan.

Reis, S.M. and McCoach, D.B. (2000) 'The underachievement of gifted students: what do we know and where do we go?', *Gifted Child Quarterly*, **44**(3), pp. 152–70.

Reis, S.M., McGuire, J.M. and Neu, T.W. (2000) 'Compensation strategies used by high ability students with learning disabilities who succeed in college', *Gifted Child Quarterly*, Spring, **44**(2), pp. 123–34.

Rimm, S.B. (1997) 'Underachievement syndrome: a national epidemic' in N. Colangelo and G. A. Davis (eds) *Handbook of Gifted Education (2nd ed.)*. Boston: Allyn and Bacon.

Rivera, D.B., Murdock, J. and Sexton, D. (1995) 'Serving the gifted/learning disabled', *Gifted Child Today*, November/December, pp. 34–7.

Scott, C. (1993) 'Gifted children with learning difficulties', *Gifted*, August, pp. 15–18.

Shaywitz, S.E. (1995) 'Gender differences in reading disabilities revisited. Results from the Connecticut longitudinal study', *Journal of the American Medical Association*, **32**.

Silverman, L.K. (1993) *Counselling the Gifted and Talented*. Denver: Love.

Silverman, L.K. (1994a) 'Spatial learners: our forgotten gifted children', n. p.: Gifted Development Centre.

Silverman, L.K. (1994b) 'Invisible gifts, invisible handicaps', *Gifted*, April, pp. 7–11.

Silverman, L.K. (1997a) 'Counselling and teaching gifted/learning disabled children'. *N.S.W. Association for Gifted and Talented Children GLD Conference*, Sydney, July 19th.

Silverman, L.K. (1997b) 'Visual spatial learners and giftedness'. *N.S.W. Association for Gifted and Talented Children GLD Conference*, Sydney, July 19th.

Swartz, R.J. and Parks, S. (1994) *Infusing the Teaching of Critical and Creative Thinking into Elementary Instruction*. Pacific Grove, CA: Critical Thinking Press.

Thomson, M. (1984) *Development Dyslexia*. London: Arnold.

Toll, M. (1993) 'Gifted learning disabled: a kaleidoscope of needs', *Gifted Child Today*, January/February, pp. 34–5.

Vaidya, S.R. (1993) 'Gifted children with learning disabilities: theoretical implication and instructions and instructional challenge', *Education*, **113**(4), pp. 568–74.

van Tassell-Baska, J. (1992) *Planning Effective Curriculum for Gifted Learners*. Denver, Colorado: Love.

Vellutino, F.R. (1979) *Dyslexia: Research and Theory*. London: MIT Press.

Vellutino, F.R. and Scanlon, D.M. (1987) 'Phonological coding, phonological awareness, and reading ability: Evidence from a longitudinal and experimental study', *Merrill Palmer Quarterly*, **33**, pp. 321–63.

Westwood, P. (1993) *Commonsense Methods for Children with Special Needs (2nd ed.)*. London: Routledge.

Westwood, P. (1995) *Behaviour Management: Learning Disabilities*. Adelaide: Institute for the Study of Learning Difficulties.

Willard-Holt, C. (1999) 'Dual exceptionalities', *ERIC EC Digest* #E574, May.

3 Giftedness, talent and dyslexia

Diane Montgomery

Nearly 90 years ago Edith Norrie, a Danish dyslexic, taught herself to read and write using an articulatory phonic system. In the UK her method is still used by dyslexia teachers, especially those taught at the Helen Arkell Centre in Surrey, and the Edith Norrie Letter Case (1917, 1982) is available.

Edith was born into an affluent and educated family so she had every normal opportunity to become literate but did not do so although she was an intelligent child. Her motivation to learn to read as an adult was that she needed to read her fiancé's letters from the war front. If she could teach herself then it is likely that many other dyslexics since then have also learned to do so, though like her they come to literacy late. Literacy is even more prized today and very bright young children can become exceedingly upset when they see others whom they regard as much less clever easily learning to read and write.

Whenever reading or writing is about to begin these children cause disruption or refuse to work and seek by all manner of devices to evade the task. They are then seen as disruptive rather than in need of special help. Other children's frustration can lead them into passive states of evasion and withdrawal such that they can become emotionally depressed. To survive these stresses the pupil needs a very supportive family and an advocate or learning mentor in school.

While other children are learning literacy skills and all about the structure of text the bright dyslexics will be engaged in compensatory learning activities if the class environment is supportive. They can become highly talented at communicating ideas through cartoons and diagrams or by using movement and drama, or they may focus on becoming a 'technowhizz', a computer expert. If they have musical and sport opportunities and find some aspect in which they can achieve, this can help them enormously and save them from emotional and behavioural distress. It is not too much to insist that some special route to achievement needs to be found for every dyslexic while the literacy skills are being remediated and brought up to grade level.

Many dyslexics do eventually learn to read adequately, if slowly, but all too frequently their spelling remains disabled. This is perhaps not surprising as reading is easier to learn because it is a recognition activity with all the details already present, whereas spelling is a recall skill when words have to be reconstructed in their perfect form in the absence of any help. It is characteristic of gifted children that they have very good memories and they may learn to read very quickly purely based upon visual memorising. At the age of about eight when the curriculum demands magnify they will begin to have difficulties which will be seen in the reading of more technical vocabulary and in their written work with problems in spelling. Some, because of deeper learning disabilities and confusing teaching strategies, may fail to learn to begin to read until about the age of eight years. By the time they do learn, dyslexics may have lost five or more years of literacy learning and practice time or all of the primary school years, and their interest and motivation to become literate may also have been blunted by successive failures and loss of self esteem. Often the behavioural problems gain them referral for help rather than the dyslexia.

Dyslexics have many icons for forebears who have achieved greatness despite the odds, and not all have been born into famous families. A few such icons are Duncan Goodhew, swimmer; Susan Hampshire, actor; Michael Heseltine, businessman and politician. Some other famous dyslexics have been Sir Winston Churchill, Hans Christian Andersen, Leonardo Da Vinci, Albert Einstein, Oliver Goldsmith and Sir Walter Scott.

At a local level many of the shipwrights and motor engineers I know left school early and went into a skills occupation in which they are now recognised for their special gifts and talents, but their bills reveal their dyslexia. Currently 50 per cent of the students on my distance learning MA SpLD programme are 'recovered' dyslexics who have fought their way through the system mostly unidentified until late in their careers and who want to prevent young people, often their own children, avoid such distress. Dyslexia is one of the most common forms of double exceptionality and has serious educational consequences for bright children.

How dyslexia manifests itself

While a wide range of difficulties have been associated with the dyslexic condition in the school age child, the educational issues of most concern are an inability to learn to read *and* spell at a level consistent with the child's age and ability. The spelling difficulties may be compounded by additional difficulties in handwriting due to mild or more severe fine motor coordination problems (Montgomery 1997a, b). This discrepancy definition is widely used to identify those in the most need for the meagre resources on offer. In research a two year decrement between reading and chronological age is usually taken as the cut-off point to define the population. The DES (1972) recommended that the decrement for remedial provision should be 20 per cent, with reading the lower. However, many bright dyslexics by this measure read at or near their age level but with IQs in the region of 140+ do have severe dyslexic difficulties. Other dyslexics do not have and never have had reading problems and so are excluded from the help they desperately need but they do have spelling problems (dysorthographia).

At the adult level, as my teacher education courses in dyslexia unfolded, a number of 'closet' dyslexics revealed themselves. In timed examinations their condition easily revealed itself by the nature and number of their spelling errors. They would make on average between 20 and 30 errors, and write about a third less than other students as they selected vocabulary they could spell and took longer to reconstruct some of their spellings. Regression to some very basic primary grade misspellings could be seen in these scripts and in extremis mirror writing occurred in one or two cases. Some of them only realised they were dyslexic on following the Learning Difficulties course! All of them needed help with spelling rather than reading. Their reading was competent although it was usually slow and they often had to read a piece of text several times to extract its meaning. This became increasingly problematic as the texts grew more academic and complex.

Note-taking in lectures was particularly difficult. Susan could not write notes and follow the argument at the same time. Brenda found lectures as they progressed ran too fast for her. Susan's response was only to study when she had an essay or assignment to do, whereas Brenda would go over her notes from lectures, borrow those of friends and read around the subject. Susan knew she was bright but with a problem and had to avoid literacy tasks where possible; Brenda thought she was a slow learner who had done well to get so far and needed some persuading to believe she could gain an honours degree. I felt I must find a way to help them but there were no guidelines. The dyslexia programmes available were not suitable, for these students could all read and write competently for everyday purposes; something tailored to their needs was required. I therefore began to run some remedial tutorials to explore the problem. For example, using cases as markers, in Year 3 Brenda's exam script contained over 30 misspellings and Susan's 23 errors with some very basic ones. In the Year 4 exam Brenda's errors went down to 7 and Susan's to 10 but these were more adult-type misspellings that looked more like slips. The essay failures took resits and all passed with at least B grades.

Pauline was another non-identified dyslexic who gained entry to higher education by dint of hard work and perseverance. She learned her spellings by rote and got friends to proof-read her coursework. In exams she selected vocabulary she knew she could spell and of course this meant she had less time to write a complete answer so she would underperform in exams but gain A grades for coursework. She was a very bright student and an excellent potential teacher. In addition to this group of dyslexics there were also about 10 per cent of the cohorts who had significant spelling and/or handwriting problems without necessarily ever having had reading problems. Their difficulties became apparent when writing at speed and using specialised or new terminology – 'jargon'. Again they seemed to have few strategies available other than proof-reading and rote learning and their standard of work was depressed. This hidden sub-group of able dyslexics would have their counterparts in schools whose needs were never considered because they could read.

Interventions with bright adult dyslexics

Seventy-five students were due to attend the Learning Difficulties course each Thursday (108 contact hours) and there was only one specialist tutor. The interventions took place at three levels. The first was 'corrective and developmental' directly on the spelling problems, the second was in the reorganisation of the pedagogy, and the third was to provide as far as possible all the course topics in the form of study guides, lecture notes and study packs; the basic Year 4 Learning Difficulties curriculum remained the same, i.e. it took an inclusive approach, which they could model in schools.

The corrective and developmental spelling interventions

Spelling can be seen to be a *core problem* in dyslexia that would appear to be more fundamental than reading. Reading in a sense is parasitic upon spelling rather than the other way round. An analysis of student spelling errors on the exam papers showed that there were several basic error types related to base words, roots and prefixes plus problems with the four suffixing rules (in English). Most misspelling occurred at syllable boundaries and this suggested that it was syllable structure and syllable rules that should be the focus of interventions.

The syllable and affixing strategies were then taught to the students together with a writing strategy as follows:

Twelve cognitive process strategies for spelling
Most misspellings occur in relation to one letter in a word or one letter in different parts or syllables in a word. Thus the cognitive process approach focuses all the attention on the area of error to identify and correct it. This attention gives it a higher profile in the memory and at first sounds warning bells as the spelling approaches and then the strategies can be applied. After a while the pupil experiences the heightened awareness and writes through the word giving the correct spelling. Eventually the correct motor programme is automatically elicited on every occasion. Thus it is essential that all corrections are written in FULL CURSIVE to help establish the automatic motor programme. The corrective strategies are:-

1. Articulation – clear, correct speech, 'chimney' not 'chimley'
2. Over articulation – parli(a)ment, gover(n)ment
3. Cue articulation – say it incorrectly, Wed-nes-day
4. Syllabification – break it down into syllables, mis-de-mean-our
5. Phonics – try to get a comprehensible skeleton of the word's sound
6. Origin – the word's root in another language may give clues
7. Rule – the l-f-s rule and 'i before e except after c' can help
8. Linguistics – syllable structure and affixing rules govern most words
9. Family – bomb, bombing, bombardier, bombardment give clues
10. Meaning – to pare or part helps spell separate correctly
11. Analogy – 'it is like braggart' helps spell braggadocio
12. Funnies – 'cess pit' helped me to remember how to spell necessary (Montgomery 1997a, b; 2000a, b).

The first six strategies are more appropriate to beginners who are just mastering phonics levels, 'funnies' suit all.

45

The protocol to correct misspellings

- The pupil proof-reads to try to identify misspellings
- Teacher also checks for errors and makes a list
- Pupil selects with the teacher TWO spellings to work on
- The more advanced pupil looks up the words in the dictionary
- The dictionary gives clues to meaning and origin as well as spelling
- Pupil puts a ring round the area of error – the wrong letter or omission
- Teacher and pupil discuss two strategies from the list for dealing with ONE error
- Pupil applies the strategies and checks to see if they have been successful using Simultaneous Oral Spelling (SOS), writing the word three times
- Pupil then does the same with the next error and reports to the teacher on progress
- A day or two later the teacher asks the pupil to spell both of the words orally as a check
- If they are correct two more can be tackled. After a while pupils will be able to manage the process themselves.

The 12 strategies were evolved with 900 teachers and 800 undergraduates to find out the range that good spellers use. Each time the 12 came out almost in complete form. This format has now been tested on thousands of good spellers with the same results and Parrant (1989) tested them in a junior school class-room. She found that in comparison with a control class's spelling all her pupils' spelling improved significantly as well as that of those on the SEN reg-ister. Morey (2001) and a range of others on the MA SpLD and MA SEN dis-tance learning programmes since 1993 have found that the techniques were particularly appealing to bright dyslexics who made rapid progress because they especially enjoyed the challenge and autonomy it gave them and removed them from that state of 'learned helplessness'.

Changing teaching for learning in ITT – the new model

The traditional pattern of teaching in ITT (Initial Teacher Training) was to give lectures followed by seminars and occasional workshops and tutorials. A weekly lecture gave a 'Cook's tour' of the general topic. In the seminars research papers were considered in relation to practice. All students were enabled to read them and anyone might be selected within their groups of 12–15 to draw out the main points from memory first. Those who had not read the paper were asked to withdraw and go and do so. The second part of the seminar was a 'brainstorm' to put in some structure and further detail. The final section involved the students now referring to their notes, working over the paper to explain its main ideas and themes, to clarify and bring forward relevant criti-cisms, and draw out applications to and reflections on their own practice.

In these ways we were trying to teach them that if they could not explain to someone else what they had been reading then they really did not know or understand it. Similarly, brainstorming and concept mapping, reading for the main and subordinate points, and flow charting of themes, chapters and articles would be study skills strategies they could use with their pupils.

The theoretical model on which the programme was based was that underlying all teaching and learning at any level there were two primary objectives:

- to enable students and pupils to think efficiently, and
- to enable them to communicate those thoughts succinctly (Montgomery 1981b).

Learning any subject knowledge and skills was to be subordinate to these higher order processes. It was argued that teaching for the development of intellectual skills had been mainly incidental to teaching curriculum subjects and this deprived the pupils, and later the students, of the ability to learn how to learn more. If the student teachers were to be able to teach their pupils to learn how to learn then they would need to go through similar processes at their own level.

In the new model it was noticeable that students developed different strategies to enable them to cope. Some began to organise themselves into study groups of twos and threes to hold a briefing meeting before the actual seminar, others undertook shared and paired reading, stopping at intervals to discuss what they had read. Some took turns to be the key reader of a paper then brief the others on the main ideas before they undertook the reading themselves. In the seminar they had the opportunity to 'microteach' sections of the paper and be challenged. All these 'talking techniques' were particularly essential for dyslexic learners as part of a 'talking curriculum' in which to ground their literacy skills. We had been telling the student teachers about these methods and now they had the opportunity to experience and evaluate them.

An example day ran as follows:

One hour lecture – giving an outline of concepts, theories and research in a defined area. Topic: 'What makes a good test?' For example, norming, standardisation, reliability and validity.

One and a half hour practical workshop – set up by the tutor but not supervised. For example, one early task was to select one of the tests and to determine according to the criteria given in the lecture whether or not it was a good test.

One and a half hour seminar – the first half hour was a debriefing session on the workshop. This was followed by a seminar for half the tutorial group on alternate weeks so that the numbers were kept down to 12–15 to enable a proper discussion to take place.

At the beginning and end of the day tutors offered individual and group **tutorials** and held their own weekly briefing/planning meeting. The collaborative groups and positive supportive learning environment in which students' ideas were valued provided an appropriate climate for the encouragement of creativity and **motivation to learn** (Deci 1988; de Alencar 1999).

First there were some interesting learning problems. The workshop described was introduced early in the course because it could bring these problems to light. Many students left the workshop rooms after twenty minutes or so, flipping through the tests. At the debriefing session when they were given back their summary reports with D and C grades there was an outcry. Tutors were blamed for not explaining properly what had to be done and a lot of heat was generated. It was then explained to them again how they should have applied the information given in the lecture and about how to judge standardisation, reliability and validity to determine if the test was a 'good' one. They were very unhappy but were allowed to 'negotiate' the opportunity to repeat the whole workshop again the following week. They needed an opportunity to gain mastery of the situation and to prove to us we had only to explain things properly for them to be able to achieve. In the event it was the best thing we could have done. They all did the task the following week extremely well with all grades in the B+ to A range. What was more important was the strong, positive effect it had on their motivation for the rest of the term. They arrived at lectures before time, sat poised ready to make notes and catch the tiniest clue to what 'games' we would get up to next. They remained 'on alert' all day and often spent five hours at a time on the seminar preparations, especially when we posed them as a problem, such as giving them an empty flow chart of a research paper to fill in. When it came to the final examinations they reported that they had a much more satisfying time with their revision because they could remember so much of the work on which they had done the problem solving, study skills and collaborative learning. Many for the first time enjoyed an exam!

The pedagogy underlying the applied course

People are born according to Kelly (1955) as investigative problem solvers and it was argued that student learners would also be motivated by a real problem solving approach – and so it proved.

In the course of these developments a series of six teaching strategies called **cognitive process pedagogies** were defined to help them see the range of possibilities (Montgomery 1990, 1996, 1998). These were later set in the context of critical thinking theory (Resnick 1989 and Paul 1990) and redefined as part of the 'cognitive curriculum' for all learners (Montgomery 2000a).

Cognitive curriculum

This consisted of:

- cognitively challenging questioning
- deliberate teaching of thinking skills and protocols
- creativity training
- developmental positive cognitive intervention
- reflective teaching and learning
- cognitive process teaching strategies, e.g.:
    games and simulations
    investigative problem solving
    cognitive study skills
    collaborative learning
    language experience methods
    experiential learning

The study guides

Booklets had been compiled for inservice training on a range of topics and thus it was an easy matter to develop more and make these available for a small sum to the students as readers and study guides. All the articles for seminars were in folders in the library and copyright clearance was obtained for multiple copies. Study packs were assembled for the workshops and in the later sections the students themselves did the teaching and preparation as we handed the work and responsibility over to them as the course neared its conclusion. There was no formal coursework requirement in Year 4 but to our relief the examination results were transformed. Instead of the bell-shaped curve with one or two 'firsts', there was a 'negative skew' with 17 first class grades, six more very close and all the rest more or less evenly divided between 2.1 and 2.2 grades. An understanding external examiner supported our arguments about quality in teaching and learning and the grades were allowed to stand. The three dyslexics outshone their previous performance, two gained firsts and the other a 2.1.

To summarise this section on helping bright adult dyslexics, it can be seen that while their spelling errors were addressed they needed the support of a talking and cognitive curriculum in collaborative pairs and groups; their note taking was supported by having study books and guides written especially for them around the course topics – as they read them they said they could hear the lecturer's voice.

How to identify dyslexia in the early years

In the 1970s longitudinal studies were undertaken to identify factors which would predict dyslexia and the results have been confirmed by later studies. The two best predictors are: a) failure to develop symbol–sound correspondence by the methods used in ordinary classrooms, and, b) an inability to name or say the sounds of the letters of the alphabet (Liberman 1973; Golinkoff 1978). Dyslexics who finally do crack the alphabetic code do so late and then appear to become stuck at about an eight year old level of skill. Chall's (1967) research had already shown that meaning emphasis methods disadvantaged dyslexics more than phonics approaches but neither were effective with a core of about 1 per cent and this has been upheld in later studies (Clay 1979, 1992; Hurry *et al.* 1996).

The first question that arises for the teacher and researcher is how does the failure to acquire the alphabetic principle manifest itself? In studies of thousands of children's work in reading and writing the most obvious and easy record of their problems can be found in their marks on paper (Montgomery 1997a). The following sample of pupils' writing illustrates the differences between normal literacy development and that of dyslexics. The pupils are asked to write their news or a story without any help from the teacher using any spelling skills they can muster. In identification terms there is an unexpected decrement between the child's apparent higher ability and the performance on literacy tasks. This decrement widens as the child grows older unless action is taken.

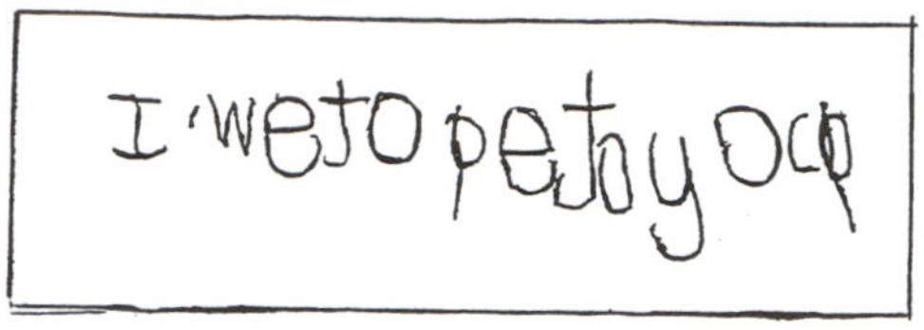

'I went to bed.' Yacob, 5 years 2 months

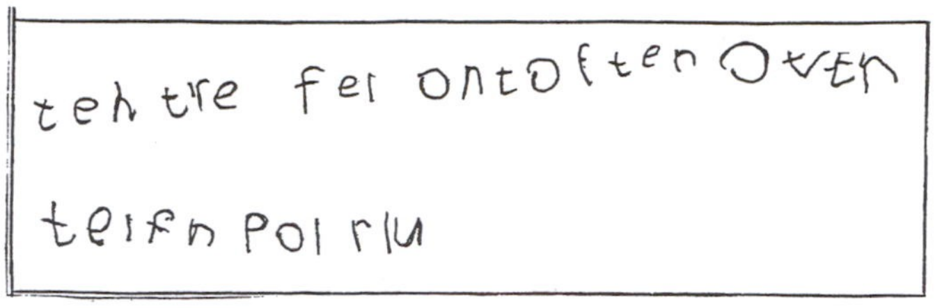

'The tree fell on top of the telephone pole wire.' William, 5 years 2 months

'She is in bed. She is sick. She has chickenpox.' Kelly B, 5 years 1 month

Figure 3.1a Writing of non-dyslexic 5 year olds after three weeks in school

```
wuns a pon tyme tcer as a
crisms fariy
```

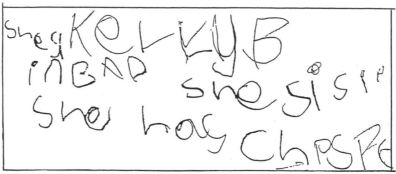

'Once upon a time there was a Christmas fairy.'

Figure 3.1b Emma K, 5 years 2 months

Emma K had a teacher who was encouraging developmental writing and who also used copy writing and tracing techniques. Emma's work was the most advanced in the class and the above was her first attempt at free writing.

The writing of the five year olds in Figure 3.1 shows that they have 'cracked' the alphabetic code and that they will not become dyslexic.

In Figure 3.2 Annette is five years 11 months and wrote the piece on woodland animals in 10 minutes. She had a memory span of 11 digits (average span at six years is about 4 items so it is likely we are seeing some photographic recall here. Her IQ score was reported to be above 145).

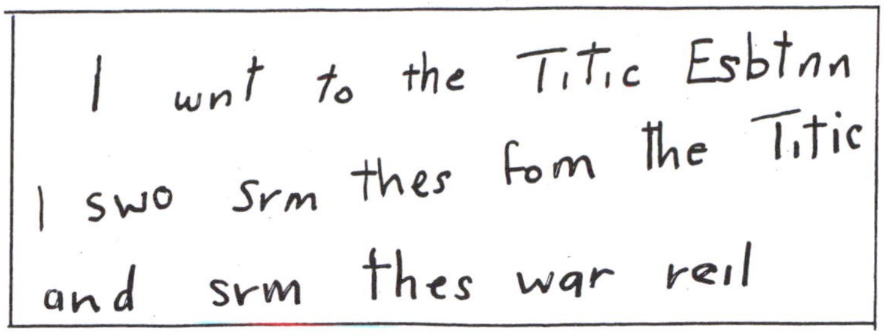

I wnt to the Titic Esbtnn
I swo srm thes fom the Titic
and srm thes war reil

'I went to the Titanic exhibition and saw some things from the Titanic and some things were real.'

Maria, 5 years 10 months. Began reading at 4 years. Good reader now, highly verbal, wide vocabulary. (⅓ size)

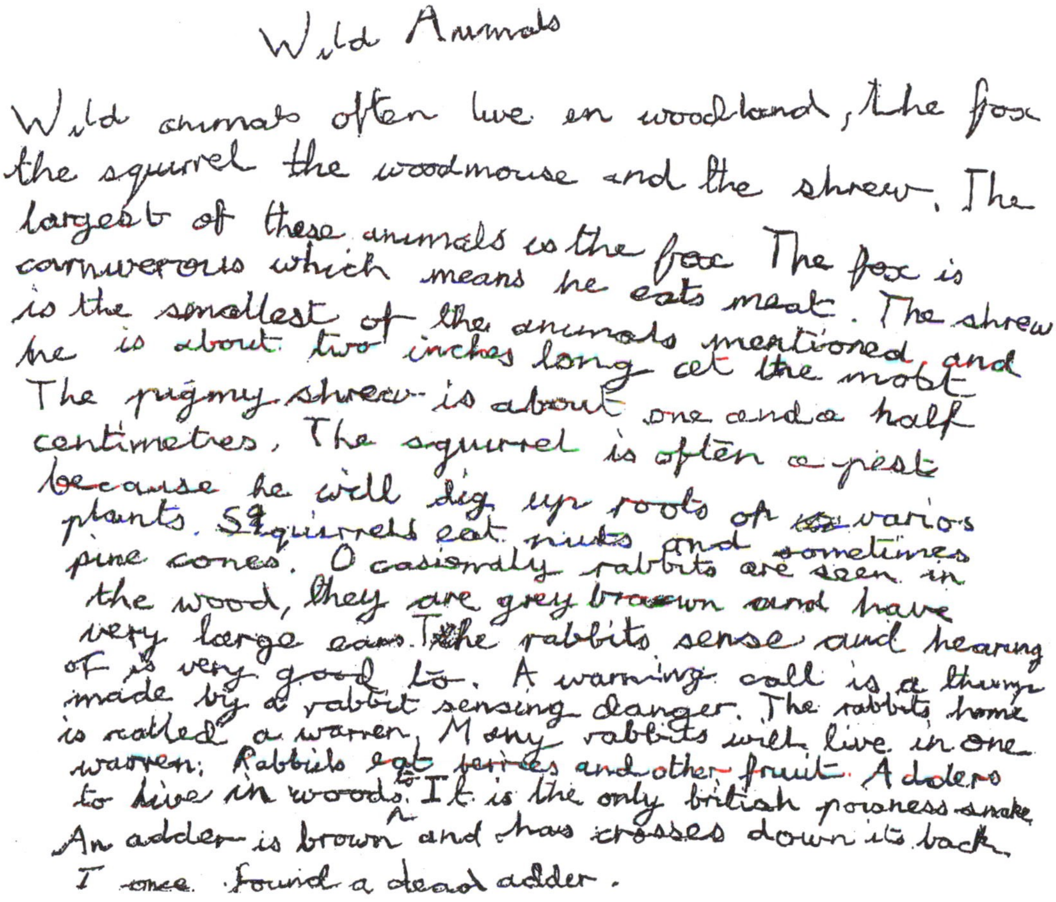

Wild Animals

Wild animals often live in woodland, the fox the squirrel the woodmouse and the shrew. The largest of these animals is the fox The fox is carniverous which means he eats meat. The shrew is the smallest of the animals mentioned, and he is about two inches long cet the most The pigmy shrew is about one and a half centimetres. The squirrel is often a pest because he will dig up roots of various plants. Squirrels eat nuts and pine cones. Ocasionally rabbits are seen in the wood, they are grey brown and have very large ears. The rabbits sense and hearing of is very good to. A warning call is a thump made by a rabbit sensing danger. The rabbits home is called a warren. Many rabbits will live in one warren. Rabbits eat berries and other fruit. Adders to live in woods. It is the only british poiness snake An adder is brown and has crosses down its back. I once found a dead adder.

Annette, 5 years 11 months (⅓ size)

Figure 3.2   The spelling of two gifted pupils

Maria (Figure 3.2) taught herself to read at four years old and is bilingual in German and English. She is a highly skilled verbaliser with a very good vocabulary. However, we can see here that she has a distinct problem with spelling in comparison with reading and is a candidate for later dysorthographic difficulties unless she is given some remedial help at this early stage.

Stephen and Caroline (Figure 3.3) have not cracked the alphabetic code

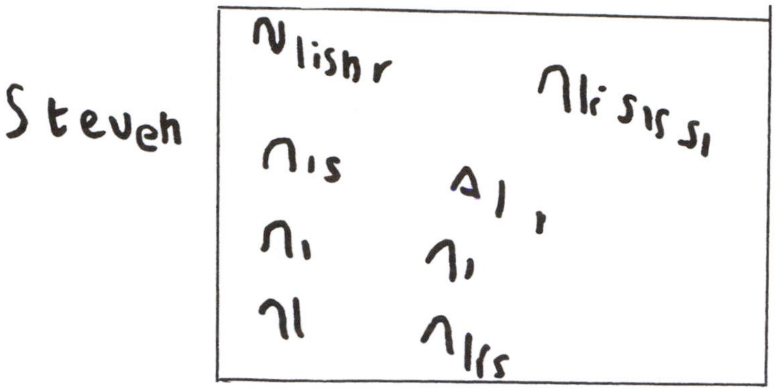

Steven, 6 years 6 months (½ size)

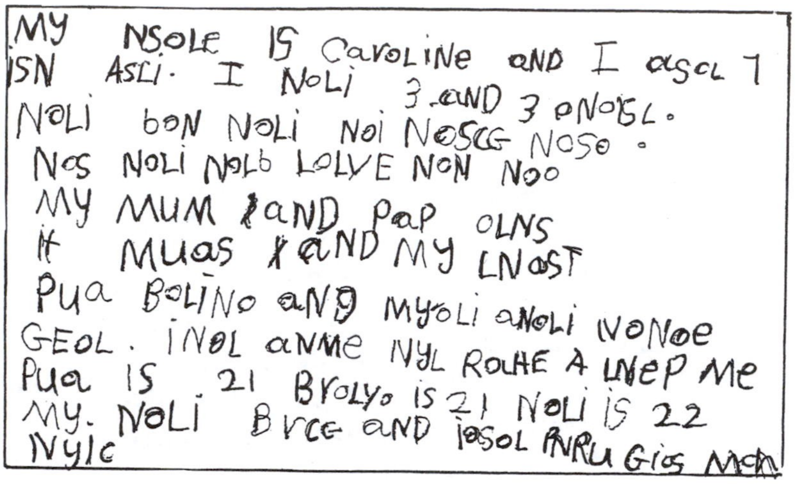

Caroline, 7 years (½ size)

'My name is Caroline and I am 7 years old. I have 3 brothers and 3 sisters. Some of them live at home and some of them do not. My mum and dad live at home and so do my goldfish. Paul, Breda and Mark still live at home. They are a lot older than me. Paul is 21, Breda is 21 and Mark is 22. My other brothers and sisters are a lot older than them.'

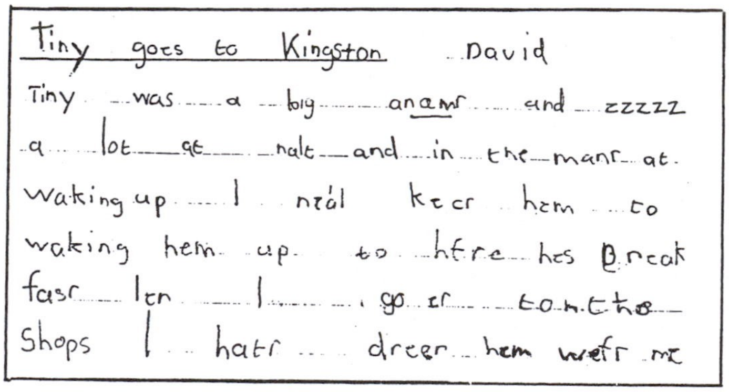

David, 8 years (½ size)

'Tiny was a big animal and slept a lot at night and in the morning I have to keep waking him up. I have to keep waking him up to have his breakfast. When I go to the shops I have to drag him with me . . .'

Figure 3.3   Writing of able dyslexic pupils across the age range

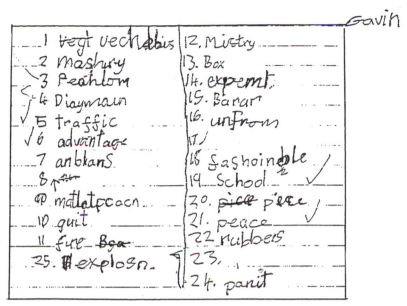

Gavin, 10 years (½ size)

A spelling test. Item 13 was the word 'parcel'

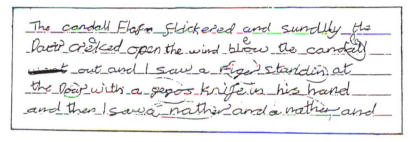

Kevin, 14 years (½ size)

'The candle flame flickered and suddenly the door creaked open. The wind blew the candle out and I saw a figure standing at the door with a gigantic knife in his hand and then I saw another and another and . . .'

Stephen's writing after 6 × 20 minutes of TRTS – cursive writing was not permitted by his school. (½ size)

Figure 3.3 (continued)

although some whole word knowledge can be seen in Caroline's writing. David has just begun to 'crack the code' and Gavin and Kevin have succeeded but they are five and nine years delayed. Gavin and Kevin also have a mild handwriting coordination problem as well as the dyslexia. Gavin has an IQ above 140 and is showing emotional and behavioural difficulties during any literacy activities, singing and shouting and swaying about on one leg of his chair.

For policymakers what we can glean from these examples is that complex tests for dyslexia are not necessarily required and that a teacher with a short course of training can do the analysis. Looking at the examples we can see dyslexics stuck in Frith's (1985) logographic stage, others in the alphabetic stage and some halfway through the orthographic stage. This suggests we need three levels of intervention but probably not three different methods. First the origin of the difficulties needs to be identified, as Kokot has pointed out in Chapter one.

What is the origin of dyslexic difficulties?

The origin of a difficulty to a large extent defines the intervention that is given to remediate it and the history of dyslexia is littered with out of date and irrelevant or plainly wrong theories. Traditional teaching wisdom was that supplying the dyslexic with phonics training would solve the problem and this was and still is the main remedial provision, to which is now added a multisensory dimension. Thus it was possible to find pupils in dyslexia centres who were failures by the usual method, failed in the extra reading and phonics tuition, failed in the remedial withdrawal multisensory phonics setting: three times failures. This led me to conclude that multisensory phonics teaching was necessary but not sufficient for the dyslexic to develop basic literacy skills. If the alphabet was the key then it was a total mystery that, for example, a pupil with an IQ of over 150 could not learn the names and sounds of 26 letters of the alphabet when he or she could at the age of five discuss quasars and planetary motion. It could not be a memory problem though that was and is a popular theory.

The alphabet apparently has only been invented once and by the Phoenicians, who were maritime traders. The key turned when it was learnt that the Phoenicians spoke a Semitic consonantal language made up of 22 letters! It must be the consonants that are crucial in linking sound and symbol. Both sound and symbol are, according to researchers such as Ehri (1980), abstract perceptual units that change and vary within words, making them difficult to tag. But every one of them has a distinct and concrete pattern of feel in the mouth so that when we say 'l' or 't' or 'k' we can feel the differences and learn to associate this with the sound and symbol as we articulate for reading and spelling. Thus if dyslexics had an articulatory awareness problem they would not be able to use this feel pattern and would become very confused by the alphabet's arbitrary symbols. It would make any list learning of arbitrary units difficult, such as the names of the alphabet, left and right, 'b' and 'd', days of the week, months of the year, tables, digit span and so on. From this it became obvious how Edith Norrie had taught herself to read; she had cracked the code using an articulatory phonics method. Dyslexics who learn to read and spell eventually do so too. It is possible that their articulatory awareness develops late or there is a lag or temporary block in development, which seemingly clears up at about eight years of age.

In a series of case analyses and experiments the articulation awareness (AA) hypothesis was developed and tested (Montgomery 1981, 1990, 1997a) with the following results:

Table 3.1   To Show Articulation Awareness (AA) and Phonological Segmentation (PS) Mean Scores in Controls and Dyslexics

	Chron. Age	WISC Full	R. Age	S. Age	PS (10)	AA (10)	M:F
HIGHLY ABLE Ds N =30	10.2	126.8	8.5	8.5	8.0	5.3	5:1
DYSLEXICS N = 288	10.1	109.6	7.8	7.4	7.8	5.2	5:1
CONTROLS N = 94	8.05	108.7	8.7	8.7	8.7	8.2	1:1

As can be seen the now popular theory of phonological processing difficulties (Vellutino 1979, 1987) was also put to the test using phonological segmentation (PS) items (for example, saying stimulus words without their initial sounds). AA was tested by getting pupils to identify articulatory features such as mouth open or closed, teeth open or closed and where the tip of the tongue was touching or its position in the mouth in relation to 10 key initial sounds and two dummy items. The results were interesting, as all the dyslexics were on a remedial programme of some kind and were on average 10 years old, they were overcoming any articulation awareness problems they may have had but the AA score can be seen to be significantly depressed in comparison with the younger controls. PS scores in dyslexics appear to be at a level consistent with their spelling. This suggests that phonological difficulties are more a result of failing to learn to spell rather than a cause of dyslexia itself with segmentation a sub-skill of spelling.

There would also appear to be neurological support for an articulation awareness hypothesis in the work of Geschwind (1979), who associated dyslexia with problems in the angular gyrus, where articulatory information is linked to the auditory and visual. We can hypothesise that in some pupils the delay is temporary and clears up by itself, in others direct articulatory awareness training is required, in some it may be part of a more fundamental set of difficulties involving deeper and broader areas of the cortex. In the sample discussed this was 30 per cent, where the literacy difficulties were associated with handwriting coordination difficulties or dysgraphia. Some also had gross motor coordination problems or dyspraxia.

An articulatory training procedure was devised called Multisensory Mouth Training and was incorporated into the specialist remedial programme called Teaching Reading Through Spelling (TRTS; Cowdery *et al.* 1984, 1994). Some results were spectacular with one pupil gaining two years in reading and spelling in a fortnight. The policy implication to be derived from this is that to help learners crack the code all Reception Year teachers need to be trained to use Multisensory Mouth Training in association with the other developmental strategies they normally use. In AA screening at five years and one month, only a handful of 200 children had AA problems.

Another feature of the results was that when the able pupils were separated out (at least one WISC score over 130) the highly able were seen to have much higher literacy scores than the other dyslexics. In policy terms this leads to them being referred later, if at all, although their needs are equally great. Thus IQ scores must be included as a consideration in any referral procedure. The records showed that most of the more able group were referred because they were developing EBD (emotional and behavioural difficulties).

Girls, and particularly able girls in the same study (Table 3.1) who had learned to copy neatly, were at risk of being excluded from specialist help. Girls as a group were referred at least a year later than boys and in a lower ratio than the national average of 4:1 (Rutter *et al.* 1970). More recently Shaywitz (1995) has reported the ratio difference was gender biased and maintained that it was closer to 1:1.

Research by Tallal (1994) has found that dyslexics are slower than controls at processing auditory information, which may have implications for learning to read. However, the slow processing may be a result rather than a cause of dyslexia, as identification of dyslexia does not occur until the students are at least nine or ten years old. Similar problems exist for the eye movement studies. If, however, we focus upon developing spelling, speed of auditory processing and eye movement problems need not be involved. Beginners can be seen mouthing and repeating the initial sound such as 'l-l-l-look' as they write the letter.

The fact that the human ear cannot hear the separate sounds in a syllable because they are shingled on top of each other (Liberman and Shankweiler *et al.* 1967) means that the only concrete cues are articulatory ones and the initial sounds' greater energy. This is why an onset and rime strategy for reading should accompany an articulation awareness training for spelling. It is also evident in the writing of beginners who have just begun to crack the code, for example, 'I wt t bd' (I went to bed); it shows that syllable structure needs to be directly taught once spelling begins to develop.

Effective remedial teaching programmes for dyslexics

For older dyslexics who have not fully cracked the code a specialist remedial programme which is multisensory, including Multisensory Mouth Training, and APSL (Alphabetic-Phonic-Syllabic-Linguistic) is needed to enable them to catch up with peers and fill in those elements which over the three to five years they have missed.

The most effective approach is a programme that gives multisensory training linking reading, writing and spelling developed at the Scottish Rites Hospital by Orton *et al.* (1940), and Gillingham and Stillman (1956). It was from there that

Kathleen Hickey, Beve Hornsby and others learned of it and Hickey anglicised and developed it in the UK (Hickey 1977; 2nd edition by Augur and Briggs 1991). Hickey set up the Dyslexia Institute at Staines in Surrey; her programme (DILP – Dyslexia Institute Language Programme) is widely used. Hornsby became Head of the Word Blind Institute at Bart's Hospital and later set up her own Dyslexia Teaching Centre in Wandsworth. She wrote her variant of the Scottish Rites programme with a phonic linguistic emphasis called Alpha to Omega (Hornsby and Shear 1975, 1994).

At Kingston in Surrey, Cowdery, Morse and Prince-Bruce were trained by Hickey and went on to develop their own version of the Gillingham-Stillman-Hickey programme which is called Teaching Reading Through Spelling (TRTS) and is also a multisensory Alphabetic-Phonic-Syllabic-Linguistic programme (Cowdery *et al.* 1983–1987, 1994). We wrote it down as an inservice development project.

In the tables set out below, comparisons can be made of the effectiveness of different programmes over a one year span by looking at the calculations of actual reading and spelling progress. Progress of one year or less cannot be judged as remedial success although it may launch a pupil into literacy after a period of no progress. Remediation should seek to bring the pupils' scores at least up to that of peers matched for age, preferably within two years. The more severe the dyslexia the greater the initial gains will be (the 'catapult' effect). It is then that progress often stops at about the eight year old level and it is at this point that bright dyslexics can be driven mad and refuse to participate in the overlearning training needed for automatisation. For them it is now very important to switch to the more informal and autonomous Cognitive Process Strategies.

Table 3.2 The Relative Effectiveness of Different APSL Programmes in One Year

APSL	R. Progress	S. Progress	Researcher	Numbers
A to O	1.93	1.95	Hornsby *et al.* (1990)	N=107
TRTS	2.45	2.01	Montgomery (1993)	N=38
TRTS	3.31	1.85	Webb (2000)	N=12
(H and A to O)	1.21	0.96	Ridehalgh (1999)	N=50

Table 3.3 The Relative Effectiveness of Non APSL Remedial Programmes in One Year

Programme	R. Progress	S. Progress	Researcher	Numbers
Non APSL	0.53	0.32	Hornsby *et al.* (1990)	N=?
Non APSL	1.06	0.16	Montgomery (1997a)	N=15
SME	0.69	0.65	Ridehalgh (1999)	N=50
SME	2.2	1.14	Webb (2000)*	N=12

(SME – Spelling Made Easy; Brand 1993)
* Webb used some TRTS method here in SME (ethics)

The results in the tables show the strong effect of the APSL programmes in remediating dyslexic difficulties based upon two lessons per week in matched pairs. The entries need some qualification in that in the use of the APSL programmes in Ridehalgh's research and in Webb's using TRTS, the lessons were shortened by the timetabling structure and this often caused the spelling pack work and the dictations to be omitted. Of course these are crucial components of the APSL structure.

According to Goulandris (1994), research shows that teaching a child how spelling patterns represent sound patterns improves eventual spelling *and* reading ability. Teaching phonological skills in isolation is less effective, as 'they must be explicitly linked to spelling patterns to effect improvement of literacy skills' (p. 413). The research of Hatcher and Hulme *et al.* (1994) showed that remedial instruction needed to forge alphabetic links in which the sounds in words and letters used to represent them in written language are explicitly taught.

Because of their detailed and complex nature specialist APSL remedial programmes cannot be taught within other lessons and by non-experts. They need to be taught in withdrawal sessions, preferably of 50 minutes' length to **matched pairs** of pupils at least twice a week (Ridehalgh 1999). It is not difficult to work out why the pairs teaching was more effective in relation to learning theory and metacognition. We all need thinking and mental rehearsal time – the too close attention and interaction between teacher and single learner does not always allow this. Another feature of the results is that the APSL approaches directed equally, but differently, to spelling and reading transfer to reading and promote it more than spelling. However, the reverse is not the case; approaches orientated to reading do not directly become transferred to spelling. In policy terms specialist intervention is required in Reception or Year One. Although some false positives may occur in identification they will easily be discovered and the literacy difficulties resolved. Although specialist intervention will involve additional tuition costs these will be counterbalanced by the savings in the long term. It will keep many out of units and special schools for the behaviourally disturbed and also out of prison (Alm *et al.* 2002). Double exceptionality can make literacy failure doubly distressing but an entrepreneur in a legitimate or criminal career can always pay for a clerk.

High ability and spelling difficulties in schools

If recovery to grade level can be achieved before entry to secondary schools this will ensure students can cope with the typical writing curriculum there. As they approach the later stages of secondary education they may need a top up course directed to spelling and study skills to help them cope with the examinations.

Highly able pupils may be dyslexic but mask this by having very good visual memories and so read at the level of age peers but have 'severe problems with spelling'. At the age of about eight years, as text vocabulary rapidly increases, they suddenly begin to fall behind. When their spelling is examined, however, it is clear that the problem could have been remedied earlier.

Recently, the British Dyslexia Association has suggested that the incidence of dyslexia in the UK is 10 per cent and this would seem to be borne out by my most recent studies of spelling samples of some whole school cohorts as set out in Table 3.4. But there could well be an even larger number who are suffering spelling difficulties alone. Silverman (1989), for example, found that 17 per cent of 1200 students were both gifted and learning disabled.

Table 3.4   A Comprehensive School Cohort, Year 7 (12 year olds) Showing Spelling Errors in a 20 Minute Essay in 2000

Standard Deviation SD Errors:	0–6/7	7–13	14–20	21–27	28–36	Total number
SET 1 (top)	17	8	1	(2)	–	28
SET 2	7	12	4	–	–	23
SET 3	10	5	(1)	(2)	–	18
SET 4	13	5	4 (2)	–	–	22
SET 5	5	5	3 (1)	–	(2)	15
TOTAL	52	35	13	4	2	106
%	49.10	33.02	12.26	3.77	1.89	100.00

(Sets 2, 3, 4 are parallel sets for ability)   SD: 6.65   Mean Errors: 8.76
Dyslexic: N = 10 (9.43%) (18+ errors and type, in brackets in table)
Proportion of 'good' spellers (0 – 1 S.D.) N = 52 (49%)
Proportion of 'poor' spellers (– 2 – 5 S.D.) N = 54 (51%)

These results show that some 50 per cent of pupils in this year group have substandard spelling skills for 12 year olds. Whereas an undergraduate might be expected to misspell three or four words before a tutor would express concern, we might expect that school pupils on average are allowed a bit more leeway. Here the cut off point used is one standard deviation with all borderline cases given special attention. Only different errors were counted in the scripts, not repeated misspelling of the same word. The pupils were writing about their favourite topic and so were on familiar ground and working within a known vocabulary as part of a handwriting speed test. More able students were grouped in Set 1 and were better spellers on the whole.

Two case example interventions with more able students follow, showing how they gain control of the process and how Cognitive Process Spelling Strategies (CPSS) could be taught to all children.

Case study of Maia by Karen Morey (2001), Head of Learning Support at a School in Nairobi

Maia was taken into the Learning Support programme at seven years one month, and at eight years eight months her spelling was 15 months behind and reading was four months behind the level where she was at the former age. She was a highly articulate child, in the high average range of ability, from a linguistically rich social background but was not making progress, especially with spelling. She was put on the first level of the Teaching Reading Though Spelling programme

(Cowdery and Montgomery *et al.* 1994) and given Multisensory Mouth Training as she seemed unaware of the feel of blends she was making. She received two 35 minute individual tutorials per week during the autumn term and at times made progress. She would then regress as she seemed unable to see the relevance of segmenting the sound for spelling. Onset and rime strategies did not work either unless she was interested. As an experiment, in the spring term of 2000, she was switched to the CPSS. Immediately there was an overwhelming change in the relationship between the teacher and the student. Maia began arriving at the lessons announcing which areas were giving her difficulty. This required some careful negotiation and rethinking on the part of the teacher who was using a structured programme and who had to decide whether to continue with any of this or involve herself fully in the latest concerns of Maia. By March 2000, although there were still problems with the spelling, Maia had become much more effective in the use of her literacy skills and there had been a dramatic improvement in her reading ability – it had jumped to five months above her chronological age. The spelling deficit had reduced from 15 months to 12 months. She had become reflective about her literacy work and interested in words and their construction, whereas before she had used mainly visual strategies and some phonics to no good effect.

Case study of Carl by Juliet Wraith (2001)

Carl was nine years eleven months old with a spelling age of eight years four months and had been diagnosed as 'moderately dyslexic' by an educational psychologist. Carl was a keen fan of Harry Potter and was given a dictation from one of the books to encourage his interest in proof-reading for the errors.

He found the following errors: monning (morning); itsalf (itself); bewiching (bewitching); foled (followed); terbern (turban).

He missed these errors: cristmas (Christmas); midde (middle); coverd (covered); sevulal (several); soled (solid); punshed (punished); thay (they).

Each lesson followed the format below:

Lesson 1
Christmas – Carl missed the 'h' in this word and said that he sometimes missed the 't' as well.
Cue articulation: we pronounced the word 'Christ mas'
Meaning: we talked about the fact that Christmas is all about Jesus i.e. Christ. We looked up 'mass' in the dictionary and discovered it can mean a meal or a body and that at Christmas we have a big meal to celebrate that Jesus came to earth in a human body. Carl had never realised that the word 'Christ' was in Christmas. Funny: as soon as I spelt this word correctly for him Carl said 'Oh look, my brother's name'. He has a brother called 'Chris' whose name he can spell quite happily so it really helped him to remember that the name Chris is in 'Christmas'. Simultaneous oral spelling (SOS): he found it quite hard to make himself use cursive writing at first but said it got a lot easier as he repeated the word. He also found it easier to remember the spelling if he shut his eyes.

Followed – Carl spelt this as 'foled'

Syllabification: He needed help to see how this word can be broken down into syllables then he spotted the word 'low'

Analogy: he was able to think of a rhyming word for 'foll': 'doll'. As soon as past tense was mentioned he remembered he needed an 'ed' ending.

SOS (Simultaneous Oral Spelling)

Lesson 2

Carl was able to spell both 'Christmas' and 'followed'; without difficulty, he just needed to be reminded that Christmas should have a capital letter. In the lesson 'monning' and 'coverd' were tackled and so on.

At the end of the six sessions Carl redid the Harry Potter dictation. The writing was much more joined than on the first occasion and all the 12 target words were spelt correctly. Initially he resorted to his incorrect spellings of 'covered' and 'punished' but in both cases he immediately realised his error and self corrected; he was hesitant over 'several' but after some thought wrote it correctly. At first he wrote 'terban' but immediately corrected it to 'turban'.

These mini lessons took place over a period of only two weeks and throughout them it was interesting to see Carl becoming far more involved in the process of selecting strategies and also becoming more conscious of the way in which words are made up. He became particularly adept at recognising syllables and found cue articulation and funny ways of remembering things most memorable. His class teacher has noted an improvement in his written work and has observed him using the strategies on a wider scale than in the tutorials. The corrected spellings have stayed corrected.

Summary and conclusions

In the majority of cases dyslexia is associated with verbal rather than visual processing difficulties. Contrary to general belief it is more than a reading difficulty, at its core is a severe spelling difficulty. In cases where the condition is not pervasive and complex, it is possibly the result of a developmental delay which can be remedied in Reception class so that the reading and spelling difficulties do not have the opportunity to arise. It would appear that many gifted children with this learning difficulty eventually overcome the problem by themselves but the delays to literacy development can be very damaging educationally. Most do learn to read satisfactorily and some never have any reading difficulties at all. Their spelling, however, remains disabled unless they are given a specialist APSL multisensory programme. As soon as progress is made on this it will be necessary to switch to a cognitive set of strategies for spelling to maintain their interest and motivation. The strategies automatically transfer to reading.

At undergraduate and adult level most gifted dyslexics read and spell adequately for everyday purposes but as text becomes specialist and complex their difficulties are revealed. Their spelling becomes deficient and their understanding of the meaning and deep structure of text is slowed or deficient because of the years of missed practice. This means that there is frequently a serious mismatch between their potential ability and their academic attainments. Because the giftedness can mask the dyslexia the difficulties may not be identified and help given. The difficulty then remains as a disabling condition and the students are regarded as of just average ability and come to see themselves as such. They then miss out on many more challenging and appropriate learning and career opportunities.

The incidence of dyslexia across the ability range would appear to be about 10 per cent with at least two per cent of these being in the gifted category. However, it would seem that in the population at large most of the gifted and dyslexic students go unnoticed and undiagnosed and there are possibly 10–20 per cent more of them, a silent, sleeping majority.

References

Alm, J. and Kaufman, A. S. (2002) 'The Swedish WAIS-R factor structure and cognitive profiles for adults with dyslexia', *Journal of Learning Disabilities*, **35**(4), pp. 321–33.

Augur, J. and Briggs, S. (eds) (1991) *The Hickey Multisensory Language Course: 2nd Edition*. London: Whurr.

Bradley, L. and Bryant, P. (1985) *Children's Reading Problems*. Oxford: Blackwell.

Brand, V. (1993) *Spelling Made Easy 14th Edition*. Baldock: Egon.

Chall, J. (1967) *Learning to Read: The Great Debate*. New York: McGraw Hill.

Clay, M.M. (1979) *The Early Detection of Reading Difficulties*. London: Heinemann.

Clay, M.M. (1992) *By Different Paths to Common Outcomes*. Maine: Stenhouse Publications.

Cowdery, L.L., Montgomery, D., Morse, P. and Prince-Bruce, M. (1994) *Teaching Reading Through Spelling (TRTS)*. Clwyd: TRTS Publishing, Frondeg Hall.

Cowdery, L.L., McMahon, J., Montgomery, D. (ed.), Morse, P. and Prince-Bruce, M. (1983–87) *Teaching Reading Through Spelling (TRTS): Series 2A-2F*. Kingston: Learning Difficulties Research Project.

de Alencar, E.M.L.S. (1999) 'Developing creative abilities', Keynote presentation, European Council for High Ability Conference, Istanbul, August.

Deci, E. L. (1988) 'Motivating the gifted to learn', Presentation at the 10th International Conference on Education in Plovdiv, Bulgaria, October.

DES (1972) *Children with Specific Reading Difficulties: The Tizard Report*. London: HMSO.

DILP (1993) *Dyslexia Institute Language Programme*. Ed. Walker, J. and Brooks, L. Staines: Dyslexia Institute.

Ehri, L.C. (1980) 'The development of orthographic images' in U. Frith *Cognitive Processes in Spelling*. London: Academic Press, pp. 311–38.

Frith, U. (1985) 'Beneath the surface of developmental dyslexia' in K. Patterson and M. Coltheart (eds) *Surface Dyslexia*. London: Routledge & Kegan Paul, pp. 303–32.

Geschwind, N. (1979) 'Specialisations of the human brain', *Scientific American*, **241**(3), pp. 158–67.

Gillingham, A.M. and Stillman, B.U. (1956) *Remedial Training for Children with Specific Disability in Reading, Spelling and Penmanship*. New York: Sackett and Williams.

Golinkoff, R.M. (1978) 'Phonemic awareness skills and reading achievement' in F.B.

Murray and J. J. Pikulski (eds) *The Acquisition of Reading*. Baltimore: University Park Press.

Goulandris, N.K. (1994) 'Teaching spelling. Bridging theory and practice' in G. D. A. Brown and N.C. Ellis *Handbook of Spelling*. Chichester: John Wiley, pp. 407–23.

Hatcher, P., Hulme, C. and Ellis, A.W. (1994) 'Ameliorating early reading failure by integrating the teaching of reading and phonological skills: the phonological linkage hypothesis', *Child Development*, Vol. 69, pp. 41–57.

Hickey, K. (1977) *Dyslexia: A Language Training Course for Teachers and Learners*. (19 Woodside, Wimbledon, SW19.) 2nd edition by Augur and Briggs (1991).

HMI (2000) *The National Literacy Strategy: The Second Year*. London: The Stationery Office.

Hornsby, B. and Farrar, M. (1990) 'Some effects of a dyslexia centred teaching programme' in P.D. Pumfrey and C.D. Elliott (eds) *Children's Difficulties in Reading, Spelling and Handwriting*. London: Falmer Press, pp. 173–96.

Hornsby, B. and Shear, F. (1975) *Alpha to Omega: 2nd Ed.* London: Heinemann.

Hornsby, B. and Shear, F. (1994) *Alpha to Omega: 4th Ed.* Oxford: Heinemann.

Hurry, J., Sylva, K. and Riley, J. (1996) 'Evaluation of a focused literacy teaching programme in Reception and Year 1', *British Educational Research Journal*, **22**(5), pp. 617–30.

Kelly, G.A. (1955) *The Psychology of Personal Constructs*, Vols 1 and 2. New York: Norton.

Liberman, A.M., Shankweiler, D., Cooper, F.S. and Studdert-Kennedy, M. (1967) 'Perception and the speech code', *Psychological Review*, **74**(6), pp. 431–61.

Liberman, I.J. (1973) 'Segmentation of the spoken word and reading acquisition', *Bulletin of the Orton Society*, Vol. 23, pp. 365–77.

Montgomery, D. (1981a) 'Do dyslexics have difficulty accessing articulatory information?', *Psychological Research*, Vol. 43, pp. 235–43.

Montgomery, D. (1981b) 'A model of modern teaching: education comes of age', *School Psychology International*, Vol. 1, pp. 2–5.

Montgomery, D. (1984) 'Multisensory mouth training' in Montgomery, D. (ed.) *Teaching Reading Through Spelling: The Foundations of the Programme*. Kingston: Learning Difficulties Research Project (2nd Edition 1994), pp. 81–8.

Montgomery, D. (1990) *Children with Learning Difficulties*. London: Cassell.

Montgomery, D. (1996) *Educating the Able*. London: Cassell.

Montgomery, D. (1997a) *Spelling: Remedial Strategies*. London: Cassell.

Montgomery, D. (1997b) *Developmental Spelling: A Handbook*. Maldon: LDRP.

Montgomery, D. (1998) *Reversing Lower Attainment*. London: Fulton.

Montgomery, D. (ed.) (2000a) *Able Underachievers*. London: Whurr.

Montgomery, D. (2000b) 'Supporting the bright dyslexic in the ordinary classroom', *Educating Able Children*, Spring, Issue 4, pp. 23–32.

Morey, K. (2001) 'Casework with an able dyslexic in Nairobi', *Educating Able Children* **5**(1), pp. 27–30.

Norrie, E. (1917) Cited in the *Edith Norrie Letter Case Manual*. London: Helen Arkell Centre 1982.

Norrie, E. (1982) *The Edith Norrie Letter Case*. London: Word Blind Institute, 1946, Reprinted Helen Arkell Centre.

Orton, S.T., Gillingham, A.M. and Stillman, B.U. (1940) *Remedial Training for Children with Specific Disability in Reading, Spelling and Penmanship*. New York: Sackett and Williams.

Parrant, H. (1989) 'Investigation of the relative effects of cognitive process strategies'. Unpublished dissertation, Kingston Polytechnic.

Paul, R. (1990) 'Critical thinking', chapter 3 in *Critical Thinking Handbook*. Sonoma: Sonoma State University, Centre for Critical Thinking and Moral Critique.

Resnick, L.B. (1989) *Knowing, Learning and Instruction: Essays in Honour of Robert Glaser*. Hillsdale NJ: Lawrence-Erlbaum, pp. 1–23.

Ridehalgh, N. (1999) 'An evaluation of the relative effectiveness of three different remediation programmes', Unpublished MA SpLD dissertation. London: Middlesex University.

Rutter, M. L., Tizard, J. and Whitmore, K. (eds) (1970) *Education, Health and Behaviour*. London: Longman.

Shaywitz, S. E. (1995) 'Gender differences in reading disabilities revisited. Results from the Connecticut longitudinal study', *Journal of the American Medical Association*, Vol. 32.

Silverman, L. K. (1989) 'Invisible girls, invisible handicaps', *Roeper Review* **12**(1), pp. 37–42.

Tallal, P. (1994) 'New clue to cause of dyslexia seen in mishearing of fast sounds. An interview with Dr Tallal' by S. Blakeslee, *New York Times*, 16th August, p. 24.

Vellutino, F.R. (1979) *Dyslexia: Theory and Research*. London: M.I.T. Press.

Vellutino, F.R. (1987) 'Dyslexia', *Scientific American*, **256**(3), pp. 20–7.

Webb, M. (2000) 'An evaluation of SEN provision to improve literacy teaching at N School', Unpublished MA SpLD Dissertation. London: Middlesex University.

Wechsler, D. (1998) *WISC-111*. Oxford: The Psychological Corporation.

Wraith, J. (2001) 'Cognitive process strategies case study', Unpublished portfolio work, MA SpLD. London: Middlesex University.

4 Non-verbal learning difficulties
Diane Montgomery

Research into non-verbal learning difficulties (NLD) has a long history, like that of dyslexia. The term does not mean that the child cannot speak but that verbal skills superficially do not appear to be affected or causing problems. The difficulties lie primarily in skill acquisition and development and those abilities governed by the right hemisphere in 95 per cent of the population. The difficulties observed range from those who, left alone, get lost in Woolworth's; to the clumsy and disorganised; those whose handwriting is illegible; those with poor social skills; those who cannot sing in tune or draw and those with attentional, impulsive and hyperactive conditions, ADHD and ADD.

Patricia was a classic case. At 12 she was already a gifted linguist, and good at maths and English with a very good memory for facts and strong at all subjects requiring them. She was not so good at science, could not sing in tune and painted lollipop trees and stick persons in art with the skill of a five year old. Her movements were ungainly and twitchy and she was not at all good at sport or PE and was never chosen for a team. Her voice was a rather strangely pitched monotone and her social skills were somewhat limited. She showed a range of what are called 'soft neurological signs'. With her linguistic gifts she obtained a place to read languages at Oxford University. At first she became a teacher of modern foreign languages but, not surprisingly, had difficulty in class control and so was obliged to change career.

Not all children with NLD are as fortunate as Patricia and their difficulties can be more broadly based and more deeply disorganising and dysfunctional. Each pattern will be different. Characteristically the neurological impairment is more identifiable than in dyslexia, where most often no neurological difficulties are found except in complex cases and these are often where they are linked to coordination and/or language difficulties.

Neurological difficulties/disorders

The underlying condition in NLD is said to arise from problems in the myelination of particular tracts of nerve fibres in the brain (Rourke 1989). Thus although the brain functions they serve may be intact, the connections between them may be disrupted to a greater or lesser extent. Rourke argues that as there are larger areas of the right hemisphere given over to these fibres (white matter), complex connections are upset, as are pathways between areas and hemispheres and through to the cerebellum, which contains the 'programmes' for learned movements such as walking, swimming, writing, playing the piano and so on. When we learn a new skill the frontal regions of the cerebral cortex are heavily involved, where they are responsible for organising, controlling and learning new voluntary movements. While they are busy developing more and more efficient skilled movements for the required purpose, the cerebellum shadows this process and lays down the programme that will eventually allow us to operate the skill with minimal perceptual and cognitive input. This enables us, for example, to drive a car and talk at the same time. When we perform a complex reversing car movement we frequently have to suspend talk while we concentrate on the task. Doing two tasks at the same time is particularly problematic for children with NLD. It is also characteristic of infants; they have to develop proficiency in walking, for example, before they can do another task at the same time.

Duane (2002) considers Asperger Syndrome, Tourette Syndrome, Attention Deficit Hyperactivity Disorder (ADHD), Attention Deficit Disorder (ADD) and Epilepsy all to have characteristic neurological NLD patterns in common, as well as unique differences. In a sample of 200 10 year olds he found more boys affected in the ratio of 2 or 3 to 1 girl. He found 45 per cent of samples with ADHD had depression and when he discovered that 36 per cent of those with dyslexia had depression he began to suspect they had a gene for mood disorder in common. One third of those with reading disorder also had ADHD.

The history of the study of NLD has been dominated by neurology. In the early 1900s the term 'congenital maladroitness' was used and the condition came to be regarded as due to Minimal Brain Dysfunction (MBD). The term MBD according to Clements (1966) referred to children of near average, average, or above average intellectual capacity with certain learning and or behavioural disabilities ranging from mild to severe that are associated with deviations of function of the central nervous system. The characteristics are: short attention span; distractibility; hyperactivity or hypoactivity; impulsiveness; labile emotions; poor motor integration; deficits in perception of space, form, movement and time; disorders of language or symbol development, often delay in talking and learning to read and spell. Repeated drills appear to create learning but then fade; they know them today but not tomorrow.

In 1979 in the UK, Blythe and McGowan introduced the term Organic Brain Dysfunction (OBD) to describe a range of difficulties with neurological involvement and produced a lengthy questionnaire to help identify their cases. Some key questions were:

Is there any evidence of:

1. Headaches that are aggravated by stooping and/or physical stress?
2. Finding bright lights disturbing?
3. Finding noise disturbing with higher or lower than normal tolerance?
4. A tendency to rock at times of stress or anxiety?
5. Difficulties at time differentiating between right and left – says left and puts out right hand?
6. Handwriting deteriorates while writing, spelling ability deteriorates in the process?

They identified two 'perceptual problems' in OBD. The first was an increase in 'nystagmus'. (Close eyes and rapidly spin in a circle. Stop and open eyes and the world reels the opposite way. The eyes flick rapidly in the opposite direction as you recover.) Disturbance in the neural pathways makes this sensation worse and the child may jerk and fall over. Nystagmus is regarded as a 'soft' neurological sign. The second condition was a lack of 'yoking' of latent strabismus. This is an inability to ignore irrelevant stimuli within a configuration – a 'stimulus bound' difficulty and poor scanning ability that will interfere with visuo-motor integration (VMI) tasks such as in learning to write. Their remedial programme is called Reflex Developmental Patterning. The training returns the child developmentally to the stage where the reflexes failed to be inhibited, modified and transformed. They are also returned to stages of motor development that may have been missed in part or in whole. This gives the individual a second chance to correct an aberrant pattern and continue development. When they are put through regression in the physical dimension they are also seen to regress emotionally too and this allows unresolved conflicts to be ventilated (p. 83). The programme involves identifying the critical reflex not inhibited, purposely eliciting it to give the individual sufficient time and practice so that it can be inhibited. A continuously elicited reflex will gradually give a weaker and weaker response. This is the inhibition process at work. Blythe and McGowan (1979) report simultaneous gains in reading skills in their patients with dyslexia when RDP is given without any extra reading coaching. It can be seen how their programme might well be suitable for a sub-population with their pattern of OBD and dyslexia but not for dyslexics without OBD.

Neurological screening

A physician will be likely to carry out a clinical assessment for 'soft neurological signs' or MBD/ABD (Atypical Brain Development). This is not so far from what the observant teacher will also note and the following activities will be checked for speed and efficiency:

- hopping on one foot, toe-heel walking, balancing on one foot then the other
- skipping (ages 7–10)
- touching fingers with thumbs in sequence
- slapping knees alternately with palms and backs of hands – slow, fast, separately and together
- tapping index fingers on thumbs
- observing mirroring or spreading movements in tasks 1–5
- right–left confusion, touch left ear with right hand etc.; point to examiner's left ear etc.; stand feet together and turn right, turn left, left again etc.; turn only head or torso; lean to one side then the other (this latter is significant of immaturity if not mastered by seven years)
- eye tracking – watch examiner's finger, head still (observe quality of tracking, there are problems if jerky or flicks/jumps of eyes as the mid-line is crossed)
- writing to dictation on unlined paper, note reversals, confused letter sequences, laboured writing, spelling errors, and reckless speed, often associated with ADHD.

In school the teacher can also note drawing and copying and jigsaw completion. The child with visuo-motor difficulties will show difficulty with activities involving crossing the mid-line and in not making mirroring or contra-lateral movements while doing a task one-handed. If pencils or pieces to use are placed on the left the child with problems, for example, will reach for them with the left and then transfer them to the right. Balance on apparatus, and coordination in PE and in ball skills and games can all be observed for signs of immaturity and dyssynchrony.

As a rough indicator of ability and/or visuo-motor skill the 'Draw a Person Test' (Harris 1963) can be used as part of everyday classroom activities up until about the age of 10 years to give some indication of potential problems. At five, holding a pencil with the full fist rather than between thumb and fingers can be considered immature. When such delays and immaturities are observed, or the persistence of them and reflex movements beyond the standard periods, then remedial intervention is recommended. Blythe and McGowan (1979) address the reflexes, Laszlo *et al.* (1988) the proprioceptive feedback and Kokot (Chapter one) the vestibular system.

The term Atypical Brain Development (ABD) was proposed for wider use when referring to children's difficulties by Kaplan (2000). She argued that the disease model presented by MBD and OBD does not fit well with developmental problems. In ABD the 'atypical' emphasises and can include areas of excellence; it can include sub-types and is not a unitary condition; there is no evidence of brain trauma and it is not pejorative.

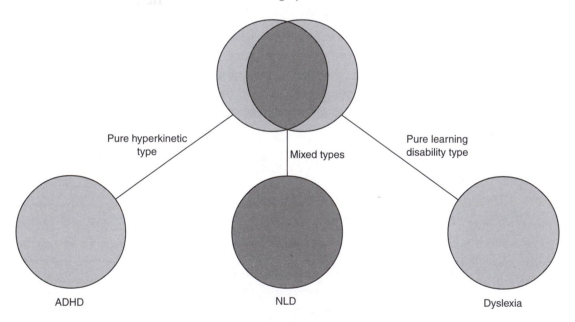

Figure 4.1 Venn diagram to show patterns of overlapping conditions in and between NLD and other conditions

There are a number of patterns of NLD that can cause pupils in school to underfunction, despite having recognisable gifts and talents in other areas. It is the disability which gets focused upon and masks the talents. If no supportive help is given and the child becomes the subject of bullying then there is loss of self esteem and motivation. Because the difficulties only affect 'non academic' school subjects then it may not be deemed important enough to give support and serious underfunctioning may be missed. However, they may overlap with verbal learning difficulties such as dyslexia (see Figure 4.1).

Physical impairment from brain injury

It is important before investigating dysfunctional difficulties to look briefly at physical impairment and giftedness. Nowadays it is common for children with a physical impairment, for example limbless, very small in stature, paraplegic or with disabling medical conditions to be educated in mainstream schools with assistance from trained staff with their welfare and mobility. While they can function at their intellectual level with minimal support and are expected to do so, the same is not true if they are immobile and/or with impaired speech and they are treated as intellectually limited as well. Gifted children with profound physical disabilities desperately need the intellectual challenge of mainstream and gifted education, which it is almost impossible for them to obtain in a special school setting.

Joey was in a large hospital for the mentally handicapped before the doors were opened. He had Cerebral Palsy as a result of severe brain damage at birth. He was strapped into a wheelchair and occupied a corner of the room where he could see all that was going on and greet everybody as they arrived. However, it was extraordinarily difficult to understand anything he said. He was tiny, thin, very much alert and with a keen sense of humour. Mike was his friend and would push him around in the wheelchair and feed him and so on. They were inseparable. Mike also had a severe language impairment, however, quite extraordinarily, he could understand everything that Joey said. Mike would translate Joey's howlings into a form closer to English, some of which could be grasped. More understanding was possible as the listener gained practice. One day when an old typewriter was left for the residents, Joey developed a plan. He would dictate his life story to Mike, who would spell it to their friend Dave, who typed it up with one finger. Joey's book was published and with the money from it they were able to have a bungalow built in the grounds of the hospital with all the services and supports the three needed and they lived out their lives happily. They did not want to move away from the only place they had known and all the people there who were their friends.

Christy Brown, an Irish poet, was similarly locked away in a damaged body but his mother knew somehow he was intelligent and wanted to communicate. She was right and with the support of computer assisted technology he was eventually able to write via movements of a toe.

Developmental dyspraxia

Praxis is the ability to motor plan, and 'dys' means difficulties with this. Praxis implies that there is a motivation to plan, an ability to produce the skilled hierarchies of movements, satisfactory functioning of the brain at neocortical, basal ganglia, cerebellar and brainstem levels; adequate kinaesthetic and proprioceptive feedback; and storage ability. Developmental dyspraxia indicates that the function has never normally developed because of some impairment of innate cerebral mechanisms or understimulation due to faulty input or feedback pathways. It is sometimes characterised as a 'dysfunctional difficulty' that may be possible to remedy or overcome by the right sort of training or therapy. In the USA the term Developmental Co-ordination Disorder (DCD) is used (APA 1994).

It takes only a small amount of disturbance of the nervous system to disrupt the smooth functioning of a motor skill. This can lead to difficulties in coordination of gross locomotion functions that in the past was termed the 'clumsy child syndrome' (Gubbay 1975). Clumsiness is a relative term, for the newborn is clumsy and a teenager may temporarily become so during growth spurts. A child does not have a motor impairment but a dysfunction in planning and integrating movement (ideational difficulties) if s/he can use a key to open a door but cannot pretend to do it when the key and door are absent.

Developmental dyspraxia is characterised by difficulties in some or all of the following:

- Ideational difficulties – impairment or immaturity in planning and carrying out complex movement
- Movement – hesitant, inefficient, uncontrolled, twitchy
- Language – uncontrolled rhythm, volume, sequencing of sounds – some have speech difficulties, delayed speech and articulatory problems
- Perception – copying patterns, letters
- Attention and concentration deficits
- Thought – organising, sequencing difficulties
- Memory – especially difficulties following instructions
- Emotionally sensitive, lability – over reaction
- Poor motivation, fear of failure
- Visuo-motor and perceptual difficulties
- Abnormal behaviours
- Often overactive
- Educational difficulties

According to Henderson and Sugden (1992) the most commonly occurring cases are where children have movement difficulties but these are not accompanied by intellectual retardation, rather by educational or behaviour problems.

Among this group are children who find it difficult to concentrate at school and become the class nuisance, children who are unhappy in school because they are bullied or socially isolated, children who cope with their clumsiness by becoming the class clown and children who withdraw completely from participation and remain unnoticed until it is too late to help them. (Henderson and Sugden 1992: 6)

Dyspraxia may arise in a number of different ways such as developmental immaturity; inherited or family difficulty; anoxia at birth; brain damage;

deprivation of stimulation such as is caused by spina bifida and extensive hospitalisation and immobilisation periods. The difficulties may range from severe and profound right along a continuum to mild and circumscribed.

Anna was delivered after a long and difficult birth and had been almost buried in the placenta. As she developed there was just a mild, right-sided lack of coordination. It did not stop her learning to ride a bicycle, although she fell off more times than other children. Because she was very determined she learnt to dance, play tennis and play the piano to grade eight standard and beyond. She had a beautiful singing voice and joined various choirs and concerts. Her IQ was 137 and beyond. What hampered her progress in the early years in school was bead threading, pencil control, drawing and sewing. Later the problems were manifested in handwriting and spelling and they were never entirely overcome through her life, leading to many job applications being turned down. It was only as an adult that the diagnosis of motor impairment was realised, too late to go on those application forms and only discovered when one employer explained why she had been turned down. Obviously she should have word processed the forms and recorded the difficulty. However, there is still little sympathy for such disabilities if you do not use a walking stick or write neatly.

In motoric terms developmental dyspraxia may affect not only locomotion but also dressing and other organisational skills. It may affect learning to swim and ride a bicycle, and learning to play a musical instrument or participate in ball skills and team games. It may be accompanied by difficulties in fine motor skills. Alternatively it may only be observed under stress and fatigue.

Ben had suffered some brain damage at birth. This had affected his locomotion, which was awkward and ungainly and his fine motor skills in handwriting, cutting and drawing. At seven he was managing in the mainstream setting very well, although he had to be delivered to the school and helped to the classroom and only participated in some PE activities. He was intellectually very bright but was beginning to become extremely upset by his teacher's continual complaints about his untidy handwriting. At home he would spend hours trying to write out his work neatly and carefully to please this teacher but he would become exhausted and anxious. The whole situation was affecting his mental health and stability and he was becoming depressed and fearing to go to school. With specialist advice the parents found that Ben was in fact gifted and needed to stay in mainstream education and perhaps be accelerated when things stabilised. They managed to insist that he should be permitted to use a lap-top in class to present his work. Reluctantly the school agreed as the parents paid for it. Relieved of the pressure Ben was keen to get back to school. It is typical that while the school could recognise and accommodate his general coordination difficulties they did not recognise their effect and permeation into the area of handwriting and make allowance and provision for this (see Figure 4.2).

Chesson *et al.* (1991) found that in their sample of children with coordination difficulties, over 50 per cent had had speech therapy. Some of the group were only identified on entry to school. Half their sample were doing well at maths but the rest had spelling and handwriting problems that were hampering their

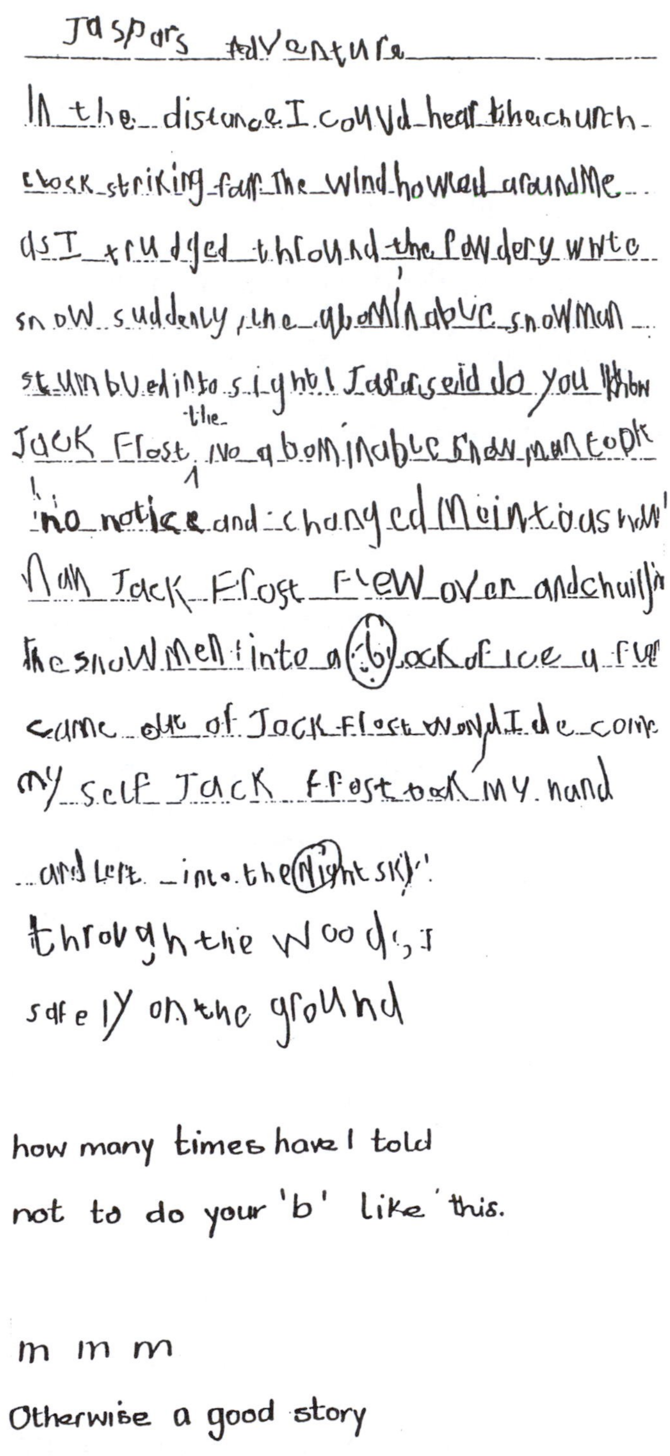

Jaspars Adventure

In the distance I could hear the church clock striking far The wind howled around Me as I trudged through the Powdery white snow suddenly, the abominable snowman stumbled into sight I Jasper said do you know the Jack Frost, no abominable snow man took no notice and changed Me into a snow man' man Jack Frost flew over and chuill'n the snow men into a (b)ock of ice a fire came out of Jack Frost would I de come My self Jack Frost took My hand and left into the (Night sky)' through the woods, I safely on the ground

how many times have I told
not to do your 'b' like 'this.

m m m

Otherwise a good story

Figure 4.2 An example of Ben's best writing (½ size)

progress in school. Primary schools are the best place to address the needs of such children but since the imposition of the rigid approach to 'academic studies' in the National Curriculum in the UK, the opportunities for movement education have radically diminished and teachers who always felt a little underskilled in this area now receive even less training.

The screening test by Gubbay (1975) shows how easily teachers may assess and monitor children's motor coordination using everyday items and school tasks. Gubbay's test items for clumsiness in 8–12 year olds included:

- whistle though parted lips (pass or fail)
- make 5 successive skips without skipping rope (pass or fail after 3 attempts – 2 demonstrations allowed)
- throw a tennis ball, clap hands up to four times, catch ball with two hands, then dominant hand
- roll tennis ball with dominant foot in spiral fashion around six matchboxes set at 30 cm intervals (18 seconds allowed)
- thread 10 beads in 18 seconds (beads 3 cm diameter, bore of 0.8 cm, string stiffened at each end)
- pierce 20 holes in graph paper in 24 seconds (use hat pin, 2 rows in 0.1×0.1 cm squares)
- posting box – fit six different plastic shapes into appropriate slots in two seconds each (fails if takes longer than 18 seconds).

He identified children as clumsy by six or more failures at eight years; five or more at nine years; four or more at 10 years; three or more at 11 and two or more at 12. A condition known as 'oral dyspraxia' is identified by difficulties in yawning, whistling and teeth chattering.

Developmental dysgraphia

In some individuals the dyspraxia may only be manifested in fine motor skills. When this is the case the condition is usually called 'developmental dys-graphia'. It is this seemingly minor difficulty that can cause major educational problems, for dysgraphia prevents them getting enough spelling practice. They will engage in elaborate avoidance strategies whenever they are required to write something down. Their school reports always bemoan their lack of effort and motivation when the reverse is usually the case.

At least a third of dyslexics have dysgraphia in addition to the dyslexia. In the population at large, surveys indicate that the incidence is five to 10 per cent for dyspraxic difficulties in general (Gubbay 1975; Laszlo *et al.* 1988; Henderson and Sugden 1992) but estimates of handwriting difficulties vary. Alston found from 40 to 60 per cent of pupils in her survey in local schools complained of pain when writing. Roaf (1998) found 25 per cent in her school unable to write faster than 15 words per minute. These were the pupils who were struggling in all lessons where a lot of writing was required. A close link between self-concept and handwriting presentation was found. The majority of the slow writers showed difficulties with motor coordination, spelling and letter formation. A speed of 25 words per minute was regarded as a successful rate. Recently I found that 50 per cent of a Year 7 cohort had handwriting difficulties.

Thomas (1998) described a policy adopted in her Kent infant school in which the creative aspect of expressing children's thoughts was developed only orally. They spent a longer time than before on developing an automatic joined hand. As a result they have seen a new quality in the creative written work. The teachers did not act as scribes and the pupils did not engage in copy writing. She compared the usual system in the UK with that which operates in France, where teaching cursive writing is a lengthy process, has high priority in schools and teacher training, begins on entry to school and takes precedence over reading as it once did in the early part of the twentieth century in the UK. Following a research study of handwriting speed in her own school, Allcock (2001) became concerned that many did not have adequate speed and fluency to take advantage of their secondary school demands. She devised a 20-minute test of writing speed and then obtained further samples of some thousands of pupils across the age range. She found that the average speed in free writing was one word per minute more than the age of the pupil so that at 12 years the average speed was 13 words per minute and so on. 25 per cent of pupils at 16 had a speed of less than 12 words per minute and it was recommended that they be given 25 per cent extra time in examinations to make up for their difficulties. Such difficulties are often associated with dysgraphia (Montgomery 1997a, 1998, 2000). Table 4.1 presents handwriting and spelling data from three different schools using Allcock's (2001) 20-minute free writing test format.

Table 4.1   To Show Spelling and Writing Scores of Year Cohorts in Three Different Schools

AGE/YEAR	NUMBER	Writing speeds		Spelling errors	Spelling errors per no. of wds
		av. words	av. w.p.m.		
School A (2001)					
SET 1 YR 7 (More able 12 years old)	28	317.20	15.86	7.11	44.75
SETS 2/3/4 YR 7	63	278.00	12.04	8.65	32.13
SET 5 YR 7	15	217.60	10.88	12.73	17.1
School B (2001)					
SET 2/3 YR 6	16	130.13	6.56	10.01	17.00
SET 1 YR 5	29	196.25	9.81	14.76	13.3
SET 2/3 YR 5	28	134.43	6.72	10.07	12.6
School C (Pre NLS 1998)					
YR 2	17 (+7 no score)	84.83	7.84	17.71	4.79

In Table 4.1, as spelling errors decrease handwriting speed increases. The final column shows the frequency of spelling errors in relation to words written. The more able Set 1 in Year 7 make on average one spelling error every 44 words, whereas Set 5 make one every 17 words and the Year 2 pupils make one error approximately every five words. This was in a school where spelling SATs were very low and for whom the *Developmental Spelling Handbook* (Montgomery 1997b) was written. Within two terms the spelling SATs had improved by 40 per cent, reading by 10 per cent and maths by 5 per cent. They already had a cursive writing policy from Reception but it was not linked with teaching of spelling.

Handwriting difficulties are distributed across the ability range but wherever they occur there is little sympathy in schools; children are told they *must* write neatly, never how to do so or why they have problems. Some become frightened of putting pen to paper because of the sharp criticism they will get, the content can be regarded as worthless if the child 'cannot even be bothered to write it legibly'. Of course this is unfair and it seriously damages the child's confidence and motivation when a little help is all they need. Gifted children's thoughts may run much faster than their writing skills can cope with and so they will be criticised too and again content can be ignored. It is only when a piece of work arrives word processed and appears to be deeply thoughtful that the busy teacher may realise the potential there. Sadly, it may be assumed that the lengthy thesis has been copied from the Internet or is the parent's work and it is back to handwriting again.

Subjects use a range of strategies to cover up their spelling problems; they repeat the same words and phrases, they select from a vocabulary they know they can spell which slows down the writing speed, and some use illegible squiggles as they scribble away at speed. Slow handwriting may arise for a number of other reasons. The pupil may write in an elaborate and florid manner or use a style such as Gothic or Italic which requires careful execution. Others lack practice and write in a slow and laboured fashion; some have difficulties assembling their spellings and this slows the writing process; in some writing is too large and consumes not only space but time; those who have not been taught a fluent and easy letter form will waste time on inefficient strokes, and finally some types of writing such as print script are slower to produce than a fluent, running, joined hand. However, the most serious difficulty is that of fine motor coordination, which can underlie and undermine all handwriting activities. Most of these can be overcome with handwriting training but where there is a deeper cerebellar involvement, an ataxic type problem, or wider coordination disabilities then a lap-top should be used from pre-school onwards for all except name signing.

Fluency and a well-formed hand take time to develop and so beginners cannot be expected to achieve this. At Year 7, however, we should be able to expect that all the pupils have developed a serviceable running hand. Unlike the rest of the world, in the UK a print script is generally taught first, such as is found in children's story books, and then a cursive but half joined form is introduced after about two or three years. This means that one set of motor programmes have been laid down and then these have to be replaced by another set. It is not surprising that some children refuse to change, some half change and others with coordination difficulties develop further problems.

Pupils on the whole do not deliberately write poorly and untidily. Instead illegibility is an indication of their handwriting problems and various squiggles may also help conceal spelling difficulties. Pupils with handwriting coordination difficulties experience little practice and this of course also inhibits their ability to spell. Each spelling may have to be thought out instead of appearing automatically. As all this engages a considerable amount of brain processing power, it results in the content of the narrative being diminished and fatigue setting in very quickly. It is therefore crucial that all pupils very quickly learn a fluent style. Wedell's (1973) research showed that pupils with a co-ordination problem *must* use a joined script. For a beginner, the high precision skills of positioning the pencil on an imaginary line, starting each new letter afresh and making them all lie in the same direction with equal spaces between them are not available. Likewise pupils with even a mild coordination difficulty can find this perceptuomotor task well-nigh impossible. Being made to use a print form until they can 'write neatly' results in them never acquiring a running hand and so they are handicapped by the writing curriculum and this handicaps spelling – both problems damage learning in all subject areas where writing is required. Even the gifted pupil's good oral abilities may be overlooked in the drive for neat writing. Girls tend to be better at this and more persistent than boys and so neat writers with little talent gain the highest marks because their scripts are easy to read. In later years girls who write neatly can be handicapped and thought to be rather dull because their work is so legible! Sassoon (1989), for example, found that 40 per cent of boys and 25 per cent of girls at age 15 said that writing was actually painful and avoided it whenever possible, whilst 21 per cent of nine year olds in some Cheshire schools were found to be ill-equipped for the writing demands of secondary schools (Alston 1993).

However, there is no need for writing to be painful as a significant proportion of such difficulties are brought about by bad posture, incorrect writing positions, inappropriate furniture, and wrong positioning of the paper. Minor handwriting difficulties can be resolved by teaching cursive from the outset. Even so there will be the rare occasion when a pupil with spidery, shaky writing cannot improve whatever style is used because the underlying difficulty is not amenable to training. This may be the case in motor impairment when the effort needed to write is excessive and then the pupil should be given a lap-top computer to use from entry to school.

The following piece of writing contains a number of clues to a pupil's mild motor coordination difficulties.

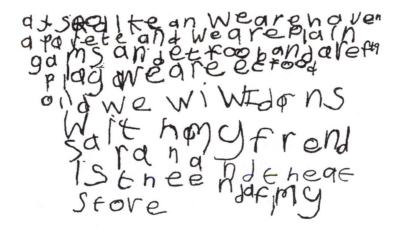

Figure 4.3   Sarah's unaided writing, 7 years 6 months (½ size): 'Our Christmas Party'

(Chronological age: 7.5 years; Reading age 7.2; Spelling age 6.75 years). It took her three quarters of an hour to write and she copied most words from the dictionary in front of her. Sarah is well above average in intelligence.

The signs of motor coordination difficulties in writing are:

- writing pulling in from the margin towards the mid line
- 'rivers' of spaces running down through the writing
- apparent capital letters spotted about but which are really large forms of the lower case out of control, especially of s, w, k, and t
- writing which looks scribbly or spiky
- shaky and wobbly strokes on close examination of letters
- writing that varies in 'colour', sometimes dark and in other places very faint, indicating variation in pressure
- writing that produces ridges on the reverse of the paper and even holes in it due to the pressure exerted
- inability to maintain the writing on the line
- difficulties in copying fluent letter shapes in one fluid movement

Dyslexics and dysgraphics *must be taught full cursive writing* from the outset to support their spelling and overcome any handwriting coordination difficulties. In this system all letters must begin on the line with a lead-in stroke. An ovoid cursive has been found to be the most natural and easy to learn. The APSL programmes of Hickey (1977, Augur and Briggs 2nd edition 1991) and Cowdery *et al.* (1983–87) demand cursive in order to reinforce the sound, symbol and kinaesthetic links and establish the automatic syllable and whole word motor programmes (see Figures 4.4 and 4.5).

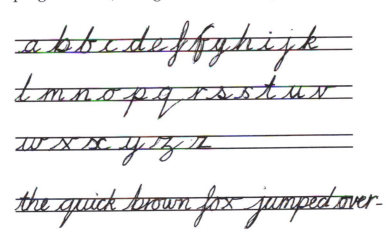

Figure 4.4 An example of the Learning Difficulties Research Project (LDRP) ovoid cursive (Montgomery 1997b)

The specific reasons for teaching cursive handwriting are that it:

- aids left to right movement through words across the page
- eliminates reversals and inversions of letters
- eliminates the need to relearn a whole new set of motor programmes after the infant stage
- induces greater fluency in writing, which enables greater speed to be developed without loss of legibility

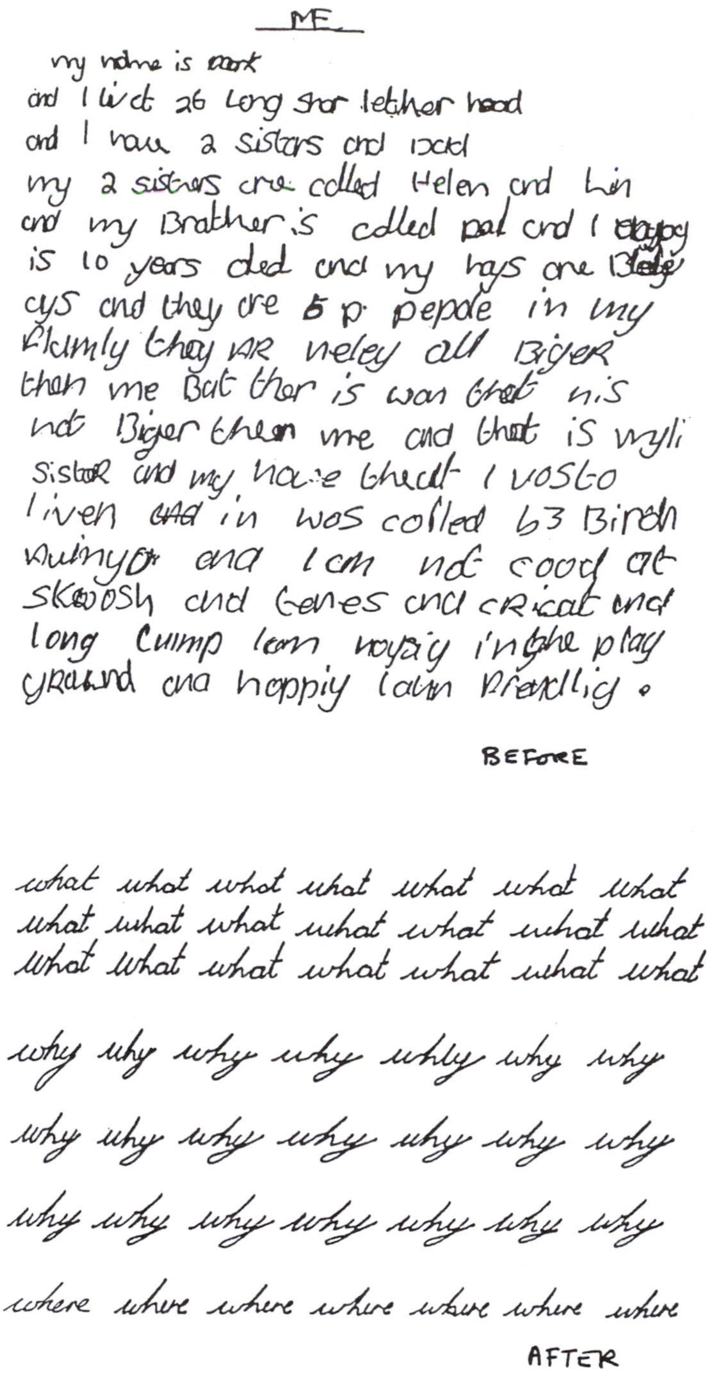

ME

my name is mark
and I lict 26 long star letther head
and I have 2 sistars and 1 dad
my 2 sistars are colled Helen and Lin
and my Brather is colled pal and I
is 10 years ded and my has one
cys and they are 5 p. pepole in my
Flamly they are neley all Biger
than me But ther is wan that his
not Biger then me and that is myli
Sistar and my nave that I vosto
liven and in wos colled 63 Birch
walnyor and I am not cood at
skwosh and Games and cricat and
long cump lam royaiy in the play
grawnd and happiy lam Prexllig.

BEFORE

what what what what what what what
what what what what what what what
what what what what what what what

why why why why whly why why

why why why why why why why

why why why why why why why

where where where where where where where

AFTER

Figure 4.5a Mark's writing before and after intervention, age 10 years

- helps store the motor programmes for spelling whole words, bases and affixes and so spelling accuracy is improved
- makes spaces between letters and between words orderly and automatic
- helps develop a more efficient, fluent and personal style
- causes less pain and difficulty as speed and fluency increase
- improves legibility of writing
- reinforces multisensory learning, linking spelling, writing and speaking.

Thus it can be seen that handwriting and spelling are intimately related in the remediation of dyslexia. Reading, a pattern recognition skill, is more parasitic on the writing process and also responds to different strategies to promote its development. In many cases there are symptoms of handwriting difficulty, which if addressed, will clear up in a few weeks and spelling will improve as well.

Jack needs more training in finger painting and finger strengthening exercises to support his writing development.

Figure 4.6   Jack's writing, age 5.1 years

Tourette Syndrome (TS)

Jim was my laboratory assistant and seemed unaware that during a series of instructions for setting up apparatus he would interrupt with a set of explosive bursts of 'Excuse me', and 'Yes, yes' and other repetitive noises. It was often accompanied by body twitches and occasional snaking arm movements and groping himself.

He was small and rounded in stature with an obsessional interest in small arms and gun clubs or so it seemed, but was good at his job. He would disappear at intervals muttering to himself and engage in serious bouts of handwashing. There seemed little point in telling him about Tourette unless he broached the subject. One day he rushed into my office flushed with triumph and announced he had read an article in a Sunday magazine all about him, he was 'a Tourette', a 'gifted child', then poured out his life story, which was a cavalcade of bullying, intimidation, misunderstanding and special schooling. After this he developed a new sense of self-confidence and was much more relaxed, less prone to bouts of depression and illness.

TS is a neurodevelopmental disorder that is much less rare than we have supposed. In a study of Year 9 pupils in an Essex secondary school nearly three per cent of pupils were found to have signs of TS (Mason and Banerjee *et al.* 1998). The APA (1994) diagnostic criteria are that the children have multiple motor tics and one or more vocal tics. A tic is an involuntary, rapid recurrent non-rhythmic motor or vocal action. They can be simple as in blinking, grimacing, throat clearing or shoulder shrugging. A complex tic would be twirling, bending or touching self or others. The vocal tics like Jim's comprise of out of context utterances such as 'shut up'. This can upset teachers greatly, as can be imagined, unless they know about the condition. The onset is usually at about seven years but may be earlier and to confirm the diagnosis the tics have to have lasted for more than a year and occur many times a day. Adults may have complex vocal tics involving swearing – coprolalia – which are obscene but this is more rare in children.

The prevalence of ADHD in Tourette is thought to be at least a third, and TS is often co-morbid with Obsessional–Compulsive Disorders (OCD). Some children have rage attacks or explosive outbursts, all of which contribute to them being regarded as behaviour problem cases rather than having NLD. None of these combinations is good for their school work and they perform poorly (Chowdery and Christie 2002). They also have social skills deficits that cause them to misinterpret the interactions of peers and this leads to further disruption and isolation. Treatment involves medication such as Clonidine (Robertson 2000), which also helps with any hyperactive symptoms. Other treatments involve talking through the difficulties and the syndrome and, before key events, giving the tic massed practice to weaken it before an exam; converting it into a socially appropriate gesture such as stroking one's hair or pulling one's jacket together; relaxation therapy; and physical exercise (Mansdorf 1995). In a recent conference keynote presentation the distinguished speaker engaged in 37 left arm tics and about five facial tics. The number of tics diminished as he warmed to the subject, 'Intelligence and test measurement'.

Treble exceptionalities

Dyslexia and dysgraphia often co-occur and frequently are accompanied by ADHD and giftedness all in the same individual. As most individuals with NLD also have coordination problems and some with dyslexia do too, it can be seen that it will be necessary in these cases to address the underlying symptoms as well (see Kokot, Chapter one).

Nicholson and Fawcett *et al.* (1995) have located dyslexic difficulties as a cerebellar problem in the failure of the automatisation processes in articulation, reading, writing and spelling and thus advocate the inclusion of multisensory training in specialist remedial programmes as the means by which automatisation is achieved. But it can be tedious and time consuming especially in the early stages, after which the progress does speed up. 'Audiblox' (Strydom and du Plessis 2000) is a multisensory programme addressing a multiplicity of difficulties in non-verbal and verbal learning areas. Its name is based upon 'auditory' because it enhances auditory skills among other things and 'blox' because the main materials are little coloured blocks. The training covers patterning, sequencing, audition and attention, logical thinking, directional coordination and balance exercises, using an arrows card, shoe box, bean bags and paper crumpling. Finally, there are mathematical exercises using counting and the blocks again.

The extent to which the principle of repetition is built into Audiblox is best illustrated in the language training element. A five-chapter book has to be read by the tutor onto five separate tapes and each chapter repeated many times on each tape. The student with language disabilities is then required to put the first tape on a 'Walkman' and listen to it for at least three hours each day for several months, or until his or her own language structure and vocabulary matches that on the tape. The listener then progresses to Chapter two. As can be imagined great persistence is required.

If we add 'intellectually gifted' and 'creative' into this framework we have a potentially explosive situation. The giftedness and the creativeness do not mix well with repetition, hence the HANDLE interventions are very short. Gifted learners in particular need to see the rationale behind what they have to do to 'engage brain' with the process and they need targets by which they can assess progress. It is then that it can become more effective or be stopped and changed if it is not working. The children do know best. Forcing them into rigid routines, even school, can make them become disturbed and depressed, or consigned to waste time by day dreaming school away and losing valuable years of learning and much of their enormous capability as they learn to underfunction.

Attention Deficit Hyperactivity Disorder (ADHD)

Interest in the condition was first aroused in the United States in 1918 following an epidemic of encephalitis. Many children who had recovered from the disease showed catastrophic changes in personality. They became irritable, unruly, distractible, destructive, antisocial and hyperactive. It was then discovered that similar symptoms could occur in cases of brain injury after accidents and anoxia at birth when the mechanisms of inhibition were disrupted. The condition came to be named 'hyperactivity' after its most overt symptom and at first it was thought to be a brain damage syndrome. However, when most children with hyperactivity were found to have no history of brain injury it was labelled an MBD. Later it became linked with visuo-motor difficulties and was termed the 'Strauss Syndrome' and not only did parents complain but teachers reported that the child *could not* sit still (Strauss and Lehtingen 1947). Estimates of the incidence vary from three to five per cent in the USA to one to two per cent in the UK with two to three boys to one girl (Rutter 1975). The narrower definition of ADHD in the UK has led to finding a lower incidence (Cooper and Ideus 1995). In the 1970s and early 1980s as the condition became more widely known, every other overactive child was labelled 'hyperactive'. We have seen this again in the late 1990s in the renamed ADHD condition. An increase in numbers does appear to have occurred in this cycle, but as yet the origin is unknown and may be due to better information and diagnosis. For example, in 1993 in the USA, 900,000 children were diagnosed with the condition but in 2001 5.5 million were given the diagnosis. This could be due to the recognition of ADD without hyperactivity for impulsivity and inattention and 'oppositional defiant disorder'.

Cooper and Ideus (1995) make the point that in the UK children with ADHD would have previously been included in the grouping of those with Emotional and Behavioural Difficulties (EBD) as a category of special educational need: an educational rather than a medical and psychiatric definition. They list from the Elton Report (DES 1989: 31) a survey of teachers' views on discipline in schools, behaviours about which teachers are concerned:

- talking out of turn, calling out, distracting others, chatting
- calculated idleness or work avoidance, not having books and equipment
- hindering other pupils, distracting and interfering with their work
- making unnecessary non-verbal noises, banging and scraping chairs, whistling, humming
- persistently infringing school dress codes and rules
- leaving seat without permission
- verbal abuse to pupils and teacher
- cheeky or impertinent remarks or responses

Not only are these behaviours characteristic of children with EBD, each of the behaviours could also be categorised under the headings of impulsivity, hyperactivity and/or inattention.

Therein lies the danger of course that all problem pupils become ADHD and are administered Ritalin. To the characteristics we have to add the dimensions of morbidity, pervasiveness and severity in cases of ADHD, i.e. the disorder is manifested across all lessons and both at home and at school and does not respond to the ordinary teacherly management behaviours such as reasoning, ignoring aversive behaviour and punishment.

Sam at six is bright, drives his father's tugs, runs the family about in the dory, sails and rows and plays at the boatyard. He has tea with the men and discusses boats and sails like a little old man. During the week he has to go to school and finds sitting about all day tedious and tells his teacher so. He is used to managing his own time and learning and continues this at school to the annoyance of the teacher. He is easily bored and wanders off to do his own thing as well as deliberately disobeying to see how far he can go. The teacher is at her wits' end with him as he is out of her control, 'cheeky', overactive and disobedient. The parents are called in and told he is hyperactive and needs Ritalin medication. Of course he did not need Ritalin and was not hyperactive, just different, used to talking with adults on equal terms.

In 1970, Stewart in a study of 37 'patients' and 37 six year old controls from matched backgrounds found that there were significant differences between them. 81 per cent of the patients were unable to sit still at meals as opposed to eight per cent of controls and 84 per cent were unable to finish projects compared with 0 per cent of controls. The patients showed many forms of antisocial behaviour such as fighting with other children, irritability, defiance, lying and destructiveness, and 50 per cent were unpopular with other children. Stewart found that the condition was always evident by the time the child was three or four years old. Mothers usually noted unusual behaviour before the age of two years where this was not the first child.

One hundred years previously Heinrich Hoffman (cited in Stewart 1970) wrote about such a case of ADHD as follows:

Fidgety Phil,
He won't sit still;
He wriggles
And giggles, . . .
The naughty restless child
Growing still more rude and wild

As the studies into hyperactivity progressed it became clear that the underlying difficulty was not the hyperactivity but an *inability to maintain attentional set* either posturally or in eye movement and in its second incarnation it has come to be known as Attention Deficit Hyperactivity Disorder (ADHD), in which there are three main symptoms contributing to the diagnosis:

1. Inattention – this includes behavioural, ocular and postural set
2. Hyperactivity – extreme and incessant mobility and restlessness
3. Impulsivity – shouting and calling out and cannot take turns.

When the symptoms are present without the hyperactivity the diagnosis is made of Attention Deficit Disorder (ADD). The ADD condition is frequently overlooked as it can appear as a case of dreaminess, disorganisation and quiet withdrawal, an easy child to manage in a busy classroom, but little learning takes place. The overactivity does not always continue into adolescence and may be replaced by underactivity, inertia and lack of motivation. In the USA in ADD three subtypes are identified (APA 1994). The first subtype is characterised by all the symptoms (ADHD – Combined), the second subtype consists of inattentiveness without impulsivity or hyperactivity (ADHD-I) and the third type is hyperactivity with impulsivity (ADHD-HI). Studies show that those with hyperactivity are more likely to show aggressive behaviours whilst those without show a sluggish, cognitive tempo. However, individuals will have their unique patterns depending on levels of arousal, temperament and rearing techniques (Baum and Owen *et al.* 1991).

ADHD and ADD are one of the group of specific learning difficulties and co-occur with dyslexia and other SpLDs (Knivsberg *et al.* 1999). In extreme forms, i.e. chronic, pervasive and severe hyperactivity, biological causes are strongly implicated. Where there are less severe forms the biological aspects of the condition are inconclusive (Cooper 1997: 6). However, in this area there is a tension between pathology and ecological models of deviance. In terms of gifted children, those with ADHD tend to show precocious motor development, intense interest in certain topics, problems following up school work, and difficulties with peers.

A typical profile is as follows:

Richard, aged 13, was diagnosed with the condition ADHD after pulling a knife on a friend. His father said, 'It is like walking on eggshells. You are constantly on your guard, always looking over your shoulder. To be honest there is a constant tension because the slightest thing will set him off into a tantrum. He will rip his clothes, bang his head or drop to the floor and writhe around. Sometimes he will run away or dash in front of cars, and on one occasion he set fire to the carpet and wrecked the house' (www.adders.org/story21.htm 6/7/2001). His father had been working as an insurance broker in the City until Richard was four but then had to give up work because his wife could not cope alone. Schooling was erratic because of his disruptive behaviour, and even the special school he was referred to expelled him after three days. For the last 10 years his father has been sleeping fully dressed in a sleeping bag on the couch because the boy gets up very early – any time after midnight – and the father has to be ready in case he runs out of the door or tries to burn the house down. Richard is now on medication, Ritalin, which has not helped his behaviour but has improved his concentration so that he can catch up with his school work. He now attends a special needs unit but has to be taken there each day. He is a bright child, well into computers, and has his own web site although he is still behind in educational attainments.

At one extreme is the view that ADHD is a postmodern social construction resulting from a modern technological system and media driven society. A system unsympathetic to the social and psychological wellbeing of humans, such as television lives where families never sit down to eat and talk together but 'graze', shout and 'zap' through television programmes. This life style is thought by some to induce ADHD in vulnerable children. At the other extreme it is regarded as a pathological condition which has to be medicated. In reality it is possible that both extremes can evoke the condition and it is not uncommon to find highly able children, bored and frustrated at school, earning the diagnosis, as may abused children acting out their distress. It is the treatment paradox which is most prominent in ADHD studies. Although it might seem logical to prescribe sedatives for a hyperactive individual it was found that these made the condition worse. Instead stimulants such as Ritalin, the commercial name of particular amphetamines, was found to improve the child's behaviour, calming the hyperactivity and increasing attentional set. Amphetamines release the neurotransmitter noradrenaline from the nerve endings; this has a calming effect in specific areas such as the reticular formation and the frontal lobes. The drug has to be used very carefully and is usually only used to help the child settle back into school in case drug dependency develops. The dose effect is temporary: four hour, six to eight hour or slow acting doses can be obtained. Administration needs to be coupled with a behaviour management programme to help the child gain control of the behaviour. Clonidine is also often prescribed to decrease the aggressive behaviour.

In 1999, Fischman and his colleagues reported on research that showed abnormally high dopamine transmitter substances in the brains of those with long standing ADHD. Dopamine is a facilitator at the synapses. Because of the fleeting attention and the classroom disruption it is frequently found, as in Richard's case, that there are accompanying difficulties in reading and writing secondary to the main problems. In the period of administering the drug a remedial programme for literacy teaching needs to be implemented. Because of the good memory skills of highly able children, reading is usually easy to remediate but handwriting and spelling remain very problematic.

In the same period a behaviour management programme needs to be implemented which both teachers and parents learn to follow. This would consist of:

- keeping the child close to the teacher so that the teacher has prior attention and can use touch to calm, or quietly name or point the finger
- setting up low stimulus areas to reduce distractibility: carrels, carpeting and headphones all help
- structuring the child's day very carefully so there is a known routine and no sudden changes and upsets
- limiting instruction about tasks to small steps making sure the child is attending
- asking the child to repeat the instructions to help programme the behaviour
- allowing frequent breaks for physical activity
- avoiding over stimulation and excess fatigue
- establishing clear and firm limits on behaviour and what will not be accepted; a prearranged signal can be used to give a warning
- trying to CBG (Catch the pupil Being Good, Montgomery 1989, 1999) rather than nag or punish
- rewarding any desirable behaviours or their close approximations
- anticipating outbursts and tantrums and redirecting attention to positive events
- having a 'time out' space, cushion or chair where there is quiet and time to collect oneself and calm down.

Ritalin treatment does not work in a significant number of cases and then other treatments and models are sought. One of these is the allergy model. A number of children have been identified with hyperactivity who have an allergy to preservatives and tartrazines – additives in foods such as sausages, soft drinks and crisps, all things that children enjoy. Yet others are allergic to chocolate, cheese, flour or milk protein and an appropriate diet has to be constructed. In the light of this some schools have replaced sweets and crisps in their tuck shops with fruit and have found significantly calmer and more attentive behaviour in classes in the afternoons.

In ADD without the hyperactivity a pattern of uninhibited curiosity and meddlesomeness is seen in pre-school. There tends to be continual trial and error learning, wandering away from the guarding adult, rash acceptance of strange adults and proneness to accidents. It is a form of impulsive inconsequential behaviour.

Creativity and ADD

What researchers tend not to see is the other side of ADHD and ADD. Johnny was a colleague in the science department, he taught physics, much of it learned in the Services. By day he was a teacher, at night and weekends he was a demolition worker. It was the only way he could use up his surplus energy and fulfil the need to be constantly on the move. Jack, like Johnny, had a wild youth, became a boxing champion, talked his way into university without the proper grades and later became the head of a Mercantile Exchange, earning millions of dollars a year (Jaksa 1999). Jaksa reported other cases who manage and use their ADD to advantage such as Phil, who insisted that it made him a more exciting speaker, comedian and motivator. He claimed it was a gift although he admitted that at school teachers took early retirement when they found he was going to be in their class.

An association is beginning to be made between creativity and ADD. For creativity to occur the conditions needed are a willingness to take risks, intrinsic motivation, tolerance of ambiguities, independence of thought and a belief in oneself despite what others say, the ability to redefine and look at problems from different perspectives – lateral thinking, skills of insight in which unusual connections between things can be made – and the strength of motivation to overcome barriers and obstacles (Hartmann 2000). Gifted individuals are frequently reported to have high levels of energy and creativity along these dimensions and these are shared to some extent by the person with ADD. The constant switching of attention assists in refocusing in problem solving and so on. In fact, it might be suggested that many of the creative, energetic and successful figures in a range of fields have ADD. Those on Ritalin often stop taking it at key output times because they enjoy the 'buzz' they get and the high energy released, which they learn to channel into their work.

Typically those with ADD succeed in adulthood but not in school, where the daily routines and static nature of classrooms drive them to distraction. If the programmes of teaching and learning were made more flexible and offered greater potential for direct participation, activity and creativity by learners then more underfunctioning pupils with such disabilities might find success.

Summary and conclusions

Non-verbal learning difficulties are the result of atypical brain development and are neurodevelopmental difficulties. If correctly identified there are a range of remedial programmes and strategies that can be used to overcome them and compensatory strategies that can relieve the pressures. In most NLD there is a motor coordination problem.

In schools in particular the needs of pupils with non-verbal learning difficulties have not always been understood. Some types of difficulty such as handwriting and gross motor coordination attract a great deal of criticism and bullying. The child is blamed for carelessness and fault and little help is given. All this is very demotivating and undermines the self concept and progress in school. Any giftedness and talent is then masked.

Attention deficit hyperactivity disorder is also one of the non-verbal learning difficulties and the lack of time spent on tasks can prevent the easy acquisition of basic skills and the learning of school subjects. This increases the frustrations of gifted learners as the disparity between their abilities and their achievements grows. This, coupled with their problem behaviour and inability to get on with peers, can make them early candidates for exclusion from school and thus very vulnerable. In all these cases the educator needs to be able to understand the disability and recruit the necessary support, therapy or treatments which improve all the time, and then the giftedness can be promoted. Sometimes educators can also be therapists and education can be therapy.

At time of publication, educational systems seem to be doggedly opposed to educating to the needs of pupils with non-verbal learning difficulties. Their strengths and their difficulties frequently go unrecognised, leading to disaffection and exclusion because they are regarded as lazy, defiant, awkward and problematic.

References

Allcock, P. (2001) 'The importance of handwriting skills in Keystage 3 and GCSE Examinations of more able pupils' *Educating Able Children* 5(1), pp. 23–25.

Alston, J. (1993) *Assessing and Promoting Writing Skills*. Stafford: NASEN.

American Psychiatric Association (APA) (1994) *Diagnostic and Statistical Manual of Mental Disorders* DSM IV (4th edition). Washington DC: American Psychiatric Association.

Augur, J. and Briggs, S. (eds) (1991) *The Hickey Multisensory Language Course* (2nd edition). London: Whurr.

Baum, S. M., Owen, S. V. and Dixon, J. (1991) *To Be Gifted and Learning Disabled: From Identification to Practical Intervention Strategies*. Mansfield CT: Creative Learning Press.

Blythe, P. and McGowan, D.J. (1979) *An Organic Basis for Neurosis and Educational Difficulties*. Chester: Insight Publications.

Chesson, R., McKay, C. and Stephenson, E. (1991) 'The consequences of motor/learning difficulties in school age children and their teachers: Some parental views' *Support for Learning* 6(4), pp. 172–77.

Chowdery, U. and Christie, D. (2002) 'Tourette syndrome: a training day for teachers' *British Journal of Special Education* 29(3), pp. 123–26.

Clements, S.D. (1966) *National Project on Minimal Brain Dysfunction in Children – Terminology and Identification Monograph No. 3; Public Health Service Publication No. 1415*. Washington, DC: Government Printing Office.

Cooper, P. (1997) 'Biology, behaviour and education: ADHD and the bio- psycho – social perspective' *Educational and Child Psychology* 14(1), pp. 31–9.

Cooper, P. and Ideus, K. (1995) 'Is attention deficit hyperactivity disorder a Trojan horse?' *Support for Learning* 10(1), pp. 29–34.

Cowdery, L.L., Montgomery, D. (ed), Morse, P. and Prince-Bruce, M. (1983–87) *Teaching Reading Though Spelling Series*, Vols 2A–2F. Kingston: Learning Difficulties Research Project. Reprinted by TRTS Publishing, Clwyd, 1994.

DES/Elton Report (1989) *Discipline in Schools. The Elton Report* London: HMSO.

Duane, D. (2002) 'The Neurology of NLD', Policy into Practice Conference on Dyslexia. Uppsala, Sweden, August.

Fischman, A. (1999) 'Human clinical study using diagnostic radioimaging with Altropane in ADHD' *Boston Life Sciences Inc. Press Release* (NASDAQ: BLSI). Boston MA.

Gubbay, S. S. (1975) *The Clumsy Child*. London: W.B. Saunders.

Harris, D. (ed.) (1963) *The Revised Version of the Goodenough Draw-a-Man Test*. New York: Grune and Stratton.

Hartmann, T. (2000) 'Creativity and ADD: A brilliant and flexible mind' in K. Kay (ed.) *Uniquely Gifted: Identifying and Meeting the Needs of Twice Exceptional Students*. Gilsum NH: Avocus Publishing Inc., pp. 163–66.

Henderson, S. E. and Sugden, D. A. (1992) *Movement Assessment Battery for Children*. Oxford: Psychological Corporation.

Hickey, K. (1977) *Dyslexia: A Language Training Course for Teachers and Learners*. 19 Woodside, Wimbledon, SW19. 2nd edition by Augur and Briggs (1991) London: Whurr.

HMI (2000) *The National Literacy Strategy: The Second Year*. London: The Stationery Office.

Jaksa, P. (1999) 'The flowers and the thorns'. FOCUS Reprint Newsletter of the National ADDA, pp. 1–4 (www.add.org.com).

Kaplan, M. (2000) 'Atypical brain development'. Paper presented at the 27th International Congress in Psychology, Stockholm, August.

Knivsberg, A.-M., Reichelt, K. L. and Nedland, M. (1999) 'Comorbidity, or co-existence between dyslexia and attention deficit hyperactivity disorder' *Support for Learning* **26**(1), pp. 42–7.

Laszlo, M., Bairstow, P. and Bartrip, P. (1988) 'A new approach to perceptuomotor dysfunction. Previously called clumsiness' *Support for Learning* **3**, 35–40.

Lie, K. G. and O'Hare, A. (2000) 'Multidisciplinary support and the management of children with specific writing difficulties' *British Journal of Special Education* **27**(2), pp. 95–99.

Mansdorf, I. (1995) 'Tic disorder' in R. Ammermann and M. Hersen (eds) *Handbook of Child Behaviour Therapy in the Psychiatric Setting*. New York: Wiley.

Mason, M., Banerjee, S., Eapen, V. and Robertson, M. M. (1998) 'The prevalence of Tourette syndrome in a mainstream school population' *Developmental Medicine and Child Neurology* **40**, pp. 292–96.

Montgomery, D. (1989) *Managing Behaviour Problems*. Sevenoaks: Hodder and Stoughton.

Montgomery, D. (1997a) *Spelling: Remedial Strategies*. London: Cassell.

Montgomery, D. (1997b) *Developmental Spelling Handbook*. Maldon: Learning Difficulties Research Project.

Montgomery, D. (1998) *Reversing Lower Attainment*. London: Fulton.

Montgomery, D. (1999) *Positive Appraisal Through Classroom Observation*. London: David Fulton.

Montgomery, D. (ed.) (2000) *Able Underachievers*. London: Whurr.

Nicholson, R. I. and Fawcett, A. J. (1995) *Dyslexia Screening Test*. London: Harcourt, Brace and Co., Psychological Corporation.

Roaf, C. (1998) 'Slow hand. A secondary school survey of handwriting speed and legibility' *Support for Learning* **13**(1), pp. 39–42.

Robertson, M. M. (2000) 'Tourette syndrome, associated conditions and the complexities of treatment' *Brain* Vol. 123, pp. 425–62.

Rourke, B. P. (1989) *Nonverbal Learning Disabilities: The Syndrome and the Model.* New York: Guilford Press.

Rutter, M. L. (1975) *Helping Troubled Children.* Harmondsworth: Penguin.

Sassoon, R. (1989) *Handwriting: A New Perspective.* Cheltenham: Stanley Thornes.

Smith, P. A. P. and Marx, R. W. (1972) 'Some cautions on the use of the Frostig test' *Journal of Learning Disabilities* **5**(6), pp. 357–62.

Stein, J. (2000) 'Visual processing problems in dyslexia'. Paper presented at the 27th International Psychology Congress, Stockholm, August.

Stewart, M. (1970) 'Hyperactive children' *Scientific American*, April **222**(4), pp. 94–99.

Strauss, A.A. and Lehtingen, C.E. (1947) *Psychopathology and Education of the Brain – Injured Child.* New York: Grune and Stratton.

Strydom, J. and du Plessis, S. (2000) *The Right to Read: Beating Dyslexia and other Learning Disabilities.* Pretoria, South Africa: Remedium CC.

Tanguay, P.B. (2002) *Nonverbal Learning Difficulties at School.* London: Jessica Kingsley.

Thomas, F. (1998) 'Une question de writing. A comparative study' *Support for Learning*, Vol. 13, pp. 43–5.

Wechsler, D. (1998) *WISC – 111.* Oxford: The Psychological Corporation.

Wedell, K. (1973) *Learning and Perceptuomotor Difficulties in Children.* New York: Wiley.

PART TWO:
SENSORY DISABILITIES

There have always been a few acknowledged high achievers, or the gifted and talented with sensory difficulties such as Beethoven, who became deaf as he grew old and Helen Keller, who was deaf-blind as a result of an early Rubella infection. Today there are a number of well-known deaf icons such as Emma Nicholson and Jack Ashley, politicians, and Evelyn Glennie, musician. Representing the blind there are Peter White, broadcaster; José Feliciano and Ray Charles, musicians and David Blunkett, former Secretary of State for Education and now at the Home Office. Before these people came to prominence in such careers the blind might more frequently have been met as masseurs and piano tuners and the deaf as switchboard operators using special visual cueing equipment – careers thought to be suitable for them by sighted and hearing persons. Now we can see from the achievements of these exceptional people what any other student with sensory disabilities/difficulties might aspire to. What we have to do when looking at these high achievers is to question how many more might and should be taking their place in a wide range of careers with the rest of us. Are they represented in all fields of endeavour and are there sufficient of them given the numbers with sensory difficulties? The answer to both these two questions would seem to be no, not yet. In fact the discrimination that still operates is so strong that it was only recently (2002) that a Disability Discrimination Act was placed on the UK statute books, more than three decades after the Race Relations Act and nearly three since the Sex Discrimination Act.

The talent and ability of these highly successful people in the face of all this prejudice must have been prodigious and their determination extraordinary to have succeeded against such odds, even with a supportive family around them. In the next two chapters Rosemary Starr explores visual difficulties and giftedness – a rare condition because of the few born with severe visual impairment – and Carrie Winstanley examines the needs of the doubly exceptional in the deaf population and the long-standing issues raised by deaf culture and teaching and learning methods in ordinary schools.

It has not proved easy to find authors who would be prepared to think about double exceptionality and find research in any of these areas and it makes me wonder if in education we have adopted the somewhat patronising approach to disability where we are more concerned to do good to than promote the good of individuals.

It seems especially important to listen to these exceptional individuals and learn from them.

5 Show me the light – I can't see how bright I am: gifted students with visual impairment

Rosemary Starr

Interest in this topic began in the 1970s. The limited studies conducted during this period continued into the mid-1980s, when sporadic discussion then emphasised the need to correctly identify students and alert teachers and parents to the possibility of a student being both gifted and having visual impairment. Some programmes were established in the US, generally in universities or medical research centres. The need for appropriate programmes to meet the specific needs of gifted students with visual impairment was raised again in the 1990s. Few educational programmes appear to continue, despite their established need. Recent books about giftedness now have chapters on gifted children with disabilities, but despite this, there are few published studies about reliable and valid instruments to identify these children and their cognitive and behavioural characteristics.

Definitions can vary according to the priorities regarding the type or types of abilities a system is most concerned with developing. Budgetary constraints also play a very important role as these affect the eligibility criteria and limit the scope of the definition. Generally the more limited the funds, the higher the level of giftedness that is required for participation in special programmes, therefore students with disabilities would tend to be overlooked.

Definitions

Visual impairment

Hardman, Drew, Egan and Wolf (1993) maintained that visual impairment is associated with three groups of eye problems – refractive eye problems, which includes cataracts; muscle disorders, which includes nystagmus (uncontrolled eye movements that may move sideways or up and down); and receptive eye problems, including retrolental fibroplasia, which often results from too much oxygen being administered to premature babies. Visual impairment includes the educationally blind, those who are partially sighted/have low vision and those with limited vision, according to Pagliano (1994).

Gifted children with disabilities

Those children with potential giftedness/talents who showed some evidence of underlying ability, which had not been observed earlier through lack of opportunity, due to the focus on their disability, should be classified as gifted. The functionally talented were defined as having demonstrated ability beyond that of their peers with the same disabilities in one or more domains. Hackney (1986) maintained that there were no guidelines in the literature to identify gifted students with visual impairment, and the differential education for gifted children with disabilities was still at developmental stages. It was suggested by Hardman *et al.* (1993), that even though adaptive uses of computers and related technologies were becoming more widespread, there is little known about the service delivery systems and materials that are best suited for these individuals. It was estimated by Corn (1986) that three to five per cent of the general population are gifted. People with visual impairment constitute one per thousand of the school population, or 0.1 per cent, therefore, to be gifted with visual impairment would occur in one per twenty thousand. However, Braggett (1988) maintained that there may be proportionally as many gifted among those with a disability as among the general population, but their gifts may be obscured by their disability. Teachers may, for example, attribute atypical behaviour to the disability rather than to giftedness.

For purposes of the research to be described, intellectual giftedness was defined as having a Verbal Scale score of 130 or above on the WISC-111.

Educational needs of gifted children with disabilities

It was not until the 1970s that suggestions were being made about the educational needs of gifted children with disabilities. But even in 1987, Minner *et al.* found teachers reluctant to include gifted students with disabilities in gifted programmes, fearing the student would be unable to cope. For some, the identification itself is a huge hurdle, but that is only the beginning, as much prejudice needs to be overcome before a student can be included in an appropriate gifted programme.

There are numerous problems involved in being identified as gifted with any disability, according to Johnson (1987) and Maker (1977). In relation to the visually impaired gifted students some of the problems included stereotyping, developmental delays (particularly in spatial awareness) and often incomplete information. For example, opportunities are not always available to those with disabilities to show their high abilities in an appropriate environment, coupled with stereotypic expectations and test limitations that usually restrict the numbers of atypical gifted students identified. Measures generally used to aid identification tend to recognise ability and not potential. To overcome this, Baldwin (1987) stressed that programmes need to be differentiated for all gifted students and therefore gifted students with disabilities could be included and appropriately accommodated. A further problem is that the gifted with disabilities were still being treated under a medical model with the greater emphasis on the disability rather than giftedness. However, the shift towards more school-based provision of programmes was becoming increasingly important in the 1980s.

In 1988, Braggett stated that there were no programmes in Australia catering specifically for gifted children with disabilities. A current literature review indicates that as no published studies are available concerning programmes for gifted children with disabilities, the situation has not changed since Braggett's statement. Vialle and Paterson (1996) raised the issue of lack of provision in Australia for appropriate programmes and the need for identification of gifted children with hearing impairment.

The difficulties encountered by visually impaired gifted children in gifted programmes would be the same as for any group of minority students being included within a gifted programme, according to Gallagher and Courtwright (1988), and they need the same type of provision as other gifted students (Yewchuk and Lupart 1993). There is no evidence for teachers' fears that they may not be able to cope. Caton (1985) proposed that visually impaired students be educated in mainstream settings with children of similar abilities. The visually impaired need the same academic curriculum and would need to learn adaptive skills for improved orientation and mobility, and the use of tape recorders and other equipment to develop the use of listening to facilitate adaptation. It is critical that they learn to use any residual vision efficiently. Seeley (1989) maintained that gifted students with visual impairments use their strengths to learn compensation skills.

Whitmore and Maker (1985) discussed at length the behavioural and emotional adjustments that the gifted with a disability frequently have to face. Often these children have to cope with mixed messages from others that accentuate their abilities and differences. They are different from other children with disabilities, children without disabilities and also from other gifted children. The intellectually gifted with a disability are vulnerable to lowered self esteem. Sensitivity and perfectionism is common with all gifted individuals, but those with a disability also have extreme desires for independence. Often these students experience communication problems with their sighted peers. According to Corn (1986), visually impaired gifted students often stated the need to be better than gifted students without disabilities in order to be recognised.

Gifted children, as a whole, are usually self-critical. However, the gifted with disabilities are considered to show even greater sensitivity according to Corn (1986) and Maker (1977) and believe that they have to prove themselves by being better than other gifted students. The findings of Cohen and Ambrose (1993) would support this and they continued to caution that the gifted with disabilities often have unrealistic expectations as to what constitutes giftedness and, as a result, often experience depression and intensity of emotions.

Identification

Karnes and Johnson (1986) claimed that identification of gifted students with disabilities gives them an opportunity to excel, raises their self esteem and leads to changed perceptions of peers and teachers. As a result, parents become more accepting of the disability and are often more optimistic about the future for their child. In order to identify giftedness in these students with visual impairment, Anastasi (1988) advocated using the Verbal Scale of the Wechsler Intelligence Scale for Children (WISC), as high verbal ability can often be associated with high intelligence, and concluded that the results were reasonably satisfactory. It is suggested in the literature that those with visual impairments tend to score higher on verbal fluency, verbal flexibility and verbal originality. Johnson and Corn (1989) suggested that some of the difficulties with identification were due to the checklists of characteristics of giftedness being used but not adapted for children with visual impairments. Another difficulty involved with identification was that frequently the group making the decision about inclusion in gifted programmes would contain teachers with qualifications in giftedness, but not also in special education. Davis and Rimm (1985) suggested that gifted students with disabilities frequently underachieve so it is necessary to encourage them to see the worth of their achievements.

Four obstacles to being identified as gifted with a disability were listed by Johnson and Corn as follows:

1. Parents and professionals often had a limited knowledge about potential – most found it hard to understand that a child could co-function with two areas of exceptionality.
2. Due to the small percentage of gifted children with disabilities, teachers have not always had experience of teaching children with disabilities and may, therefore, not have a positive attitude towards such a child being included in a programme for the gifted.
3. Inappropriate methods or instruments for identification are used which may not highlight the student's strengths.
4. Funds are often limited and the costs of accommodating a child with a disability into a gifted programme by the provision of spoken output computers for the visually impaired, magnification of materials etc., may be too great for the budget.

Research study in Victoria, Australia

Selection of the students for the study

The children were selected through enquiries to the Directorate of School Education, Catholic Education Office, Royal Victorian Institute for the Blind and the Visiting Teaching Service for Students with Visual Disabilities. The five students in this study met the dual selection criteria of having visual impairment and possibly being gifted. Participants in this project were a sample of five children (four girls and one boy), ranging in age from three years 10 months to 16 years one month. Four of the students had nystagmus, a muscle disorder resulting in rapid eye movements either from side to side or up and down. However, three also had comorbid visual conditions of albinism, small optic nerve hypoplasia, and congenital cataracts. The other student had retrolental fibroplasia, a receptive eye problem. The students all attended mainstream settings and had support, once a week, from the Visiting Teacher Service for Students with Visual Disabilities.

Test instruments and checklists

The children were assessed using the following measures:

1. *The Wechsler Intelligence Scale for Children – Third Edition (WISC-111)* As the students in this project had severe visual impairments, it was inappropriate to administer the Performance Sub-tests. The Verbal Scale requires skills in understanding verbal information, thinking with words, and expressing thoughts in words. The Verbal Scale provides an objective measure of Verbal Intelligence.
2. *Piers-Harris Children's Self Concept Scale* (Piers 1984) was used to examine the self esteem of the participants in this study.

The parents were required to complete the following measures and checklists:

1. *The Parents' Identification Checklist* was the one recommended by the Victorian Directorate of School Education in the Bright Futures Policy Statement, published in 1995.
2. *Multiple Intelligences Parent Inventory* (Adapted from *In Their Own Way – Seven Intelligences Inventory* (Shannon 1991) by L. G. Kronborg, Krongold Centre, Monash University).
3. *Social Skills Rating System – Parent Form* (Gresham and Elliott 1990).

The teachers were required to complete the following checklists:

1. *The Renzulli-Hartman Scale for Rating Behavioural Characteristics of Superior Students* (Renzulli and Hartman *et al.* 1971).
2. *The Social Skills Ratings System – Teacher Form* (Gresham and Elliott 1990).

Findings from the study

WISC-111 profiles

The students in this project were not homogenous in terms of age, grade level and school attended, although they shared two characteristics in common. They all had a visual impairment and were gifted. From a survey of the literature, it was anticipated that certain characteristics may be shared, apart from visual impairment and giftedness. According to Tillman (1973) and supported by Maker (1977), gifted students with visual impairment present a WISC Verbal Scale sub-test profile where Digit Span and Information are elevated and Comprehension and Similarities are lowered. Maker (1977) asserted these results were due to those with visual impairments reaching their maximum capacity somewhat later than people with sight. Maker (1977) proposed that children with visual impairments may have difficulties with abstract conceptualisation problems at a concrete, functional level, especially if tested using the Stanford Binet Intelligence Scale, where the gifted tend to perform at the level of older children. Whitmore and Maker (1985) would support this viewpoint. The profiles from the Verbal Scale of the WISC-111, therefore, were expected to show elevated scores on the Information and Digit Span sub-tests and lowered scores on the Similarities and Comprehension sub-tests. The following table shows the students' results on these subtests.

Table 5.1   WISC-111 Sub-Test Scaled Scores or Age Equivalent Scores

	Digit Span	Information	Comprehension	Similarities
Case A	25	84	99.9	99
Case B	84	95	99	99.9
Case C**+	6.0	5.10	7.10	6.6
Case D	37	37	99.6	84
Case E	99.6	75	98	95

**Age equivalent scores are presented for Case C, as the WISC-111 norms begin at 6 years 0 months.
+ Chronological age at time of testing: 3 years 10 months

As can be seen from the above table, none of the students in this project shares the profile proposed by Tillman (1973) and Maker (1977). All of the students had raised scores on Comprehension sub-tests and demonstrated highly developed understanding of societal rules and conventions with thorough explanations. All the students also had elevated scores on the Similarities sub-test, and were able to conceptualise verbal information with a high degree of abstraction.

Case A had lower than expected Digit Span scores, when compared to A's other sub-test scores on the Verbal Scale. However, Case D was the only student with lowered Information and Digit Span sub-test scores, which is the opposite of the profile of the Verbal Scale scores on the WISC, according to Tillman (1973) and Maker (1977). This is contrary to their suggested hypothesis in expecting raised scores on the Information and Digit Span sub-tests. It could be an indication of a verbal processing deficit characteristic of dyslexics (Montgomery 1997; and see Chapter three), suggesting double disability and giftedness each masking the other, or triple exceptionality.

Lin Shan Ping and Sikka Anjoo (1992), in a review of the literature, concluded that both Comprehension and Similarities sub-test scores would be lower for those who are gifted and have visual impairment. They thought a lower Comprehension sub-test score could be due to a limited visual input and a restriction on the range of experiences for the comprehension of concepts. Slower development in abstract thinking could be caused by generally restricted interaction with the environment, fewer opportunities for learning through imitation, and fewer experiences for the development of abstract concepts, but this is not borne out in the case details here. Perhaps they were placing too much emphasis upon the importance of visual input in the construction of higher mental processes in visual impairment, or it is not so relevant in gifted cases.

The expected elevated Digit Span and Information sub-test scores could be attributed to those with visual impairments relying more on other sensory avenues. More specifically, according to Maker (1977), auditory memory should be weighted in predicting intellect with the visually impaired. Although Caton (1985) had maintained that often visually impaired gifted children have exceptional auditory memory, advanced problem solving skills and superior verbal communication, Hardman *et al.* (1993) stated that there was no empirical evidence that those with visual impairment develop greater capacity in other sensory areas. In fact the alternative hypothesis would seem more apt. We might expect a higher level of achievement in Comprehension and Similarities in these gifted students, for they are obliged to focus upon auditory and verbal learning, making it a strength.

Braggett (1988), Hardman *et al.* (1993) and Pagliano (1994) asserted that there may be deficits in meaningful verbal learning and students with visual impairments have a tendency to reach maximum levels of achievement at a slower rate than their sighted peers. But the evidence here for gifted students suggests a different profile.

For example, Cases B, C, D and E had elevated scores in all the four sub-tests identified by Maker (1977) and Tillman (1973) as likely to be lower. It is interesting to note that another student who was visually impaired, but who only achieved a Verbal Scale IQ of high average and therefore could not be formally included in this project, also presented with a profile where scores on the Information, Similarities and Comprehension sub-tests were elevated and the Digit Span sub-test score was lower.

One possible reason for the different profiles in this study, when compared to those of the literature, could be that these students are all gifted as well as having visual impairment and therefore their processing skills are superior. Another contributing factor may be due to the changes in education methods since the 1970s, where greater recognition is made of the different learning styles of children. Modification in teaching strategies is now made through greater use of sophisticated computer technology, combining auditory and visual input with visual techniques. There may be greater awareness that students with visual impairment may have difficulties with the concepts in the Comprehension and Similarities sub-tests of the WISC-111.

Since the 1980s, there has been greater emphasis on students with visual impairment attending mainstream schools with support from the visiting teachers for the visually impaired. These students are taught techniques relying on more visual concepts in the learning of language. In the mainstream schools, students with visual impairment would be more exposed to their sighted peers and therefore would have more opportunities to adapt and learn other techniques with the help of the visiting teachers.

Freedom from Distractibility was not looked at in earlier studies of WISC profiles as WISC-111 has only been available since the early 1990s (see Table 5.2). Freedom from Distractibility was considered to be a worthwhile aspect of

Table 5.2   Freedom from Distractibility Scores on the WISC-111

Case A	Average
Case B	Superior
Case C	Very Superior
Case D	Average
Case E	Very Superior

the students' verbal profile to investigate as Freeman (1991) and Klein (1992) and other researchers had shown that gifted students had superior memory and the ability to concentrate and attend to a task for extended periods of time. The gifted with visual impairments would be more likely to have better verbal communication skills than their sighted peers and better memory function, which could be an indicator of their giftedness, according to Caton (1985).

Arithmetic and Digit Span sub-test scores comprise the Freedom from Distractibility score. The Arithmetic and Digit Span sub-tests rely on ability to remember auditorally presented digits and require attention and concentration. The Arithmetic sub-test also involves mental arithmetic knowledge. Anxiety and verbal processing problems can contribute to lowered Arithmetic and Digit Span sub-test scores. Cases B, C and E obtained Freedom from Distractibility scores within either the superior or very superior range. Cases A and D scored Freedom from Distractibility scores within the average range. Thus it is suggested that either these two students did not find the retention of digits in isolation a task that was motivating for them and, therefore, did not attend as fully as in other circumstances where their interest was fully engaged, or that they had a mild verbal coding deficit. It was noted that Cases A and D were anxious during those particular sub-tests. Even though Case B's Freedom from Distractibility was within the superior range, Case B was distracted during the Digits Forward part of the sub-test, was able to re-focus for the Digits Backward part of the sub-test and still obtained a percentile score of 84 for the Digit Span sub-test. This was a relative weakness for Case B, when compared to Case B's other Verbal Scale scores. Case B's Arithmetic sub-test score was within the very superior range and therefore contributed to raising B's Freedom from Distractibility Scale score to within the superior range.

In all five cases, the students' mothers indicated a broad attention span and ability to concentrate well. This may give some support to a possible explanation for Case A's and Case D's scores being lowered because of anxiety, or their ability to pay attention and concentrate is more focused in other activities that hold greater interest for them. There seemed no other indication of a learning disability, however.

For gifted students with a disability to succeed, Caton (1985) asserted that they needed an intense desire to reach goals and a recognition of their strengths and weaknesses. Their self esteem was often fragile and motivational factors were very important in enabling these students to reach their potential. In a study conducted by Beaty (1991), investigating the self esteem of visually impaired and non-visually impaired adolescents, it was found that the self esteem of the adolescents with visual impairment was significantly lower than that of adolescents without visual impairment. However, the students in

Beaty's study and those in the Pagliano study (1994) were not classified as being gifted.

Self esteem

Table 5.3   Piers-Harris Children's Self Concept Scale Scores

Cases	Behavioral attributes	Intellectual & School status	Physical appearance	Anxiety	Popularity	Happiness & satisfaction
A	A	AA	AA	A	BA	AA
B	AA	AA	BA	A	A	BA
C*	—	—	—	—	—	—
D	BA	A	BA	BA	BA	BA
E	AA	AA	AA	A	AA	AA

BA = Below Average   A = Average   AA = Above Average
* (C was not administered the Piers-Harris Children's Self Concept Scale due to age constraints.)

In this group overall the self concept ranged from above average to below average (see Table 5.3). Ludwig and Cullinan (1984) cautioned against generalising findings that attempt to link self esteem and giftedness, as being consistently high or low. Feldhusen (1986), however, suggested that gifted children record a higher overall self concept particularly when successful affective relationships are established with other highly able people. All of the students in the current study have participated in extension programmes and therefore it could be expected that this exposure to like minds would eliminate one aspect of difference that these students have. Due to the small numbers of students who are gifted with visual impairment, chances of making contact with other gifted students with visual impairment would normally be slim.

Case D was in early adolescence and, at the time of the assessment for this study, was in the first year of secondary school. The other students who were administered the Piers-Harris Children's Self Concept Scale were older and more established in secondary school. This transition from primary to secondary school may have accounted for Case D's lowered self concept when compared to the other students in the study. This supposition had support from Milgram and Milgram (1976) for in their study, changes in self concept became less positive as children approached adolescence. This may account for the students in this current study rating themselves as within above average to average range, except for Case D.

In all four cases, Intellectual and School Status was rated as within the above average or average range, so that these students acknowledge their academic abilities. This was the only domain where there was consistency between the students. The work of Kelly and Colangelo (1984), Loeb and Jay (1987) and Ross and Parker (1980) supports the consistency of raised academic concept in such cases. Loeb and Jay (1987) discussed the need to differentiate between the generally raised academic self concept of the gifted and the lowered social self concept. Ford (1989) found that on self report, gifted students described themselves as being at least within the average range, if not better. In this project, each of the students rated themselves as being within either the above average or average range in academic self concept. With Case D, this was the only domain rated above the below average range. This may have been due to acknowledgement by Case D that placement in extension programmes was appropriate, even though Case D was unable to accept positive aspects of the other domains.

According to researchers such as Ross and Parker (1980), gifted students maintained that they were different from their peers and were insecure in the social sphere. This was because, according to Davis and Rimm (1985), the gifted students with visual impairments may not have well-developed social skills. Research by Hardman and Drew *et al.* (1993) confirmed this. They found that generally, students with visual impairments had poor social skills.

Cases B and E rated their Popularity as either within the above average or average range. Popularity was rated as being below average in Cases A and D. Case A mentioned to the examiner that there were often feelings of social isolation due to the family's financial circumstances and A's visual disability, which A stated interfered with the active participation that A would like with sighted peers. Case D explained that currently relationships with peers were good, although this was different to what had occurred in primary school. This was not borne out in the self ratings on the Popularity domain. In this sample there does not seem to be consistent confirmation of the findings of Davis and Rimm (1985) and Hardman and Drew *et al.* (1993) relating low social skill development and visual impairment. Both Cases B and D give an appearance of being confident and happy. However, both rated Happiness and Satisfaction as within the below average range.

Whitmore and Maker (1985) maintained that once students are identified as gifted, when they already had a disability, their abilities and differences are accentuated. In addition to such problems the gifted with disabilities often have unrealistic expectations and can as a consequence experience depression (Cohen and Ambrose 1993). Anxiety was rated as between above average to below average in all four cases. Anxiety was a common factor for all the students, either actually stated during the interview and assessment process, or evident through mannerisms such as wringing hands or the possible fluctuating levels of attention and concentration with Cases A and D. All the students who completed the Piers-Harris were adolescents and coming to terms with their new roles in the home, school and general community. This transition can often contribute to greater levels of anxiety. The students in this study stated that they experienced a level of difference compounded by their giftedness and the difficulties of coping with visual impairment.

Social skills

There is little consistency in the literature about the level of social skills of gifted students, particularly when compared to age peers. Davis and Rimm (1985) and Hardman and Drew *et al.* (1993) suggested that the gifted with visual impairment may have more poorly developed social skills than sighted peers. Davis and Rimm (1985) proposed that the social skills of gifted students with disabilities may not be well developed as they would have had few opportunities to mix socially with the gifted. However, all the students in this study attended mainstream schools so they would have had more opportunities to mix with sighted peers. For those gifted students with visual impairments, poor understanding of body language and non-verbal communication skills, with frequent mismatch of the words used and body language, could lead to social difficulties, according to Hardman and Drew *et al.* (1993).

There was consistency however, between the parents' and teachers' ratings of social skills. Both parents and teachers rated Assertion, Cooperation, Responsibility and Self Control as either above average or average, except Case C, who was rated by the teacher as being below average in Self Control and Cooperation. The teachers' and parents' ratings of the students' social skills ranged from above average to average. However, the students self-rated Popularity on the Piers-Harris Children's Self Concept Scale as ranging from above average to below average.

Each teacher rated each student as being within the average range for Externalising and Internalising Behaviours. Case A's mother rated Externalising Behaviour as being below average. Case B's mother rated Internalising Behaviour as being below average. Apart from these two exceptions, parents rated Externalising and Internalising Behaviours as generally within the average range. Case C was the only student in the sample who was rated as having Internalising Behaviours within the above average range. A possible explanation for this may have been that Case C's IQ was higher than others in the sample and the asynchrony experienced by Case C contributed to a greater awareness of difference from age peers. It was expected that more of the students would be rated as having elevated levels of Internalising Behaviours due to the sensitivity of gifted students generally, as stated by Freeman (1985), Mendaglio (1995) and Schnitz and Galbraith (1985) and because of the levels of anxiety noted during the interview and assessment. The gifted with disabilities displayed even greater sensitivity than their gifted peers without visual impairment, according to Cohen and Ambrose (1993), Corn (1986) and Maker (1977). There was no evidence to support this in the current study, as the Social Skills Rating System is not a measure of sensitivity. Anecdotal evidence from the parents would suggest that these students are very sensitive.

Multiple intelligences

The Multiple Intelligences Inventory is based on the model proposed by Gardner (1983) that each individual possesses seven intelligences in varying degrees of strength. Each person exhibits a unique intellectual profile with preferred methods of approaching and solving problems. The seven intelligences include: Verbal/Linguistic, Logical/Mathematical, Visual/Spatial, Bodily/Kinaesthetic, Musical/Rhythmic, Interpersonal, Intrapersonal. There was no pattern found in this study that was common to all students in relation to the intelligences most likely to be used.

Musical/Rhythmic Intelligence was rated by parents of Cases A, B and C as either the intelligence most likely to be preferred or equally preferred. This is despite all students playing musical instruments, and the musical ability of the students was mentioned with pride by the parents. It is possible that parents may have valued either Linguistic or Mathematical Intelligence as being more appropriate as a first choice of intelligence rather than Rhythmic/Musical Intelligence.

It was expected that as all the students involved in this study had some form of visual impairment, Spatial and Bodily/Kinaesthetic Intelligences would be the least likely to be favoured. This was the case for all students except C. Perhaps C's young age may be a factor in this situation.

Therefore more consistency was evident about the intelligences least likely to be preferred by the students in this project.

Parents' nominations

There are a number of common characteristics indicated by parents of the students in this study. The following cases obtained a top rating on each of these questions. The results obtained are shown in Table 5.4.

Table 5.4   Characteristics and Ratings

Characteristics	Parental ratings
Recalls facts easily.	A, B, C, D, E
Has a broad attention span that allows concentration on and perseverance in problem solving and pursuing interests.	A, B, C, D, E
Has advanced vocabulary, expresses self fluently and clearly.	B, C, D, E
Is an avid reader.	A, B, D, E
Has a great deal of curiosity.	A, C, D, E
Reasons.	A, B, D, E
Seeks own answers and solutions to problems.	A, C, D, E
Follows complex directions.	A, B, D, E
Likes 'grown up' things and to be with older people.	B, C, E
Has a good sense of humour.	A, C, E
Tends to dominate others if given the chance.	A, D, E
Shows initiative.	A, C, E
Sets self high goals.	A, D, E
Is independent and self sufficient.	A, C, D
Thinks quickly.	C, E
Wants to know how things work.	C, E
Is persistent – and sticks to tasks.	D, E
Enjoys complicated games.	A, C
Is adventurous.	A, C
Has a wide range of interests.	A, C
Is a leader.	A
Puts unrelated ideas together in new and different ways.	C
Asks reasons why – questions almost everything.	C
Has a great interest in the future and world problems.	C
Continually questions status quo	C

(A = Case A; B = Case B; C = Case C; D = Case D; E = Case E)

As can be seen, the recalling of facts easily and a broad attention span are characteristics shared by each of the students. This is despite Case A scoring within the average range on the Information sub-test and both Cases A and D scoring within the average range for Freedom from Distractibility. Advanced vocabulary, being an avid reader, showing a great amount of curiosity, reasoning skills, seeking own solutions to problems and an ability to follow complex instructions were characteristics shared by at least four of the students. Therefore, this subjective instrument confirms the objective scores on the Verbal Scale of the WISC-111, where each of the students performed within the superior or very superior ranges.

Behavioural characteristics of superior students

Table 5.5   Renzulli-Hartman Scale Scores for Each Case Rated by Teachers

CASES	A	B	C	D	E
Leadership Characteristics	VS	S	HA	HA	S
Motivation Characteristics	HA	HA	VS	A	S
Creativity Characteristics	S	HA	S	HA	HA
Learning Characteristics	HA	HA	HA	HA	HA

A= Average; HA = High Average; S = Superior; VS = Very Superior

It is interesting to note that only one parent rated their child as having leadership characteristics on the Parent's Nomination Form (see Table 5.4). However, teachers have presented a range of Leadership Characteristics as being from very superior to high average (see Table 5.5), suggesting that these students are giving indications of leadership qualities in the school setting that are not being recognised fully at home.

It would have been expected that the creativity characteristics would have been rated higher as parents had rated seeking own solutions to problems, a great deal of curiosity and advanced vocabulary in four of the five students. It may be possible that the students' creativity is not being developed fully at school. However, in the literature review, it was revealed that researchers had indicated limited valid measures of creativity.

Ratings on Motivation Characteristics ranged from very superior to average. Except for Cases C and E, the other students may not be producing to their potential at school because of limited educational stimulation.

The relatively low scores for all students on Learning Characteristics could indicate that these gifted students are not being appropriately accommodated and stimulated to ensure development of their full potential, despite the fact that all students are being included in extension classes of some kind.

All families were very cooperative about participation in this project, despite some hesitation as to the attribution of giftedness. They all stated that perhaps some of the difficulties the children and their families experienced could be avoided by others through increased awareness as to the possibilities for children with visual impairments who are also gifted.

Summary and conclusions

The literature review suggested that the use of the Verbal Scale of the WISC-111 would present some indication of the cognitive functioning of the students. No single measure on the WISC-111 was considered to be appropriate in the identification of these students. Objective and subjective input from parents and teachers was necessary to present a picture of the wider strengths and abilities of the children. Each of the five students scored a Verbal Scale IQ within the superior range, which was set at 130 or above. The scores on the Comprehension and Similarities sub-tests of the Verbal Scale of the WISC-111 were consistently elevated in each of the five students. Greater variability was shown with the Digit Span sub-test scores, ranging from average to very superior. Information sub-test scores ranged from average to superior. Freedom from Distractibility scores on the WISC-111 ranged from average to very superior. The results of the Comprehension, Similarities, Information and Digit Span sub-tests on the WISC-111 were not consistent with those suggested in the literature.

Three of the students rated their self esteem as either average or above average. The other student rated self esteem as below average. Each student rated Intellectual and School Status domain as either average or above average and this was the only domain where there was consistency for each student.

It had been suggested in the literature that the gifted with visual impairment may have poorly developed social skills. However, both parents and teachers rated Assertion, Cooperation, Responsibility and Self Control as either above average or average, except Case C, who was rated by the teacher as being below average in Self Control and Co-operation. Social skills were rated as above average or average by both parents and teachers.

Parents nominated top ratings for all the students on the recalling of facts easily and broad attention span. Advanced vocabulary, being an avid reader, a great amount of curiosity, reasoning skills, seeking own solutions to problems and an ability to follow complex instructions were characteristics shared by at least four of the students at the top rating student level. None of the other characteristics shared by gifted children were consistently rated at the top level.

Not all students had the same learning styles, with different 'Intelligences' being indicated as preferred, by the parents. However, there was more consistency about the intelligences least likely to be preferred by the students in this project.

On the Renzulli-Hartman Scale for Rating Behavioural Characteristics of Superior Students, there was consistency presented in the scores on leadership characteristics, creativity characteristics and learning characteristics, with each of these scales ranging from high average to very superior. More variability was shown on the motivation characteristic scale with scores from average to very superior.

The perception of the learning styles of these students, indicated by both parents and teachers, revealed that some aspects of the students' abilities are more obvious either in the home or school environments, but not necessarily in both. Justification, therefore, is provided for the use of parent and teacher checklists in the identification of gifted children as a contribution to the knowledge about the students' strengths gained by use of objective measurement on the WISC-111. Useful information is thus gained and can help ensure appropriate programme provision for these gifted children with visual impairment.

Another aim of this project was to compare the cognitive and behavioural profiles of the students in this study with findings from other studies. Due to insufficient available information in the literature, this aim was only partially fulfilled.

The early identification of these children through appropriate, ongoing evaluation using valid instruments, adapted specifically for children with visual impairments in order to optimise opportunities, is needed. This would enable children with visual impairment to be compared to others in this sub-group and their giftedness more easily identified. This would involve input from special education staff, skilled in teaching those with visual impairment, and specialist psychologists who are involved with identification of the gifted. Objective measures and student observation and checklists, completed by teachers and parents, would assist in gaining a full assessment of skills and adaptive behaviours.

There may be reluctance to establish specific programmes for the gifted with visual impairments, due to the small numbers. However, each child is entitled to an education that will enable him or her to fulfil their potential.

Exceptional children are provided with Individual Education Plans, and these must also be developed for visually impaired gifted children. Children with visual impairments who are also gifted should be included in existing programmes for gifted children, modified to accommodate their impairment. Emphasising strengths rather than impairments would raise the self esteem of these children, and in the context of programmes with other gifted children, provide much needed opportunities to establish social contacts.

References

Anastasi, A. (1988) *Psychological testing (6th edition)*. New York: Macmillan.

Baldwin, A.Y. (1987) 'Undiscovered diamonds'. *Journal for the Education of the Gifted*, **10**(4), pp. 271–286.

Beaty, L. (1991) 'The effects of visual impairment on adolescents' self concept'. *Journal of Visual Impairment and Blindness*, **85**(3), pp. 129–30.

Braggett, E.J. (1988) *Education of Gifted and Talented Children, Australian Provision*. Canberra: Commonwealth Schools Commission.

Caton, H.R. (1985) 'Visual impairments', in W. H. Berdine and A. E. Blackhurst (eds) *An Introduction to Special Education* (2nd edition). Boston: Little, Brown & Co., pp. 235–82.

Cohen, L.M. and Ambrose, D.C. (1993) 'Theories and practices for the differentiated education for the gifted and talented', in K.A. Heller, F.J. Monks and A.H. Passow (eds) *International Handbook of Research and Development of the Gifted and Talented*. Oxford: Pergamon, pp. 359–63.

Corn, A. (1986) 'Gifted students who have a visual difficulty. Can we meet their educational needs?' *Education of the Visually Handicapped*, **18**(2), pp. 71–84.

Davis, G.A. and Rimm, S.B. (1985) *Education of the Gifted and Talented*. New Jersey: Prentice-Hall Inc.

Feldhusen, J.F. (1986) 'A concept of giftedness', in R. J. Sternberg and J. E. Davidson (eds) *Concepts of Giftedness*. Cambridge: Cambridge University Press, pp. 112–27.

Ford, M.A. (1989) 'Students' perception of affective issues impacting the social-emotional development and school performance of gifted and talented youngsters'. *Roeper Review*, **xi**(3), pp. 131–34.

Freeman, J. (1985) 'Emotional aspects of giftedness', in J. Freeman (ed.) *Psychology of Gifted Children: Perspectives of Development and Education*. Chichester: John Wiley & Son, pp. 247–64.

Freeman, J. (1991) *Gifted Children Growing Up*. London: Cassell.

Gallagher, J.J. and Courtwright, R.D. (1988) 'The educational definitions of giftedness and its policy implications', in R.J. Sternberg and J.E. Davidson (eds) *Concepts of Giftedness*. New York: Cambridge University Press, pp. 93–111.

Gardner, H. (1983) *Frames of Mind: The Theory of Multiple Intelligences*. New York: Basic Books Inc.

Gresham, F.M. and Elliott, S.N. (1990) *Technical Manual: Social Skills Rating System*. Circles Pines, MN: American Guidance Service.

Hackney, P.W. (1986) 'Education of the visually handicapped gifted: a programme description'. *Education of the Visually Handicapped*, **28**(2), pp. 85–95.

Hardman, M.L., Drew, C.J., Egan, M.W. and Wolf, B. (1993) *Human Exceptionality in Society, School and Family*. (4th ed.) Boston: Allyn and Bacon.

Johnson, L. (1987) 'Teaching the visually impaired gifted youngster'. *Journal of Visual Impairment and Blindness*, **81**(2), pp. 51–2.

Johnson, L. and Corn, A.L. (1989) 'The past, present and future of education for gifted children with sensory and/or physical disabilities'. *Roeper Review*, **12**(1), pp. 13–28.

Karnes, M.B. and Johnson, L. (1986) 'Identification and assessment of gifted/talented handicapped and non-handicapped children in early childhood'. *Journal of Children in Contemporary Society*, **18**(3–4), pp. 35–54.

Kelly, K.R. and Colangelo, N. (1984) 'Academic and social self concepts of gifted, general and special students'. *Exceptional Children*, Vol. 50, pp. 551–4.

Klein, P.S. (1992) 'Mediating the cognitive, social and aesthetic development of precocious young children', in P.S. Klein and A. J. Tannenbaum (eds) *To be Young and Gifted*. Norwood, New Jersey: Ablex Publishing Co.

Lin Shang Ping and Sikka Anjoo (1992) 'The gifted visually handicapped child: a review of literature'. Paper presented at the annual meeting of the Mid South Education Research Association, Knoxville, Tennessee. July.

Loeb, R. C. and Jay, G. (1987) 'Self concept in gifted children: Differential impact on boys and girls'. *Gifted Child Quarterly*, **31**(1), pp. 9–14.

Ludwig, G. and Cullinan, D. (1984) 'Behaviour problems of gifted and non gifted elementary school girls and boys'. *Gifted Child Quarterly*, **28**(1), pp. 37–9.

Maker, C. J. (1977) *Providing Programmes for the Gifted Handicapped*. Virginia: Council for Exceptional Children.

Mendaglio, S. (1995) 'Gifted sensitivity to criticism'. *Our Gifted Children*, **3**(1), pp. 34–5.

Milgram, R.M. and Milgram, N.A. (1976) 'Group versus individual administration in the measurement of creative thinking in gifted and non-gifted children'. *Child Development*, **47**, pp. 563–5.

Minner, S., Prater, G., Bloodworth, H. and Walker, S. (1987) 'Referral and placement recommendations of teachers towards gifted handicapped children'. *Roeper Review*, **9**(4), pp. 247–9.

Montgomery, D. (1997) *Spelling: Remedial Strategies*. London: Cassell.

Pagliano, P. (1994) 'Students with visual impairment', in A. Ashman and J. Elkins (eds) *Educating Children with Special Needs*. New York: Prentice Hall, pp. 345–85.

Piers, E.V. (1984) *Manual of Piers-Harris Children's Self Concept Scale*. Los Angeles: Western Psychological Services.

Renzulli, J., Hartman, R. K. and Callahan, C.M. (1971) 'Teacher identification of superior students: an instrument'. *Exceptional Children*, **38**(3), pp. 211–14.

Ross, A. and Parker, M. (1980) 'Academic and social self concept of the academically gifted'. *Exceptional Children*, **47**(2), pp. 6–10.

Schnitz, C.C. and Galbraith, J. (1985) *Managing the Social and Emotional Needs of the Gifted: a Teacher's Survival Guide*. Minneapolis: Free Spirit Publishing Co.

Seeley, K. (1989) 'Underachieving and handicapped gifted', in J. Feldhusen, J. Van Tassel-Baska and K. Seeley (eds) *Excellence in Educating the Gifted*. Denver CO: Love Publishing, pp. 29–37.

Tillman, M.H. (1973) 'Intelligence scales for the blind: a review with implications for research'. *Journal of School Psychology*, **11**(1), pp. 80–7.

Vialle, W. and Paterson, J. (1996) 'Constructing a culturally sensitive education for gifted deaf students'. Australian Association for the Education of the Gifted and Talented. Conference Proceedings. www.nexus.edu.au.

Wechsler, D. (1992) *Technical Manual of the Australian Adaptation of the Wechsler Intelligence Scale for Children (Third Edition)*. New York: The Psychological Corporation.

Whitmore, J.R. and Maker, C.J. (1985) *Intellectual Giftedness in Disabled Persons*. Rockville MD: Aspen.

Yewchuk, C. and Lupart, J. L. (1993) 'Gifted handicapped: A desultory duality?', in K.A. Heller, F.J. Monks and A.H. Passow (eds) *International Handbook of Research and Development of the Gifted and Talented*. Oxford: Pergamon, pp. 709–25.

6 Gifted children with hearing impairment

Carrie Winstanley

The DfES website (2002) reports the following about deaf people and their education:

> There are 8 million people in the UK with some form of hearing loss. Deafness at birth or in childhood has significant effects on the learning of basic skills and this affects 180,000 people in the UK. A further 500,000 people become severely or profoundly deaf later in life. For them, deafness does not in itself create a need for basic skills, but those who wish to acquire basic skills might find it difficult to access appropriate provision. There are two important sub-groups of deaf learners: those who use British Sign Language (BSL) as their preferred language and those who use speech and lipreading. Although the best medium of instruction is different for each group, the required strategies for teaching and learning are similar. The last survey of deaf school leavers was in 1979. It found that the average reading age for all deaf learners was 8.6. This situation has not improved. (paragraph 35)

And also:

> The quality of current provision is variable. . . . There is no standard nationally of what should be the minimum qualification for tutors. . . . Overall, there are too few resources for tutors and deaf students. (paragraph 37) (www.lifelonglearning.co.uk)

Research in this field is scant and in need of updating. Hunting for material about highly able children who are deaf, proved a complex task.

Defining dual exceptionality

This chapter considers issues facing highly able deaf students, their teachers and families. Before exploring the area it is important to clarify exactly who is being discussed. Both gifted and hearing impaired groups are notoriously difficult to

110

define and even deciding on terms of reference is a minefield. Such decisions are far more than empty political correctness; they are vital aspects of the discussion that strikes at the heart of the difficulties faced by high ability children with a whole range of hearing problems. There is much argument about the exact meaning of 'talent', 'gift' and 'high ability' and as these ideas have been widely rehearsed, I will merely use the terms 'gifted' and 'highly able' interchangeably, rather generally, referring to students who are capable of making connections and seeing relationships in a way that is in advance of their age peers. However, the difficulties of describing deaf people are central to this chapter and will be considered in some depth.

Such a discussion entails an explanation of the complexity of deafness and deaf culture, a phenomenon that makes deafness unique amongst 'disabilities'. Those with hearing problems do not agree on what to be called, with many rejecting the title 'hearing impairment' as a deficit model, implying the aim of normalising the deaf, to make them like the hearing. Some people are happier to describe themselves as 'hard of hearing' (HOH) and others call themselves 'deaf'. (Throughout this chapter I will be using the convention 'deaf' to describe people with any degree of hearing loss and 'Deaf' when referring to cultural aspects of deafness.) 'The Deaf community does not view deafness as a condition to be pitied and cured as is the view held by the "medical condition" construct that has characterised much of deaf education in the past' (Vialle and Paterson 1996: 1).

Deafness and deaf culture

In recent years, two different ways of categorising the deaf have been commonly used and these are defined as 'clinical-pathological' and 'cultural'.

> The contrast in orientation is obvious. The cultural provides a way to call in to question the deeply entrenched view that profound deafness is to be associated automatically with disability, and thereby inability. In a society that sought to accommodate rather than assimilate difference, to maximise potential rather than reify difference as unacceptable, the position of deaf people would indeed be different. (Baker and Cokely, cited in Brien 1981: 46–7)

In defining the notion of culture, shared language is paramount, and Deaf communities worldwide have sign languages that are sophisticated and advanced. This is often cited when arguing for granting deaf people status as a distinct minority cultural group. In the UK, British Sign Language (BSL) is most commonly used, although a simpler language, Makaton, is often adopted for children with speech and communication problems, such as those with autism. This separate cultural identity is often denoted by the capitalisation in 'Deaf'.

> Traditionally, deaf people have been classified as a disability group but as many of the educational problems they face are more closely related to their

111

communication skills, it may be more appropriate to examine their needs alongside other language minority groups. (Vialle and Paterson 1996: 1)

Hearing people often know very little about sign, and are surprised to learn just how diminished the role of speaking can be in Deaf culture. This lack of awareness can result in teachers unwittingly plunging children into conflict by asking them to 'use their voice'. 'Exaggerated speaking behaviour is thought of as "undignified" and sometimes can be interpreted as making fun of other people' (Padden 1980, cited in Gregory and Hartley 1991: 42).

Most class teachers would, of course, be unable to pick up on the complexity of sign, and are unaware even of the existence of dialects and accents. Some accents are so strong that parents have been known to move their children to different schools to avoid adopting the sign accent of those around them. In schools for the deaf that advocate an oral approach, sign is discouraged and sometimes completely disallowed. This is viewed by some members of the Deaf community as devaluing the child's home culture, and a violation of a child's basic rights. However, advocates of the oral approach argue that the deaf child is given optimum opportunity to function in a hearing world if they have developed strong speech, and that this is only really possible if sign is not taught.

Power (1992, cited in Vialle and Paterson 1996: 1) describes 'a handicapping society', and this is clearly seen in schools in which a child's first language is disallowed if it happens to be BSL. In other minority groups, it would be considered an outrage if children were punished for using their home language in the playground, but this is not unheard of in oral schools for the deaf, or in units attached to mainstream schools.

In general, 'deaf' is understood as a description of severe to profound hearing loss, and 'hearing impairment' to cover the whole range of differences in hearing, including the minimal loss that commonly accompanies the ageing process. In the hearing world, this emphasis on varying degrees of hearing loss is considered important, but such distinctions do not apply in the Deaf world. There is even some argument that hearing people can be described as 'Deaf' (but not 'deaf') as they are fully assimilated into the Deaf community but are hearing people.

> 'Deaf' is not a label of deafness as much as a label of identity with other deaf people. . . . The existence of conflict brings out those aspects of the culture of Deaf people that are unique and separate from other cultural groups. It also shows that the group of Deaf people is not merely a group of like-minded people, as with a bridge club, but a group of people who share a code of behaviours and values that are learned and passed on from one generation of Deaf people to the next. Entering into Deaf culture and becoming Deaf means learning all the appropriate ways to behave like a Deaf person. (Padden 1980, cited in Gregory and Hartley 1991: 42)

While emphasising the similarities between the Deaf and people of other linguistic minorities, it is also important to highlight the differences. Many vociferous people in the Deaf community have fought long and hard to achieve some kind of recognition of their deafness as a positive part of their identity, rather than something for which they are to elicit sympathy and pity. This is, of course, to be applauded and it is hoped that their hard work will serve to help the general public better understand what it means to be D/deaf. The recent effect of this campaigning may be seen in the media coverage of a deaf lesbian couple making a deliberate attempt to conceive a deaf baby, through the use of donor sperm from a deaf friend. Some reports expressed outrage about their gay identity, but were more accepting of their desire for a deaf child, demonstrating some understanding of the notion of the Deaf community.

The following statistics were obtained from the National Deaf Children's Society (2002). Congenital deafness occurs in around 840 babies born annually with significant permanent hearing loss. Half of all deaf children remain undiagnosed by the age of 18 months and one quarter of deaf children are not diagnosed by three years. This leads to insufficient support, with less than half of deaf children with access to hearing aids by two years of age. This is probably related to the fact that nearly all (90 per cent) of deaf children are born into families with no experience of deafness, although most children under eight (80 per cent) experience temporary deafness caused by glue ear and so raising awareness would be of use to almost all parents and teachers of primary aged pupils. 16 per cent of permanent deafness may be acquired, progressive or of 'late onset' and in these cases it is often part of a cluster of difficulties. One third of acquired deafness is caused by meningitis, and this often brings other health issues such as visual problems. Treating a student with such difficulties as if they have only some kind of linguistic difference would clearly result in a failure to address their real needs. Of course, 'deaf children face tremendous difficulties learning to read, write and communicate in the hearing world around them' and 'are more vulnerable to neglect, emotional, physical and sexual abuse' National Deaf Children's Society (2002).

Understanding deafness

In the 1960s, studies of deaf people with emotional problems tried to understand congenital and early onset deafness and the psychological aspects of such conditions (Basilier 1964). The term 'surdophrenia' was coined to describe the psychological consequences of deafness and although research emphasised that most deaf people lead happy and fulfilled lives, there were differences recorded in the dream experiences and emotional health of the deaf. Investigations concluded that the deaf are likely to suffer from isolation and detachment that can result in aggression, apparent when deaf people 'attempt to communicate'. It was also noted that emotional turmoil and difficulties cannot be easily expressed and that this could lead to the absence of diagnosis of a potentially serious problem. Clearly, these problems are caused by communication difficulties and could be alleviated by allowing deaf people access to professionals trained in the first language of their clients. The report exposed the unsurprising fact that the Deaf were not very well served by the psychological services. This has been addressed in the last 40 years, of course, but the basic premise still exists; that people who may have difficulty expressing themselves in the majority language, are likely to be mis-diagnosed, or have difficulties being allocated appropriate treatment.

A more positive and enduringly useful observation concerned the finding that a secure family unit significantly helped in the reduction of problems associated with deafness. Those working with deaf children support this, placing huge value on the contribution siblings and parents can make. There are, of course, many deaf children who are not in happy family circumstances and some cultures are ashamed of deafness, viewing it as something to hide and making it difficult for deaf family members to see themselves as Deaf. Although it would be wrong to make generalisations about different cultural groups and to isolate any one community, it is true that the incidence of deafness in Asian communities is higher than in other populations. It thus follows that Asian deaf children have a higher chance of being exposed to problems, despite the Asian community's well-documented strong family ethic. Some Asian families reject the deaf community, resulting in isolation and insufficient support for children. For a gifted, deaf Asian child this would be an even more complex group of competing forms of identity.

Add to that the influence of gender and the picture is yet more crowded. Psychological studies demonstrate that 'females with disability tend to cope with that disability better than do males'(Vernon and La Falce-Landers 1993: 431).

A sense of self

Developing a sense of identity as a deaf person seems to be very important for gifted students and the case studies from Vialle and Paterson's work illustrate this. (A selection of quotations taken from their 1996 paper is incorporated in the case study section at the end of this chapter as I feel that there is a deep resonance with the issues tackled here.) There is a clear emerging theme of:

> . . . reluctance on the part of the interviewees to be double-labelled as gifted, when many of them have struggled to attain a sense of identity as a Deaf person. Identity with Deaf community was also seen as critical factor in their successes. Nearly all the interviewees had experienced an identity crisis that had affected their ability to achieve. It was the successful resolution of such crises, through identification with the Deaf culture, that enabled them to attain their potential. (Vialle and Paterson 1996: 8)

Building a robust and positive sense of self is a key purpose of schooling; there exist some particularly critical developmental periods such as primary–secondary transfer and early adolescence. Many programmes for supporting the highly able child are aimed at secondary pupils and deaf students have been known to reject the special activities for the able as they consider this to impinge upon their developing identity as a member of the Deaf community.

> Through interaction with others, the individual is able to develop an awareness and acceptance of self. Through participation in the various organisations

that make up the community, individuals are able to acquire a sense of self-esteem which may be impossible to develop in the hearing world. (Brien 1981: 50)

Complex issues associated with adolescence, including gender aspects, the formation of enduring friendships and sexuality, are stressful enough, without having to battle with the addition of 'gifted and talented' to the group of labels already assigned. There is also a difference between the imposition of a label and the personal adoption of an identity. Generally, teachers nominate pupils to be placed on the gifted and talented register and such an accolade is expected to be welcomed. Students who are referred by peers are more likely to embrace their 'new identity', as this demonstrates endorsement from friends. It would also represent the kind of atmosphere in school that valued high ability. Commonly though, the attitude of peers means that being part of the 'gifted and talented' cohort can conflict with the desire to be perceived as popular, well-liked and 'cool'. The school ethos generally dictates the way that this issue develops.

There are very few role models for deaf children, making it difficult for them to keep their expectations and hopes high unless they are lucky enough to be surrounded by a truly understanding and supportive family. Similarly, for those who experience late onset deafness, the lack of support 'robbed them of their career, isolated them from friends, and damaged, or destroyed their family life' (Vernon and La Falce-Landers 1993: 430). This reinforces the significance of the Deaf community.

The problems of dual exceptionality

'That nearly 40 per cent required mental health treatment speaks to what happens when a brilliant intellect is confined by the double condition of deafness and inadequate opportunity' (Vernon and La Falce-Landers 1993: 433). Key problems are found among the late onset deaf group and this constitutes around three quarters of the deaf population. 'Traditionally the needs and potentials of such people have been almost totally ignored. The findings of the current study suggest that this segment of the deaf population may represent the greatest wasted potential and suffer the most widespread emotional disturbance to be found among the deaf and hard of hearing' (op. cit.).

Labelling able children through their deafness can lead to a focus on potential problems, with remediation being provided without attention being given to the exceptional ability. LEAs have stipulations about statementing and provision for special education, but there must be the flexibility to adapt to dual exceptionalities. As Vialle and Paterson (1996) note, 'the effect of labelling children as deaf results in the tendency to focus on disability so that a child with even outstanding abilities may be overlooked in the preoccupation with the child's deafness' (p. 2). Specific social and emotional needs accompany the dual exceptionalities of high ability and deafness, as noted above, and it should also be remembered that working with such students presents its own set of challenges. Teachers must be equipped to deal with such demands effectively and would benefit from a variety of support. This could take the form of networking with teachers in similar situations, and national and international fora, such as conferences and publications. Brody and Mills (1997) highlight this, noting that teachers need help with '. . . understanding the characteristics and needs of gifted students with disabilities, as well as strategies to facilitate their learning' (p. 292).

Informal discussion with the DfES (July 2002) indicated that dual exceptionality is high on the agenda for attention within the current gifted and talented strategy and it is likely that more research will be commissioned.

Deafness and learning disabilities

There is much literature on disabilities and associated learning difficulties, making it easy to slip into the thought pattern that treats the two as synonymous. It is not automatically the case, however, that sensory difference or physical disability will result in a learning disability, particularly when the student is highly able and the difficulty is mild. There is a difference between having a learning disability (such as dyslexia, dyspraxia etc.) and having a difficulty with learning. Being unable to learn because the pedagogy is inappropriate is not the same as having trouble learning, even if the teaching is adapted to take learning differences into account. The emphasis here is on the fact that deaf students are sometimes confused with other students whose needs are different. A dyslexic student may well benefit from strategies that will be of no use to a deaf child.

Compensation and masking can prevent accurate diagnosis and this usually occurs as the pupil either attempts to fit in with classmates, or just makes the best of their situation, unaware that other pupils can hear or see more clearly. Brody and Mills (1997: 282–3) present three subgroups of gifted learning disabled students, with characteristics as follows:

- behaviour problems due to lack of diagnosis of a learning problem;
- learning problems have been recognised, but not high ability;
- functioning at just below grade level and therefore assumed to be satisfactorily achieving their potential.

Gifted deaf school children often fall into the second category as many schools do not recognise dual exceptionality. While, as noted, it is not automatically the case that deaf children will have learning disabilities, communication difficulties associated with the experience of deaf children in school are almost certainly going to affect attainment. If there was a different structure in place, or a school-based culture that was more understanding of individual difference, the label of learning disabled may be redundant. However, as the school system currently stands, with the focus on tests and measurable standards, deaf children are likely to be unpopular in selective schools as they are in need of learning support if they are to keep a school's league table rating attractively high. In order to qualify for support, they will have to be assessed and labelled and as already mentioned, when this is done insensitively it can cause problems with a developing sense of identity.

Accurate assessment of needs is, of course, a positive strategy, but must be undertaken with care and be fair to a child who has a minority language. There are many deaf children who are also affected by visual difficulties and other medical issues that may make working to their intellectual potential particularly difficult. It is valid to consider that many deaf children would indeed benefit from effective support for learning disabilities as understood at present, but this should never make using the label 'deaf' tantamount to calling a child problematic.

There will also be a small number of deaf children who are gifted and who in addition have a dyslexic difficulty, and a few with non-verbal learning difficulties that handicap their ability to sign and/or to lip read. These are trebly exceptional children and need the most sensitive identification and support.

UK government strategies for the gifted

At this point it is worth mentioning some reservations about the UK governmental approach to the provision for and the identification of pupils targeted for special programmes in the year 2002. The choice of the term 'gifted and talented' adds to the difficulty as it is loaded with baggage and confusion, with teachers and academics disagreeing about the meanings of the words, making clear identification even more awkward. The target group of the top 10 per cent of school children highlights achievement, rather than potential. Of course, it is easy to see why this is so; it is difficult to make accurate predictions of possible future achievement and easy to ascertain who is already doing well, but this means that under-achieving children are often denied the benefit of provision. Many people working with the children in question prefer terms such as 'more able' to 'gifted and talented', as this allows for less focus on established academic success and keeps alive the debate about who should be in receipt of support, covering emerging talent and abilities. It also permits a wide interpretation of the definition of ability and the nature of intelligence beyond measures and test scores.

Because of the rigidity of systems, in some geographical areas, the way that support is calculated disallows children from being in receipt of help for more than one aspect of education. For example if they are on a gifted programme they may not be allowed reading support (Boodoo 1989; Baum 1994, both cited in Brody and Mills 1997).

As with many programmes for the gifted, the organisers are open to charges of elitism. The resource pot for education is small and the demands are many and expensive. Why support children who are already 'advantaged' through their high ability? The government has highlighted such concerns in recent ministerial speeches (Morris 2002) and aiming for excellence is its answer. Adjusting Local Education Authorities' Special Educational Needs definitions and requirements to incorporate able children with difficulties will help to balance the provision and silence critics (Van Tassel-Baska 1989, cited in Feldhusen and Jarwan 2000: 275).

117

A strongly egalitarian line is often taken when pupils have dual exceptionalities. This suggests that ethical reasons are the basis for allowing provision and that some needs are more deserving than others. If pupils are known to be able, and yet coping with a difficulty, they are deemed as undeserving of support. Extra help is only available if a pupil is causing problems or struggling academically, dragging down overall school achievement. An example of this was when '. . . it was ruled that a very bright young deaf girl was achieving at near grade level and so was not entitled to an interpreter' (Vernon and La Falce-Landers 1993: 433).

Government policy demands that the top group of each school are 'gifted and talented' but of course academic and other standards vary from school to school and from neighbourhood to neighbourhood. Special schools and mainstream schools with units will upset this simple cut off formula and affect the resulting provision, especially when this involves the coming together of local varied schools. Will there be appropriate resources and facilities? Will there be gifted and talented specialists who can communicate through BSL? Rittenhouse and Blough (1995) explored the problem of finding a reference group for comparative selection for gifted programmes. They raise the question: 'Is that reference group gifted students, hearing students, or other students with hearing impairments in the same school?' (p. 51). There is also the range of hearing differences to take into consideration. A profoundly deaf child of hearing parents is likely to have a very different experience of deafness from a late onset mildly hearing impaired child of deaf parents, for example. A direct comparison would be difficult to draw.

Identification of high ability

Teachers are exhorted to look out for different aspects of development at different stages of children's school careers, all of which affect the way in which the gifted are identified and their provision. Deaf students are usually excluded from gifted programmes as they 'rarely meet the rigid cut-offs of most identification procedures' (Fall and Nolan 1993, cited in Brody and Mills 1997: 283).

Even from the youngest stages, deaf children are at a disadvantage. In babies and pre-school children, alertness is considered a great indication of ability (Freeman 1991) and a child who seems to be unaware of aspects of her surroundings may be considered as not very able. That this is due to a hearing problem is not always easy to spot and such children can easily go undiagnosed, with obvious ramifications for the way in which the child is treated by those around her. Recommendations for extra stimulation are likely to be made for children, whatever their ability, but a simplification of language and concepts is typical if the child is considered less able. This limits the exposure to complexity and without the excitement of challenge, the child's response is simplified and may become dull. So begins the vicious circle.

The main forms of identification of the able make use of verbal tests or those with a verbal component, such as WISC-III or Stanford Binet. Teachers and learning support workers are becoming more familiar with the spiky score

118

syndrome, or 'subtest scatter', as literature and research focus on variety of abilities. In some places composite scores are still exclusively used, meaning that highly able children with weaknesses in one or more aspects of the test will not be selected for gifted programmes, as their low scores bring down their total and strengths may be overlooked. Increasing use is being made of Raven's Progressive Matrices tests (1983), which can be teacher administered.

Brian was a seemingly intelligent 6 year old with severe hearing loss in both ears and was in a unit for 5–11 year old deaf children that insisted upon oral communication. Brian seemed incapable of lip reading and was showing difficulties in learning to spell, read and acquire any spoken vocabulary. He communicated by gesture and mime, often in the most amusing way, which made his teacher think he was more able than his school achievements suggested. The pressure on lip reading from the unit leader, banning signing, was making Brian become increasingly frustrated and his behaviour was problematic. He had made no progress on the Derbyshire Language Scheme (Knowles and Masidlover 1982) or the Language Assessment Remediation and Screening Procedure (Crystal, Fletcher and Garman 1976) when retested. However, when he was tested on Raven's Progressive Matrices colour version he was found to have a visual-perceptual intelligence in the top two per cent of the population. He was a very bright little boy with a double difficulty: a severe hearing impairment and an oral language learning difficulty. He responded very well and very rapidly to the signing system that his teacher secretly taught him (Montgomery 2000).

Teacher referral tends to rely on one of the numerous available checklists and these almost always suggest that a wide vocabulary and a love of words and language are key indicators of high ability. Teachers who cannot sign may be unaware of a child's love of words and their meanings, if there is only minimal speech. It has already been demonstrated that the subtleties of BSL can be easily overlooked by those outside of the Deaf community. Many experts in gifted education (for example Gross 1993; Freeman *et al.* 1996; George 1998) highlight early speech as the key to identifying the able, but this does not allow for the developmental delay that often accompanies deafness.

The central focus of language as the main indication of ability needs to be shifted, not only for the Deaf, but for all groups that are linguistically disadvantaged. Bernstein's work in the 1970s concerning Restricted and Elaborated Codes can be invoked as the starting point for educators realising the importance of this area. Despite research and rhetoric, there are still many school children denied access to the full curriculum and appropriate gifted and talented programmes due to their lack of familiarity with the majority language. 'The literature over the last two decades has emphasised the need for multiple means of identification and appropriate curricula. In practice, however, use of standard English tends to be used as a de facto measure of intelligence' (Vialle and Paterson 1996: 1).

It follows, therefore, that an identification system that uses a range of indicators is clearly more useful than narrow IQ-based studies. The use of Gardner's (1993) Multiple Intelligences approach or the adoption of the Nebraska Starry Night observation schedule (cited in Winebrenner 1995) could allow for a broader range of children being identified and receiving support. Language scores are likely to bring down the overall score for deaf children and as some programmes can be enjoyed without a particularly high level of language, composite scores should be used as entry qualifications only when absolutely necessary. Other methods such as parent, peer and self nomination are also of use, but where expectations are held at a low level through a misunderstanding of the nature of deafness, these are not always useful.

Checklists focus on behaviours and personality traits and even among the hearing population there is so much variety that many lists even contradict themselves. Typical lists can contain the following 'help' in spotting a gifted child. They are likely to:

- be gregarious;
- be shy;
- have many friends;
- have no friends;
- spend long hours on the same task, completing it to perfection;
- leave things unfinished once the main thinking has been accomplished;
- be sensitive to those around them;
- demonstrate limited empathy.
  (conflated from a variety of different checklists)

With such confusion, it is difficult to build a clear picture of an able child and when the effect of deafness on behaviour in school is added there is an even more complex portrait. Other obstacles such as 'stereotypical expectations, developmental delays, incomplete information about the child . . . and lack of challenge' will only make things more difficult (Feldhusen and Jarwan 2000: 275).

What is needed, therefore, is a complex range of assessment tools encompassing cognitive abilities, some aspects of behaviour and focusing less on verbal approaches to measuring potential. The tests need to identify giftedness as well as finding areas of weakness that would benefit from support (Brody and Mills 1997; Feldhusen and Jarwan 2000: 279). Assessments will have to be regularly updated to ensure the appropriateness of provision and the development of emerging abilities, and the best current conceptions of ability and most up to date rating scales should be adopted.

Underachievement

The underachievement of the Deaf is an on-going problem, and the low attainment of deaf school children is reinforced by the associated low expectations. This cycle can, and must, be broken. It will require a rethink of the identification of the needs of the deaf child along with more effective training for teachers and a thorough programme of deaf awareness primarily among schools, but also within broader society.

DfES findings are presented at the opening of this chapter, and figures from the US note that the 'status of the education of the deaf was unacceptable and characterised by inappropriate priorities and inadequate resources' and that only 33 per cent of hearing impaired students graduate with high school diplomas. Other minority groups, such as black students, have a 75 per cent graduation record (Holdcomb *et al.*, and McLoughlin, cited in Vialle and Paterson 1996: 2). A further disappointing statistic shows that 30 per cent of deaf people able to enter the work force were unemployed (Vernon and La Falce-Landers 1993: 427).

It is important to spot children who are 'coasting' at school as early as possible. The lack of stimulation may force the child to look for another way to make school entertaining. This is often something anti-social, such as distracting peers. There is a likely prospect of a rather negative cycle of behaviours to form, worsening as the child progresses through the education system, with hearing classmates' achievement accelerating increasingly away from their Deaf peers.

Provision for dual exceptionality

There are other definitions and terms for the students, including 'gifted handicapped' (Clark 1992, cited in Feldhusen and Jarwan 2000: 275) but currently 'dual exceptionalities' seems to be in favour. Brody and Mills (1997: 287) bemoan the lack of clarity and agreement about what constitutes gifted students with learning disabilities. Their suggestions encompass more students than just the deaf, but are still relevant. They suggest:

1. there is a rationale for thinking about these students as a separate subgroup;
2. students with LD who are gifted represent a heterogeneous group with many different types of gifts/talents and disabilities;
3. a performance discrepancy is essential for identifying gifted students with learning disabilities; and
4. for appropriate intervention to take place, it is necessary to establish causal factors for the learning problems, or at least to rule out other causal factors that could lead to very different interventions.

All of these suggest that teacher education must focus on dual exceptionalities in order to make optimum provision for children. There are many disgruntled deaf students who would reinforce this view.

Anecdotes from deaf people are numerous about their teachers' inability to sign to them or children being forbidden to sign to one another. Under these circumstances, it is difficult to imagine an atmosphere that is conducive to creativity, imagination and discovery of students' giftedness. (Vialle and Paterson 1996: 1)

Alternatives to formal schooling are being considered with increasing seriousness as the development of technology allows for a more genuinely inclusive approach, catering for a far broader range of learning styles and needs. Home education is increasing and schools and colleges are being forced to adapt course materials for distributed and distance learning. Common proposals are typified by Adcock (1995), who emphasized home and resource centred learning and community based work incorporating learning institutions such as museums and galleries. He suggests a role for a 'critical pedagogue, challenging and supporting the learners in the process of learning and at the same time constantly developing and researching his/her own professional practice as an integral part of that learning process' (cited in Lloyd 2000: 149).

The National Council for Educational Technology (1995) reported that a further way of helping deaf children to become excited about learning is through technology such as CD-ROMS and websites. Since their report, the market has exploded and there is amazing choice and variety available to buy or through loan schemes (TEEM Teachers Evaluating Educational multimedia). Concerns about exclusion through the use of sound in multimedia were allayed: 'in spite of our scepticism, projects from around the country show that multimedia has captured the imagination of these pupils in a way that no other technology can' (p. 5). Particularly valuable has been the fact that '. . . it can be an almost entirely visual medium. If the authors choose, they can present their ideas entirely via BSL, animation and illustrations. For once they have a medium which plays to their strengths' (p. 6). Technology can also help to foster genuine interaction in the classroom. Software that converts speech to text allows students to participate without the presence of a note taker and for those daunted by text there is a possibility of real time signing or BSL video clips (p. 31).

Implications for classroom practice

Teacher expectation is vital in helping able pupils achieve highly. The traditional failure of deaf children in formal schooling has developed into a stereotype that can be combated through teacher education and the raising of awareness.

> Because teachers of deaf children are not prepared in their teacher education programmes to respond to gifted and talented students and, in fact, may be predisposed to teach in ways specifically determined by the child's hearing loss . . . it is likely that these specially prepared teachers miss important learning opportunities in their own classrooms. (Rittenhouse and Blough 1995: 53)

The deaf friendly school and teacher will probably have undergone some kind of deaf awareness training. In a project entitled 'Developing Deaf Friendly Schools' carried out in 2001 by the National Deaf Children's Society, deaf awareness training was provided for primary school pupils and teachers (www.ndcs.org.uk). A whole school approach guidance booklet was written and it is hoped that the successful project will secure more funding and therefore be extended. Although teachers considered the training very useful, they felt that more support was needed if they were to cope with having deaf children in the mainstream. Teachers of the deaf, however, reported that the awareness raising made a notable positive impact for deaf children in both classroom and playground settings.

Kaderavek and Pakulski (2002: 17) suggest functional and simple advice concerning specific aspects of the teacher's role:

- Ensure that heating/lights are repaired to decrease vibration and 'hum';
- Fit carpets, curtains, even egg crates to reduce sound reverberation;
- Do not speak louder over classroom noise;
- Position yourself with light on your face, in full clear view and move closer to students when addressing them, to encourage their attention on your face;
- Rephrase sentences in clear contexts when there is misunderstanding. This is preferable to shouting;
- Be aware of students' coping strategies such as bluffing and apparent lack of interest. These are commonly used to mask confusion.

Other, more general ideas include (summarised from Rittenhouse and Blough 1995: 53):

- Assume students have unique talents
- De-emphasise verbal test scores
- Evaluate your students against a local gifted programme inventory
- Individualise instruction and subject matter
- Create thematic units drawing on your students' talents.

Conclusions drawn from other projects echo these recommendations, and this signifies the generalisability of findings despite typically small sample groups. The conclusions below are summarised from Baum's project, where the emphasis was on Renzulli's Enrichment Triad Model (1986), adapting this to make use of approaches that 'bypass weaknesses in reading', undertaking 'no-fail entry activities' (Baum 1988: 227). These characteristics are wholly applicable to deaf students, and the following key points are also relevant:

- 'Focused attention should be given to the development of a gift or talent in its own right' – this should result in enrichment rather than remediation, which will help to build self-esteem.
- 'Gifted learning disabled students require a supportive environment which values and appreciates individual abilities' – students were equipped with tools for building their own research projects and so 'their disability was minimised while their strengths were highlighted'.
- 'Students should be given strategies to compensate for their learning problems as well as direct instruction in basic skills' – the use of word processing, spell checks, photography and other technology allowed these students 'to author without getting bogged down in the physical act of writing'.
- 'Gifted disabled students must become aware of their strengths and weaknesses and be helped to cope with the discrepancy between them – the students in the model programme were told that the enrichment programme was designed to focus on their special abilities whereas their learning disabilities programme would continue to provide remedial support' (Baum 1988: 230).

Case examples

Here are examples of the kinds of achievements of which the deaf children and their families should rightly be proud, as well as some instances of good school and family practice.

1. The BBC See Hear programme filmed a hearing mother and deaf daughter project designed to raise sign awareness, in which an original song was written and interpreted through sign by a 12 year old girl. This was broadcast nationwide.

2. A selective independent school in London has agreed to accept a deaf girl despite admitting that this will require training for staff as there are no specialists. They have been prepared to make adjustments (such as carpeting noisy wooden floors and changing teaching rooms) to allow a particularly able student to benefit from the academic environment and small class sizes. This child's deaf father has managed to persuade the LEA to foot the bill by pointing out that the school fees are around £19,000 less than the proposed specialist school. In this instance, having a brother and father who are both able and deaf, and an able mother, has ensured optimum educational opportunity for the child.

3. A ten year old deaf boy is in a mainstream school with a unit for deaf children where he is set across all subjects. Fairly typically of deaf students, he needs to undertake literacy classes in the unit, but is very able in mathematics and is in the top set where he completes accelerated work. This positive action has helped raise his self-esteem. Schools with less understanding of the deaf (and indeed of high ability) are likely to disallow this uneven acceleration where there are still literacy issues to be addressed.

4. The whole family of a ten year old girl moved across the country in order to facilitate her attendance at a specialist school in which signing is positively encouraged. She had argued with teachers in her oral school and despite citing aspects of the Children Act was still punished for making use of sign in school. Like a number of deaf children, this girl is likely to lose her sight and so will have to rely on hand on hand communication at some point in her life. Being taught using a combination of oral and signing methods will help to facilitate this development. Her parents are both hearing but have managed to enter into their daughter's world through celebrating her special qualities. She is considered a remarkable child, with great resilience and exemplary interpersonal abilities.

5. A deaf Asian child in a mainstream school with a unit for deaf children has exceptional linguistic skills, being able to communicate in BSL, Arabic Sign Language, English and Arabic. His parents recently flew him to Iran to attend a school where he could learn some Arabic Sign Language, with a focus on signing the Qur'an. A hearing child able to communicate in four languages would surely be recognised as highly able. This boy is subjected to the ridicule of peers when he selects to use BSL and some teachers (still undergoing training) have yet to decide whether they prefer an oral or a signing method. This would be equivalent to a bilingual school being unde-

cided about which language they will choose for lessons. It is not an environment that is obviously conducive to consistent educational achievement.

6. A six year old boy who has a cluster of difficulties characterised by developmental delay has only recently been able to express his abilities. He has been locked into a world where he was unable to communicate as the delay in gross motor skill development, part paralysis and deafness had made it impossible for the development of speech. The focus on his mobility and learning to use the Rolator he needs to get about, detracted from other areas of development, but once introduced to sign, it became clear that he is highly able, dealing with complex and abstract issues in a confident and impressive manner. People meeting him assume that he has been signing for all six years of his life, as he has a natural and fluent style despite less than 12 months of experience.

7. Ruth – a deaf child of hearing parents. 'I started mixing with Deaf people . . . I realised they've got a lot of answers to my identity. I didn't see myself as a deaf person who could achieve. I saw myself as someone who was sick, who couldn't really achieve in a hearing community; they were my answer; the Deaf community was my answer.'

8. Greg reports one particular incident when he was caned in front of the school assembly because he failed to line up when the bell was sounded! Greg does not use the term 'gifted' to describe himself or his attainment. He attributes his achievements to his identification with a Deaf community: 'I identify myself as a Deaf person and I live within the Deaf community. With identity comes pride as well and in being Deaf I feel that I'm not different to any other person.' He stated that he felt he could have achieved more if he had 'established his Deaf identity' earlier in life.

9. Jan suffered from self doubts and an identity crisis. She felt that teachers did not listen to her own beliefs about her needs and did not challenge her intellectually.

The following quotations are from Vialle and Paterson (1996):

> Alice – In essence, the teachers expected less of Deaf students, despite the fact that the school catered specifically for Deaf students. 'I think bilingual schools are excellent . . . you're not putting down sign language, you're encouraging that as a natural language.' (pp. 3–4)

> Stephen – . . . 'when I go into the education system and I teach Deaf students I act as a role model and in doing that it raises the expectations of the Deaf students themselves about what they can do and what they can't do.' (p. 5)

Summary and conclusions

This chapter has identified the immensely important role of Deaf culture in the development of able children with any kind of hearing loss. Sign language is central to this culture, whose communities have been vital in fostering the positive development of deaf individuals and their families. The formation of self identity and a positive self image is best carried out within this context, and further research into D/deafness is needed to help explain exactly why this is so.

Such research would also help to raise the profile of the doubly exceptional able deaf pupil whose related learning problems could be better helped if the government and, in turn, schools were appraised of appropriate courses of action. Controversy concerning identification of high ability and ways of dealing with under-achievement should be aired, and resolutions must be made in order to help teachers improve classroom practice. If inclusion is to be workable the tasks noted in this chapter should be prioritised.

The UK government is committed to inclusive schooling as far as possible. To engender real transformation and positive development in supporting the able pupil with deafness, there needs to be a sea change in the attitude to under-achievement in general. For such shifts it seems helpful to look beyond psychometric tests and psychological constructs to the more philosophical underpinnings and assumptions upon which these ideas rest. Schultz (2002) does this in a recent paper, in which he presents an overview of the field, considering a range of notions from a variety of disciplines. The key summary point he raises echoes ideas stated at the opening of this chapter as specific to the Deaf culture.

> Historically, underachieving gifted students in the classroom have been viewed as defective merchandise in need of repair. . . . Future research needs to move away from (this notion) . . . to . . . working *with* students to develop understanding and learning. . . . Alleviating tendencies leading to learner marginalisation and perceived underachievement is the goal. (Schultz 2002: 204–5)

As can be seen, to allow deaf able children a fair chance in school, there will have to be substantial attention directed towards their needs. A reorganisation of the training of teachers of the deaf is vital, as is the opening up of the debate about different teaching methods, particularly oral and signing. Parents and pupils should be presented with relevant facts to help them make choices, and if inclusion is to be the nationwide strategy, it must be adequately funded and honestly assessed. Policy makers should be properly aware of the issues involved, recognising that general education programming is insufficient and that teacher education is vital. (Rittenhouse and Blough 1995: 53)

These ideas are summarised in Lloyd's (2000) paper: '. . . as long as the organisation of schooling, the curriculum, and assessment and testing procedures remain unchallenged, equal educational opportunity will remain a myth' (p. 133). The paper concludes by drawing attention to the way in which policy 'reaffirms inequality and poor educational experience'. She recommends a 'considerable shift in understanding about the aims of education and its purposes' in order to provide both excellence and equity (p. 149).

At the time of writing, two pertinent stories have grabbed the headlines. The South African swimmer Natalie du Toit has made world history by swimming in both able bodied and disabled categories in the Commonwealth Games. In the second story, outrage has been expressed because Anastasia Fedetova, a profoundly deaf student, achieved six 'A' grade A levels but was rejected by Oxford on the basis of the interview, but could such a test be fair? The key benefit of the row is the raising of awareness of the difficulties faced by the doubly exceptional deaf and highly able person but there is still a long way to go. It seems there is some hope.

Acknowledgement

In writing this chapter enormous thanks are owed to an able Deaf friend, T-J Jobson, who graduated with a degree in Education and has gone on to establish and run 'Reversed', a youth club where the language is BSL. Deaf and hearing children are welcome and all have to communicate through sign. (For more information see the NDCS magazine, issue no. 186, May/June 2002.)

References

Basilier, T. (1964) 'Surdophenia: the psychic consequences of congenital or early acquired deafness', in S. Gregory and G.M. Hartley (eds) *Constructing Deafness* (1977). London: Pinter/Contiuum and The Open University, pp. 74–9.

Baum, S. (1988) 'An Enrichment Program for Gifted Learning Disabled Students', *Gifted Child Quarterly* **32**(1) Winter.

Brien, D. (1981) 'Is there a deaf culture?', in S. Gregory and G.M. Hartley (eds) (1997) *Constructing Deafness*. London: Pinter/Continuum, in association with Open University, pp. 46–52.

Brody, B. and Mills, C. (1997) 'Gifted Children with Learning Disabilities: A Review of the Issues', *Journal of Learning Disabilities* **30**(3) May/June, pp. 282–96.

Crystal, D., Fletcher, P. and Garman, M. (1976) *A Language Assessment Remediation and Screening Procedure (LARSP)*. London: Arnold.

DfES (2002) www.lifelonglearning.co.uk (DfES website).

Feldhusen, J. F. and Jarwan, F. A. (2000) 'Identification of Gifted and Talented Youth for Educational Programs', in K. Heller, Monks, F.J., Sternberg, R.J. and Subotnik, R. (eds) *The International Handbook of Giftedness and Talent* (2nd edn). Oxford: Elsevier Sciences Ltd, pp. 271–82.

Freeman, J. (1991) *Gifted Children Growing Up*, London: Cassell.

Freeman, J., Span, P. and Wagner, H. (eds) (1996) *Actualising Talent*. London: Cassell.

Gardner, H. (1993) *Frames of Mind: A Theory of Multiple Intelligences*. New York: Basic Books.

George, D. (1998) *The Challenge of the Able Child*. London: David Fulton.

Gregory, S. and Hartley, G.M. (eds) (1991) *Constructing Deafness*. Milton Keynes: Open University.

Gross, M. (1993) *Exceptionally Gifted Children*. London: Routledge.

Kaderavek, J.N. and Pakulski, L.A. (2002) 'Minimal Hearing Loss is Not Minimal', *Teaching Exceptional Children* **34**(6) July/August, pp. 14–18.

Knowles, S. and Masidlover, M. (1982) *The Derbyshire Language Programme.* Derby: Speech Therapy Services.

Lloyd, C. (2000) 'Excellence for *all* children – false promises! The failure of current policy for inclusive education and implications for schooling in the 21st century', *International Journal of Inclusive Education* **4**(2), pp. 133–51.

Montgomery, D. (2000) *MA Specific Learning Difficulties, Module 7 Study Guide: Language and Speech Difficulties.* London: Middlesex University.

Morris, E. (2002) 'Excellence across sectors', 16 May. Available at www.dfes.gov.uk/speeches/16_05_02/01.shtml.

National Council for Educational Technology (1995) *Focusing on Deaf People: A Report on the Focus on Deaf People Conference.* Coventry: NCET.

National Deaf Children's Society (2002) *Childhood Deafness – the facts.* www.ndcs.org.uk/ch_deaf/c._facts.htm.

Raven, J. (1983) *Coloured Progressive Matrices.* Oxford: Psychological Corporation.

Rittenhouse, R.K. and Blough, L.K. (1995) 'Gifted Students with Hearing Impairments', *Teaching Exceptional Children* **27**(4) Summer, pp. 51–3.

Schultz, R. (2002) 'Understanding Giftedness and Underachievement: At the Edge of Possibility', *Gifted Child Quarterly* **46**(3) Summer, pp. 193–207.

Smithers, R. and Ward, D. (2002) 'Admissions row engulfs Oxford', *The Guardian*, Aug. 20, p. 5.

Vernon, M. and La Falce-Landers, E. (1993) 'A Longitudinal Study of Intellectually Gifted Deaf and Hard of Hearing People', *American Annals of the Deaf* **138**(5), pp. 427–34.

Vialle, W. and Paterson, J. (1996) 'Constructing a culturally sensitive education for gifted deaf students', Australian Association for the Education of the Gifted and Talented. Conference Proceedings. www.nexus.edu.au

Willard-Holt, C. (1998) 'Academic and personality characteristics of gifted students with cerebral palsy: A multiple case study', *Exceptional Children* **65**(1), pp. 37–50.

Winebrenner, S. (1995) *Teaching Gifted Kids in the Regular Classroom.* Mass: Free Spirit.

PART THREE:
SOCIAL, EMOTIONAL AND
BEHAVIOURAL DISABILITIES

My interest and involvement in behaviour problems might be said to be life-long, having nearly been excluded from schools on several occasions for mis-behaviour from an early age. As a teacher I thus had experience that helped me to understand and predict when behaviour problems might arise and why they might occur. So often the origin seemed to lie in the unutterable boredom and sameness of the school day and of the teaching and learning going on there and the aversive and hostile nature of some teachers.

In initial teacher and in-service education one of the main areas of training has needed to be in the study and management of emotional and behavioural difficulties (EBD) in mainstream schools. In pursuing research and practice in this area it quickly becomes apparent that many gifted learners become labelled 'EBD' and thereafter their giftedness or talent is not addressed. In a recent study of pupils excluded from schools for problem behaviour (Smith 2002) one had unidentified Asperger Syndrome and the other 17 had unidentified dyslexic difficulties. One of the group had a non-verbal IQ well above his age level and verbal score suggesting giftedness as well as dyslexia and EBD. Three more had dyslexia with IQ scores at a level with chronological age or only six months below, suggesting that they were of at least high average ability or more, taking into account the dyslexia's effects on test performance. None of this appeared to have been considered in their reports or placements.

It can only be imagined how great the frustration and depression may have been in the presence of such discrepancies between ability and achievement. It is not unlikely that such intelligence would find its way into other interests such as 'annoying the teacher', oppositional behaviour, cheekiness, clowning and disruption every time literacy tasks were introduced or lessons became boring. How boring is not revealed until the researcher 'shadows' such pupils for a whole day to see what the educational diet has on offer.

In Chapter seven Sisk examines the problems that arise for gifted students in 'ill fitting' environments and how dyssynchronicities in abilities and competencies can make them vulnerable to emotional, social and behavioural difficulties. She shows how these difficulties may be identified and how additional stress is created and then how education as therapy can help them resolve the problems. Through applied research with gifted students she shows how education for self-understanding, counselling and the use of myth in teaching methods can all help the students achieve mastery and equilibrium in emotional and other areas.

In Chapter eight Montgomery analyses the condition known as Asperger Syndrome, which has only recently come to prominence since it was separated out from other autistic spectrum disorders. The chapter explains how isolated talents in autism can occur and how the high abilities and specific talents in Asperger Syndrome can be overlooked in concern for the social and behavioural problems and the lack of emotional empathy. She then describes how individualised programmes of behavioural, social and life skills training can be constructed to establish the students as independent learners and adults.

In the final chapter in this part McCluskey and his colleagues describe the results of an extensive series of last chance and rescue programmes run with 'at risk' groups of talented but troubled children and youths in the Manitoba area. They use Creative Problem Solving techniques as the core and combine them with other strategies such as mentoring and career awareness planning.

In the UK we have a number of successful projects run in local areas, such as Compact Club 2000, run in Birmingham by Chris Traxon, and in Portsmouth by Nigel DuPree, Director of the SMART Foundation, to develop self advocacy, literacy and social and behavioural skills. However, there is no overall coordination of such provision as yet and high ability and talent as a special dimension and dyssynchrony do not as yet figure as a major concern. This is not to say that the talents they undoubtedly uncover are not recognised: they are, and are celebrated.

Every school is required to have an agreed behaviour management policy and set of practices and these are usually based upon positive behavioural management techniques promoted by a range of trainers and authors. Nevertheless the training is not reaching into the deeper regions of classroom interactions. For many learners are becoming disaffected and alienated from school. The increase in problem behaviour perhaps arises from a number of factors including a standards based education system with its failures identified early at Key stages 7, 11, 14, and GCSEs; a teacher directed talk and writing based curriculum; the changing cultures of the educated and educators; the mismatches between promoted icons and models of success; and traditional values and the Protestant ethic and so on.

We do need a closer analysis of the origin of problem behaviours in relation to the inflexibility of the UK curriculum, giftedness and talent and emotional literacy or lack of it. The development of emotional literacy could and should be reintroduced into the mainstream curriculum, not as an add-on, but as integral to teaching and learning as described by Sisk and McCluskey. Although they were engaged in special projects, the essence of what they did can be transported into mainstream education as it once was.

References

Smith, L. (2002) 'An investigation of children having emotional and behavioural difficulties and dyslexic-type difficulties in three special schools and one pupil referral unit'. Unpublished MA SpLD Dissertation. London: Middlesex University.

7 Gifted with behaviour disorders: marching to a different drummer

Dorothy Sisk

If a man does not keep pace with his companions,
perhaps it is because he hears a different drummer.
Let him step to the music which he hears, however
measured or far away.

Henry David Thoreau

Individual differences have intrigued and challenged educators for centuries, and the understanding and application of this concept greatly motivates educators; yet, practical classroom responses to individual differences are elusive, particularly for gifted and talented students. One pioneer in gifted education in the United States, Ruth Martinson, said individual differences are positive and should be considered as a resource in schools. She stressed that effective schooling expands the differences between students, rather than restricting them. Martinson championed the idea of expanding diversity, rather than seeking conformity and inappropriate uniformity. Most gifted students would probably agree with her statement, which is no surprise since Ruth Martinson was a highly gifted individual.

Sternberg (2000) uses the term 'success intelligence' to describe the ability to achieve success in life, given individual personal standards within a given sociocultural context. The possibility to achieve success depends on the individual's ability to capitalise on strengths and correct or compensate for weaknesses through a balance of analytical, creative and practical skills. Sternberg says in order to adapt, shape and select environments, gifted people do these things at a higher level than do others. Sternberg stresses that gifted individuals have a superior aptitude to interact with their environment and to utilise their abilities. Whether the gifted maximise their strengths is dependent on their environment including the family, school and sociocultural context.

Neihart *et al.* (2002) report that there is no evidence that gifted children or youths as a group are inherently any more vulnerable or flawed in adjustment than any other group. They found no evidence of social or emotional vulnerabilities or flaws unique to intellectually gifted learners or to those with high creative potential; but they do state social and emotional problems related to giftedness occur, and they most frequently reflect the interaction of an ill-fitting environment with an individual's personal characteristics. It is this flawed interaction between the gifted individual, their family, school, peers and culture that impacts on social and emotional development. Using Sternberg's 'successful intelligence' as a focal point, the question that needs to be addressed is: What can education do to help gifted students be successful in ill-fitting environments?

Neihart *et al.* (2002) identified numerous researchers who agree that talented students are subject to unique stressors and vulnerable to difficulties with social and emotional adjustment (Genshaft, Greenbaum *et al.* 1995; Hoge and Renzulli 1993; Hollinger 1995; Silverman 1993; Webb, Meckstroth *et al.* 1982); and gifted children and youths have a similar collection of problems identified by numerous researchers (Webb 1993; Clark 1983; Silverman 1993).

Linda Silverman says gifted students have complex thought processes and emotions that are mirrored in the intricacy of their emotional development:

> Idealism, self doubt, perceptiveness, excruciating sensitivity, moral imperatives, desperate need for understanding, acceptance, and love – all impinge simultaneously. Their vast emotional range makes them appear contradictory: mature and immature, arrogant and compassionate, aggressive and timid. Semblances of composure and self-assurance often mask deep feelings of insecurity. The inner experience of the gifted . . . is rich, complex and turbulent. (1993: 84)

Dyssynchronicity

Terraiser (1985) describes dyssynchronicity as having two parts: **internal** refers to disparate rates of development in intellectual, psychomotor and affective development, such as a gifted five year old with an elaborate vocabulary and imagination and an inability to write or use the computer. The second type of dyssynchronicity is **social**, in which the gifted child feels out-of-step with the social context. An example would be a gifted child in a heterogeneous classroom keeping her advanced information or knowledge to herself because the other children don't understand, or they are not interested in her comments and ridicule her. Terraiser uses dyssynchronicity to describe the dilemma of being gifted and maintains because of advanced cognitive ability, the gifted are faced with the dilemma of experiencing different mental, emotional, social and physical ages. This phenomenon coupled with intensity creates experiences that are qualitatively and quantitatively different for gifted students.

Terman's (1931) classic study of intellectually gifted individuals addressed the issue of dyssynchronicity. Precocity unavoidably complicates the problem of social adjustment. 'The child of eight years with a mentality of twelve or fourteen is faced with a situation almost inconceivably difficult. In order to adjust normally, such a child has to have an exceptionally well-balanced personality and to be well nigh a social genius. The higher the IQ, the more acute the problem' (p. 579). As one gifted adolescent said, 'I limit myself to three responses per class, that way no one groans when I respond; although, when it appears that the teacher needs an answer, I'll sometimes add another response just to help move the lesson along.'

Another pioneer in gifted education, Hollingworth (1931), said the further removed children are from the average in intelligence, the more pressing their adjustment problems become. In her study of social adjustment, she found gifted adolescents to be much less neurotic, much more self sufficient, and much less submissive than non-gifted adolescents. Yet, she did report that as the intelligence of gifted children increases so does their difficulty with peer relations.

Selected characteristics that cause concern for gifted students

Persistence, intensity, perfectionism and sensitivity are characteristics that can cause considerable concern for gifted students. **Persistence** is viewed negatively by both parents and educators when the gifted child's persistence conflicts with established or set times for meals, household chores, assignments and school responsibilities. Parents and educators often describe this characteristic as stubbornness. **Intensity** whether intellectual, emotional, sensual, imaginational or psychomotor as described by Dabrowski (1964, 1972) usually positions gifted students in conflict with the demands and expectations of the environment at home or at school. Dabrowski called these intensities overexcitabilities, and research comparing overexcitabilities (OEs) has found a greater incidence of OEs in gifted children and adults in comparison with other populations. When parents and educators fail to understand the overexcitability of gifted students, the students' behaviour may become even more intensified and result in behaviour disorders or emotional disturbance.

Intellectual intensity can manifest itself with gifted children asking probing questions, becoming preoccupied with theoretical problems, displaying an avid desire for knowledge about a given topic and wanting to analyse material. It can also include independence of thought, a sharp sense of observation, striving for synthesis of knowledge and searching for truth. In the regular classroom in which a harried teacher is concentrating on introducing a concept with the highest hope that the students will remember the facts, the intellectual intensity of a gifted child becomes problematic. **Emotional intensity** can result in great intensity of feeling including concern with death, fears, anxieties and depression. It can also include a concern for others and a high degree of interpersonal feeling. **Sensual intensity** can be expressed as wanting to be in the limelight and seeking sensual outlets, including touching things, tasting and smelling. When an opportunity for a 'star' role arises, most gifted students step forward and volunteer. In a group of gifted students, often there are 'all chiefs and no indians'. **Psychomotor intensity** can be noted in a love of movement, rapid speech, restlessness and impulsive activity. When I first began teaching gifted students, I would look out on my class and see a 'sea of movement': some students were twisting their hair, others were finger drumming or foot-jiggling, and there were always one or two bounding from their seats with, 'I know about that.' **Imaginational intensity** can be associated with inventiveness, vivid animated visualisation, and the use of images and metaphor in verbal expression. It can be noted in poetic creations and dramatisations to escape boredom in the classroom or at home. When gifted students are given an opportunity to use a journal, they may choose to draw images rather than write. The psychologist Jung, in his later years, used images in his journal, rather than writing, saying images were quicker and more accurate.

Perfectionism as a characteristic in gifted students results in dissatisfaction with schoolwork and work around the home. One way many gifted students handle perfectionism is to refuse to try a task if they feel they cannot do it in the manner in which they want it accomplished. Perfectionism can become a stimulus for a lifetime of under-achievement. As a teacher, I learned to quickly appropriate art work or poetry from several perfectionistic gifted students before they had an opportunity to destroy their products in frustration. Perfectionism in gifted students leads them to say 'it doesn't look like I want it to'.

Importance of accurate and appropriate feedback

When gifted students receive feedback from parents and school personnel that 'they' are the problem, gifted students without appropriate coping mechanisms can begin to feel estranged from peers and school, and they may begin to exhibit behaviour disorders and be classified as emotionally disturbed. As Director of the Office of Gifted and Talented in Washington, DC, I received a call for assistance from the Pennsylvania state consultant for the gifted. She said that over 50 per cent of the students referred to the emotionally disturbed programme who were given individual assessments by psychologists could be classified as gifted students. The questions we decided to address were: Do teachers view characteristics of gifted and talented students as characteristics that they want 'fixed'? Were the students twice-exceptional students, gifted and emotionally disturbed? Had 'ill-fitting environments' of school, family and community manifested in behaviour disorders?

The answer to the first question addressing teacher perception was found to be mostly true. From a careful examination of the referral forms and anecdotal data, we found that the teachers had listed behaviours that were unacceptable, including critical, confrontational, argumentative, overly sensitive, and inability to get along with peers (who were chronological peers, rather than ability peers). The answer to question two was that the students were twice-exceptional. They manifested negative behaviours toward themselves, and were disruptive in the regular classroom; yet they contributed large funds of information to classroom discussions and demonstrated considerable creativity. The answer to question three was the most disturbing – we found that many of the students who were referred came from homes and schools in which the parents and professionals were unaware of the special needs and strengths of the gifted and talented.

A major educational goal emerged: to assist these gifted students in developing into the healthy, fulfilled and actualised young people that they were capable of becoming. The strategy we used was to help the students discover who they were, and to accept and develop positive feelings about themselves. Teachers and counsellors agreed to focus on helping the gifted students understand and accept the ways in which they were similar to less gifted students, and the ways in which they were different. They stressed that different doesn't mean better, it just means different, and that addressing the gifted student's behaviour disorder entailed capitalising on their strength, as well as considering their weakness, with an overall goal of turning problems into strengths.

Vulnerability of gifted students

Adolescence and young adulthood are times of vulnerability for all individuals, but even more so for gifted youths enrolled in colleges and universities, who are away from their families and their support. There is a common misconception in the field of gifted education that gifted and talented students suffer from few personal problems and traumas and that they don't need special guidance and counselling; nor do their teachers need training to understand their unique emotional needs. Being gifted does not preclude experiencing serious emotional trauma in interpersonal relationships or in establishing and reaching goals in education and career paths. It is important that parents and professionals become aware of the special needs and strengths of the gifted. Gifted adolescents set about the task of integrating a system of values that will give their life direction and a personal identity with great determination. In forming their personal philosophy of life, they endeavour to make key decisions relating to religious beliefs, sexual ethics and values, all of which centre around identity. They are searching for who they are, where they are going and how to get there. Conflicts can arise around role confusion and models are especially important at this time. Gifted students also experience diverse pressures from parents, peers and society, and they often find it difficult to gain a clear sense of identity. These pressures can manifest in depression, in rebellious behaviour or in some cases in the conscious decision to solve what appears to be an insurmountable problem by taking one's life.

Precursors of suicide

In examining the causes for suicide, a number of precursors have been identified by psychologists and researchers that are used to reconstruct the pressures an individual who has committed suicide may have experienced. One precursor is **perturbation**, in which the individual perceives himself or herself as a failure; **lethality** is a precursor that includes thoughts about death and discussions of thinking about suicide; there is **interpersonal disruption,** such as the disintegration of the role of a significant other in the family or disruption in relationships with peers; and **helpless failure feelings**, viewing one's life as burned out. All of these precursors impact on an individual's decision to commit suicide.

Schneidman (1985), one of the foremost researchers and theorists in the area of suicide, defines suicide as a conscious act of self-induced annihilation, best understood as a multidimensional malaise in a needful individual who defines an issue as one in which suicide is perceived as the best solution. He selected a

135

sample group of 30 individuals from the Terman study in which five of the group committed suicide as adults. Using the above precursors of suicide, Schneidman selected judges who were provided access to biographical data of the selected Terman group, and they were able to predict with accuracy the five individuals who would commit suicide.

Added stress of universities on gifted students

Many universities refer to these years as the most troubled times, or the 'decades of self destruction'. Since 1990 undergraduates at MIT have been three times more likely to commit suicide than those at other colleges. Morrisey (1994) says that when troubled youths learn that others have committed suicide, that makes suicide seem a more viable option for other students to end their own pain, as suggested in the Schneidman definition. He says even one suicide a year increases the risk that another will occur. MIT has 4,258 students enrolled in its undergraduate programme, and officials at MIT who have been investigating the suicides have found some alarming results: 74 per cent of the students surveyed reported suffering from emotional problems that interfere with their lives and studies, with some students saying they had to wait 10 days to see a counsellor. In response, MIT has added extra evening hours at its mental health clinic and assigned additional counsellors to work in the residence hall. MIT says research indicates that men take their lives more often than women, and that their suicide statistics are skewed since the MIT student body is 60 per cent male. However, the rigorous curriculum of MIT may represent a problem for perfectionistic high achieving gifted students. MIT has produced 22 Nobel laureates in 140 years.

The Student Affairs Dean said that he has never seen a suicide where the precipitating factors were not extremely complicated, and that growing up is difficult and especially so in these difficult times. He said MIT has the best and brightest students in the world (the gifted) and they often arrive with considerable psychological baggage. One student at MIT had been despondent for months, and the 19 year old sophomore biology student finally set herself on fire. She was described as having a drive to succeed, wanting to be A1, and her father said 'she didn't want to disappoint us'. She had repeatedly told residents in her dorm that she wanted to kill herself (Lethality precursor). Another MIT student ingested cyanide; she was described as absolutely brilliant, performing in Broadway musicals, and she came from an upper middle class professional family. She chose MIT because she considered it the 'best' university. At MIT she experienced interpersonal and relationship problems with a young man who was stalking her. She filed a harassment complaint, but she felt no one really cared about her anguish (Interpersonal disruption).

At Oxford University there were 21 deaths reported over a 14 year period from 1976 to 1990. Researchers found that student suicides were associated with worries about academic achievement or coursework in general (Hawton *et al.* 1995). Other factors that were problematic included relationships, health or family disruption. Nearly half of the students who committed suicide were clinically depressed, and most had been receiving treatment for depression, and negative expectations and hopelessness were important themes for them.

The Beck Hopelessness Scale has demonstrated that it can predict whether a person is at increased risk of suicide (Beck *et al.* 1990). In one study of patients, all but one of the 17 who had killed themselves scored above nine on the Beck Hopelessness Scale. People whose scores were above nine were 11 times more likely to commit suicide than ones with lower scores. Perfectionism increases the chances of suicide even more than hopelessness (Blatt *et al.* 1995). Baumeister (1990) has developed an escape theory of suicide in which suicide is viewed as an attempt to escape aversive self-awareness.

A great deal of the behaviour demonstrated by troubled university students who commit suicide falls under the Anxiety Withdrawal dimensions of disordered behaviour (Sisk 1999), and these behaviours include mood disorders listed on DSM-IV, which is used to diagnose emotional disturbance:

- Previous depression or mania
- Current mood
- Guilty feelings, self-esteem, or sense of worth
- Financial or business difficulties
- Increased sexual activity and indiscreet sexual behaviour
- Rapid switches in mood
- Hallucinations or delusions
- Previous suicide thoughts or attempts
- Change in level of energy or fatigue
- Change in pattern of sleep
- Significant weight loss or weight gain.

Prevention of suicide

The risk of suicide cannot be discounted among gifted college and university students. Konza (1999) reports that Australia has the highest rate of youth suicide in the Western world, and she says there is no evidence to suggest that being gifted can protect a young person from selecting suicide as a solution to life's problems. Dixon, Cross *et al.* (1995) agree that some characteristics of giftedness, such as excessive sensitivity, divergent thinking, excessive introspection, extreme emotionality and for some a preoccupation with negative themes can be directly associated with the risk of suicide. It is often pointed out that gifted individuals may not seek help because they feel they should be able to solve their problems.

Hayes and Sloat (1989) take a 'tough love' approach to gifted students who are thinking of suicide. They suggest a commitment be drawn from the gifted students to put aside whatever they may be thinking about until they have discussed the problem with a professional, and that we should tell them they have nothing to lose when the alternative is the loss of their life.

Indicators of suicide

Appleby and Condonis (1990) list a number of indicators of suicide that include:

- An actual suicide threat or statement indicating a desire to die
- An unsuccessful attempt at suicide
- Signs of mental depression, low energy levels and expressions of hopelessness and worthlessness
- Changes in eating or sleeping patterns, more time spent alone or less interest in previous activities
- Giving away prized objects.

Educators and counsellors need to be aware of these indicators of suicide and work to change cultural attitudes so that gifted students under stress will feel that it is acceptable to seek help rather than feeling that this shows a weakness of some kind. In times of stress, adolescents turn to one another, and peer programmes have been successful when the peers know the indicators that reflect emotional problems. Also it is important that significant others and peers listen to troubled gifted students and not trivialise their concerns. A checklist for emotional stability and maturity to help 'signal' stress and emotional problems can be used to assist students in peer programmes.

A CHECKLIST FOR EMOTIONAL STABILITY AND MATURITY

How do you rate yourself in emotional stability and maturity?
Strong (S), Not So Strong (NS), Weak (W)

___able to admit mistakes	___integrated
___able to set pointers	___open
___accepting of criticism	___predictable
___assertive	___purposeful
___calm	___responsible
___committed	___secure
___controlled	___self confident
___cooperative	___self efficacy
___dependable	___self-reliant
___ethical	___sensitive
___flexible	___sincere
___forthright	___steady
___hardy	

Interactive factors

Figure 7.1 depicts the interaction between risk or vulnerability factors, resiliency or protective factors, precipitating factors and the decision to commit suicide.

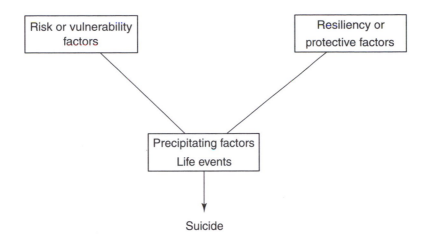

Figure 7.1 To show the interaction between factors

Importance of coping strategies

Coping strategies that counsellors, educators and parents can use with gifted students to help prevent suicide include helping them learn how to carefully plan their activities, how to set priorities to better manage the stress of school, find a close friend, and get involved in diversionary activities such as sports, music, theatre, as well as shopping, eating, etc. Rebellious behaviour can also be diversionary, and in some cases when a troubled gifted student finally rebels, this can be viewed as positive action. To maximise personality integration of gifted students, counsellors and teachers can focus on enhancing and building self esteem, reinforce their ability to 'feel in charge' and to see options, and most importantly for them, to be able to select solutions. These personality behaviours signify to troubled gifted students that they are 'in charge', which is one of their basic needs and characteristics. It is vitally important that troubled gifted adolescents do something, take that first step and perceive that they have self efficacy. The high and difficult goals that gifted students set for themselves require commitment and effort, and a feeling of what many psychologists call 'hardiness' – viewing life as a challenge and having a sense of control over one's life.

Hardiness

One coping strategy is to increase one's physical fitness, which is a component of hardiness and includes defining challenges as difficulties and perceiving oneself in control of the decisions that affect life. It is important that troubled gifted students refrain from counterfactual thinking or dwelling on alternative behaviour and thoughts such as 'if only I had' or 'it wouldn't have happened if I had . . .' When troubled gifted students become aware of their 'counterfactual thinking' it is helpful for them to note the importance of their environment and its effect on them. They can modify the environment with pleasant music, fragrance, lighting, art, supportive friends, any change that will help to improve a pessimistic mood.

Chronic depression, hopelessness, a clear plan for taking one's life and prior suicidal attempts are all clues that need to be taken seriously by parents, teachers and counsellors. Morrisey, a researcher in suicide, says that educators and counsellors need to be alert to the following eight behaviours:

1. talking about committing suicide
2. giving away prized possessions
3. taking unnecessary risks
4. being preoccupied with death and dying
5. having made previous suicide attempts
6. losing interest in hobbies, school and work
7. having had a recent severe loss
8. increased use of alcohol or drugs.

Morrisey stresses that a cry for help must be taken seriously and educators and counsellors must refer gifted students for medical and psychological assistance.

As gifted students experience risks and pressures, their abilities can become detoured toward defensive and avoidance patterns. In helping gifted students cope with their dyssynchronicity, it is essential that they develop coping strategies to manage and deal with daily life stress, and learn how to prioritise their goals, values and investment of time and energy.

Supportive strategies to minimise stress and to build self understanding

Group counselling

To meet the growing counselling needs of gifted students a group counselling technique was developed and refined at the University of South Florida that integrates the creative problem solving process and group counselling to assist participants in dealing with problems that arise as a result of dyssynchronicity (Sisk 1987). This technique proceeds in six stages, and in the first stage of **symbiosis**, gifted students engage in establishing a sense of trust and recognising group similarities and differences. A sense of trust is established by involving a group of gifted students (ideal size 11–15) in responding to open-ended questions:

If you could have the answer to any one question, what would you ask?
If you could have an extended conversation with any one person, who might it be?
If you were to describe yourself with one word, what word would you use?
If you could change one thing about yourself, what would you change?
If you could be a song, what song would you be?

As students participate in this first stage, the questions are answered round-robin and students may say 'pass' if they wish to be skipped, but it is important for the teacher/leader to come back to any student who requests a pass. This stage flows easily into the second stage of **problem identification** in which the leader/teacher says, 'Think of a problem or concern that you may have and word it in a **how might I?** format.' Each student is then given an opportunity to identify and share a concern or problem. These problems/concerns are captured on a flip chart for the group, either by the leader/teacher or an assistant, or in some cases a group member. Then the leader/teacher selects one question to focus on with the group. In problem selection it is important for the leader/teacher to select a problem that appears manageable, that is not too dramatic or stressful, and for the first go-round the leader/teacher may want to select a problem from a student who has demonstrated willingness to be open and articulate in the symbiosis stage.

After the problem has been selected, the group proceeds to the **relationship** stage in which the leader/teacher asks the group to share any similar situations that they have experienced with the student who identified the problem. The purpose of this stage is to reassure the student with the identified problem that he or she is not alone in 'owning the problem', and that other gifted students have experienced similar problems. If the group counselling session concludes at this stage, there would be positive outcomes because the student with the identified problem no longer feels isolated. The leader/teacher participates with the group and responds with suggestions. Students are always interested in how the leader/teacher interacts with the group; consequently, the modelling of open interaction is essential for the leader/teacher. When all or most of the students have shared examples of how they have experienced similar concerns, the leader/teacher then moves on to the next stage.

Alternative solutions

In this stage the leader/teacher asks the student who identified the problem to maintain a 'deferred judgement' attitude and to refrain from saying 'I have already tried that', 'That idea is super' or 'I'd never do that' – this information is shared by the leader/teacher with humour to help set the stage for open sharing of ideas for solutions. Ideas are captured in the 'exact words' of each group member, and if there are 7 students participating, the leader/teacher will write the numbers 1–8 to encourage the students to 'aim' for that number of alternatives. When the group exhausts their ideas for alternatives, the student who identified the concern is given a highlighter pen and asked to proceed to the next stage of **choice making**. In this stage, the student with the concern circles one or two suggestions that he or she will try to implement prior to the next group session. The leader/teacher then asks the student making the choice to share the criteria used in making the selection. The last stage, **implementation**, is focused upon in the next group meeting in which the successful or unsuccessful implementation of the selected alternatives is shared, and then another student concern is identified for the process to continue.

When the technique was originally developed, it was intended as a technique primarily to be used with parents of gifted children in group counselling, and was called the Child Study Technique. In using it with gifted students, they quickly suggested that it be renamed the 'PSST' Problem Solving Student Technique since it gets the student's attention. In using the technique, teachers/leaders report that gifted students demonstrate sensitivity toward one another as they engage in problem solving. Typical problems that have been discussed include: How can I convince my mother that I need to spend more time with my father, since they are divorced? How can I develop a better relationship with my maths teacher, who really doesn't like me? How can I go about getting a bigger allowance? How can I reassure my family that I'm old enough to drive? How can I improve my test-taking strategies, I get brain-dead during tests? How can I convince my parents that I can go to the school dance?

Building self-awareness: Gestalt exercises

The Growing Person: How to Encourage Healthy Emotional Development in Children (Shallcross and Sisk 1982) includes numerous self-awareness activities to use in assisting gifted students to overcome their dyssynchronicity. The Gestalt exercises are particularly successful with gifted students in building self-awareness. Gestalt is a German word meaning 'form', 'shape' or 'the whole' and in psychology vernacular it refers to 'getting it all together.' According to Gestalt psychologist Fritz Perls, when you get it altogether, there is an experience or sense of wellbeing, of being in control of yourself and capable of integrating the various parts of the whole. Perls used the idea of sub-selves and referred to them as **top dog** and **under dog**. In using this technique with gifted students, you ask them to create a dialogue that might occur between the two conflicting sub-selves. Students can move from one chair another as each sub-self talks. By way of a brief example, a dialogue might go like this:

Top dog: I know today is going to be a great day, I'm going to 'Ace' that test in Physics.
Under dog: Don't be so sure of yourself, you could go in there and blow it.
Top dog: No, I really have a positive feeling about this test today!
Under dog: That's what you said the last time.

Gifted students enjoy this technique because they are keenly aware of the numerous emotions that they experience and the range of feelings they have about themselves, and the 'PSST' technique helps to build greater understanding of their multi-dimensional personalities.

Another Gestalt technique, **talk like**, is a modified version of top dog and under dog and it uses chairs to represent dialoguing selves. Place one chair away from the other chairs in the room, ask a student to sit on the chair and to say things that the sub-self might say in the manner or way the sub-self might talk.
Talk like your smart self . . .
Talk like your loving self . . .

Talk like your useless self . . .

Talk like your jealous self . . .

Talk like your happy self . . .

When this activity is completed, the leader/teacher can help the students 'process' what they have experienced. Processing brings a completeness to activities and provides the students and the leader/teacher with an opportunity to reflect on what occurred, to clarify meanings and to more accurately interpret the significance of the activity for individual growth and understanding. It is important that the processing does not suffer from 'overkill' – there will be a natural time to conclude. Processing elevates the previous group experiences that were primarily affective to a level of cognitive awareness. By helping gifted students explore and verbalise their emotionally based responses, they gain greater insight into understanding themselves.

Stryker morphological approach

An adaptation of Gestalt work for older gifted students, who are usually more capable of identifying sub-selves in their personality structure, is the following activity based on Fran Stryker's morphological approach to story plotting. Fran Stryker is best known as the original author of the *Lone Ranger* series, and his technique for creating a different plot for the nightly radio show provides the structure for this activity. Stryker separated the four basic elements of each short story plot into **Character**, **Goal**, **Obstacle**, and **Result**:

Using Stryker's model as a format, Gestalt theory can be applied to a personal story. The characters in the original model now become the sub-selves, or the different characters within oneself. With modifications to suit this purpose, the new blank chart would be as shown in Table 7.1a.

Table 7.1a   Modifications of Stryker's model

Sub-self	Goal	Obstacle	Usual Outcome	Desired Outcome	Alternative Behaviour

This chart helps gifted students identify the roles that their sub-selves play in facilitating or hindering an integrated personality structure, and the completed chart provides a 'picture' of what is going on in their life at a given time. By identifying sub-selves and how they function, gifted students become more aware of their positive and negative personality features. The use of the Stryker chart provides gifted students with a 'grayline' view of where conflicts occur between and among sub-selves. Filling in each column for a sub-self can be revealing, for beyond identifying the sub-self, the students are able to examine how each sub-self functions to either serve or hinder in the total picture. For example, an eighth grade gifted young man who was classified as a behaviour disordered student identified 'the clown' as one of his sub-selves and completed the chart as shown below.

Table 7.1b   Completed table for Stryker's modified model

Goal	Obstacle	Result	Desired Outcome	Alternative Behaviour
To be funny, make students laugh, to be popular with the class	Sometimes it gets me in trouble with the teacher in class	I get teacher frowns, punished, not called upon or yelled at	In this class to be popular same as GOAL	Be funny, but not when it gets me in trouble

Importance of counsellors

Counselling needs to be an essential component of educational programmes for all students, but particularly for gifted students with behavioural disorders. Sensitive, caring teachers can provide a great deal of assistance and support for troubled students, but many of these students will need the assistance of a more specialised counselling programme. Two life skills that gifted students need to learn have been addressed, those of problem solving and self-awareness, that teachers can model and teach to build resilience and a positive proactive approach to daily challenges. People with resilience have an internal locus of control, that is essential for troubled, gifted children and youths engaged in struggles for power or autonomy. Effective counselling techniques can include the use of visualisation exercises and journal writing to provide opportunities for the students to express their thoughts or insights.

Using visualisation integrated with journaling to build resilience

In a session with a troubled gifted teenager, who was experiencing bouts of depression, and engaged in an ongoing power struggle with her mother resulting in abusive language and physical abuse, the student was asked to gaze at a picture of a dolphin swimming in water with a smaller dolphin nearby. After a few moments, she was asked to close her eyes and visualise the two dolphins together, and to let the images flow of their own accord. She was asked to 'be aware of any sounds that you might hear, notice the colours, and if there is dialogue between the two dolphins. Hear what they are sharing . . . gathering any insight that you might from their interaction.' Using the picture as a visual stimulus, followed by a guided visualisation, in which she was in control, she was encouraged to observe and to hear the interaction of the mother/child dolphins. This activity focused her attention on the sensual or sensory responses that are usually open to most students. Then she was offered an opportunity to project what she thinks/wants the dolphins to say to one another. This provided her with an opportunity to tap into her 'inner knowing' for information. The wording of the question: 'What knowledge or insight are you gathering from this conversation?' further stimulated her to pull the images and thoughts together, to synthesise and move from the sensual, affective experience to a more cognitive experience, resulting in an abstract thought of personal meaning.

When she was provided with an opportunity to write about her experience in the visualisation exercise in her journal, she quickly began writing very fluidly and remarked, 'The ideas come to me so quickly and I feel calm just like the dolphins.' In her journal she wrote:

> There once was a young dolphin who travelled with her family and other dolphins in the Atlantic Ocean. She thought her world was a beautiful one, but she had heard elders speak of their travels to the sea of tranquility. When she asked about travelling there, the elders told her that she must find the way herself.
>
> She swam into a cave looking for a secret passage, but found none. She swam as far as she could in one day, but to no avail.
>
> One day she came across her mother floating with her eyes closed. And when the young dolphin sounded to her, her mother did not seem to hear her. The young dolphin became increasingly upset that she could not awaken her mother. Finally a number of minutes later, her mother awakened from her trance.
>
> 'Why didn't you hear me, mother?' the young dolphin asked.
>
> 'I was in the sea of tranquility,' replied the mother.
>
> 'How is that possible?' asked the confused young dolphin. 'You were right here.'
>
> 'My child, the sea of tranquility is within me,' explained the mother.
>
> All of us have a sea of tranquility.

When she was asked for a copy of her journal to share with teachers in a graduate class in Creativity and the Gifted Child, she replied, 'Sure if it will help them understand what it means to be gifted, most of my teachers never liked me.' Her statement sounds harsh and accusatory, but many teachers and counsellors are less than enthusiastic about teaching gifted children and youths. They view many characteristics of gifted students as a challenge, such as their resistance to control, use of humour that can be scathingly direct, critical questioning, advanced vocabulary and extensive knowledge that can be somewhat intimidating.

Applied research with gifted adolescents

For the last five years, the Dabrowski theory of overexcitability has been used in an ongoing research programme with secondary gifted students in the Texas Governor's Honors Program. Dabrowski's theory is composed of two parts: five overexcitability levels and five levels of development. He theorised that the strength of overexcitabilities, along with special talents and abilities, makes up a person's developmental potential, and that overexcitabilities are developmental and can be observed in infancy. The five overexcitabilities (OEs) are psychomotor, sensual, imaginational, intellectual and emotional. Dabrowski studied gifted children and youths in Warsaw and found every one of them showed considerable manifestation of the overexcitabilities (Dabrowski 1972).

Dabrowski's theory of emotional development addresses a core of personal characteristics that distinguish the behaviour of gifted students. Dabrowski said it is in the nature of many gifted students to steadfastly uphold the principles that they believe in and to attempt to be individuals who are true to themselves (Level 3); Level 4 is where an individual is well on the way to self-actualisation and attempting to make a difference, and Level 5 is where the struggle for self-mastery has been won. Level 1 and Level 2 students are not always steadfast in upholding principles.

Students in the Texas Governor's Honors Program volunteer to take the original Dabrowski questionnaire, which requires thoughtful responses and considerable time set aside for completion of the questions during a busy three week residential session. All of the participating students scored Level 3 on emotional, imaginational and sensual overexcitabilities. In analysing their responses, the students who scored at Level 3 psychomotor were actively involved in sports, and had selected aerobics, soccer, Tae Bo, basketball, swimming, tennis or football. The students who scored at Level 3 on sensual had selected art, musical production, dance, drama, history of jazz and instrumental ensemble as activities. The students who scored at Level 3 on imagination selected advanced creative writing, British poetry, journalism, and sculpture. The students were curious about Dabrowski's theory, and when it was explained to them following the administration of the questionnaire, they enjoyed discussing the questions and their responses. They agreed with Dabrowski's contention that intensity is not a deficit. The five OEs are summarised and adapted using descriptions suggested by Piechowski (1997). Selected student responses of the Texas Governor's Honors Program students at Level 3 of all OEs are shown below:

Imaginational OE (M) is the capacity for free play of the imagination and creative vision. It is recognised through rich association of images and impressions (real or imagined), inventiveness, vivid and often animated visualisation, and use of image and metaphor in speaking and writing. Daydreaming, distractibility, predilection for fairy tales, magical thinking, imaginary companions, love of fantasy, poetic creations, dramatising to escape boredom, and a taste for the absurd and surrealistic are characteristic expressions of Imaginational. A student example:

> Sometimes when I am imagining something, I can be composing a short musical piece and my mind usually is filled with music that I have heard or performed, but it is in the moments of internal quiet that I hear new things. (Female, age 16)

Emotional OE (E) is the heightened intensity of positive and negative feelings. It is recognised in the way emotional relationships are experienced; in strong attachments to persons, living things or places; in the great intensity of feelings, emotions and an awareness of their full range. Characteristic expressions are: inhibition (timidity and shyness); enthusiasm; emotionality; compassion and understanding of others; strong affective recall of past experiences; concern with death, fears, anxieties and depressions; and occasional feelings of unreality. Intense loneliness may be combined with an intense desire to offer love, or a deep concern for others. Intrapersonal and interpersonal feeling achieve a high degree of differentiation. A student example:

> Last summer, I became involved with the Summer Special Olympics for children with disabilities. We worked hard for weeks and weeks and finally the 'big day' came. I was able to see our hard work pay off. To see this excellence in these special little children's eyes flooded my soul with happiness. I don't think I've ever had a rush quite like that. (Female, age 17)

Psychomotor OE (P) may be viewed as excess energy or heightened excitability. It may manifest as love of movement for its own sake, rapid speech, pursuit of intense physical activity, impulsiveness, pressure for action, drive or the capacity for being otherwise active and energetic. A student example:

> I feel tons of energy after I do really well in a race. If I win or improve my track times I get lots of energy. With all of this new found energy I usually annoy people. It comes out in the form of hyperness and excitement. (Male, age 16)

Sensual OE (S) is sensory aliveness and heightened capacity for sensual enjoyment. It finds expression in heightened experiencing of pleasure through touch, taste, smell, sight and sound, as well as in seeking sensual outlets for emotional tensions. Sensual overexcitability is manifested as a desire for comfort, luxury or aesthetic delights; it includes the pleasure derived from being admired, being in the limelight; it may also manifest itself as intense sexuality. Sensual outlets of emotional tension include overeating, buying sprees, and other forms of self-indulgence to soothe oneself. Sensual OE may also demonstrate itself as extreme sensitivity, and sometimes irritation to sensory input. A student example:

> All the time, I am always trying to create scenes from my surroundings. Sometimes I imagine people that I would like to talk to and, don't laugh, talk to them. Much as they did in the movie 'Tap'. I listen to the sounds around me and hear music in it. (Male, age 16)

Intellectual OE (T) is intensified activity of the mind. Its strongest expression is manifested in asking probing questions; avidity for knowledge and analysis; preoccupation with logic and theoretical problems; and striving for understanding and truth. Other behaviours include: sharp thinking, development of new concepts, striving for synthesis of knowledge, and a desire to search for knowledge and truth. A student example:

> I would first find a pattern and follow it. What goes on in my head would be how one solves the problem. Second, I would tell myself that I'm not confused. Think why do we have to understand this idea? Last, find the pattern. (Female, age 16)

Using moral dilemmas to promote social/emotional development in middle school gifted

Twenty-three gifted students who were referred to their school psychologist for disruptive classroom behaviour and as possible candidates for their school's behaviour disorders programme were provided with moral dilemmas for dialogue and discussion. The students were encouraged to engage in self-observation and self-analysis to reflect on their values and those of others. Twenty-five moral dilemmas were developed and introduced to the students. As an introductory activity, Benjamin Franklin's list of 13 values was given to the students and they were told that, at the end of each day, Franklin engaged in self-analysis to ascertain if he had measured up to the virtues on his list, noting any errors and lapses. Franklin's list included: temperance, silence, order, resolution, frugality, industry, sincerity, justice, moderation, cleanliness, tranquillity, chastity and humility. The students thoroughly enjoyed discussing these virtues and applying them to their lives and to the lives of others. They were also introduced to the concept that for a 'belief' to become your own belief, it has to follow a process of freely choosing the value; choosing it from alternatives after thoughtful consideration of consequences; prized and cherished; publicly affirmed; acted upon in reality; and acted upon repeatedly. This process was adapted from Raths, Harmin and Simon (1978). In evening sessions from 7:00 to 9:00 pm the gifted students read and discussed a moral dilemma employing a simple discussion format of **What, So What** and **Now What**. Pre- and post-tests on the Loevinger–Wessler scale were given to the students and each student kept a running daily journal for reflection. An example of one moral dilemma is the following:

Sara, who is thirteen, has a sixteen year old brother named Dylan. They share ideas and talk about almost everything, including boyfriends and girlfriends. When school started in September, Dylan began hanging around with some new kids. He began to lose weight and his personality also began to change. He had always been a happy-go-lucky person, but now he is always fearful and nervous. Sara and Dylan's parents are very concerned and worried about him. At dinner they ask if there is anything wrong, but Dylan always says that they are just being overly concerned and that there is nothing wrong.

Late one night Sara and Dylan are talking and Dylan begins to cry and says that he is taking drugs. The other kids that he hangs out with are also doing drugs, and as a result, he has become involved. He also shares that he has shoplifted to pay for drugs, which are very expensive. Dylan says that the drugs make him feel very good, but that he feels sick when he can't get any. He makes Sara promise not to tell anyone what he has said – especially their parents. He also promises to stop taking the drugs as soon as he can.

The next day Sara's mother comes to her and asks her if she knows what is wrong with Dylan. She knows Sara and Dylan talk about everything and she expects Sara to tell the truth.

What should Sara do?

1. Should she break Dylan's confidence?
2. Should a promise be kept?
3. Is there any way that Sara has a right to tell her mother what Dylan has shared?
4. If she doesn't tell her mother, is she justified in saying she doesn't know anything?

The gifted students examined the moral issues involved in the dilemmas and discussed each dilemma to bring the ethical issues into clear focus for analysis.

Findings

The pre- to post-test changes on the Loevinger–Wessler ego maturity instrument, using a 10 point scale, indicated a significant shift from Stage 3 (Conformist) and Stage 3–4 (Transition from Conformist to Conscientious) toward Stage 4 (Conscientious) Stage 4–5 (Transition from Conscientious to Autonomous) and Stage 5 (Autonomous) occurred during the twenty weekly sessions. Twenty-one of the twenty-three gifted adolescent students in the original intervention study completed the follow-up testing. A person at Loevinger's Stage 4 level of Conscientious behaviour displays complex thinking and perceives complexity, and absolute standards and rules are often replaced at this stage with ones in comparative and contingent form. The Stage 4 person views life as presenting choices and they are not pawns of fate. They feel in charge of their own destiny. Achievement motivation is at its height at this stage, along with a strong sense of responsibility and a concept of privileges, rights, justice and fairness. Self-evaluated standards, differentiated feelings and concern for communication are also manifested in the Stage 4 level. The Stage 4–5 (Transition from Conscientious to Autonomous) person evidences greater complexity in their concept of interpersonal interaction, in psychological causality and in their concept of individuality. Clearly, we would want gifted students to operate at Stage 4–5, and to be capable of using their potential in positive, constructive endeavours that are fulfilling to them and helpful to society. The scores of the students on the Loevinger–Wessler scale are shown in Table 7.2.

This study indicates that it is possible to promote positive socio-emotional growth in troubled gifted and talented students through linking discussion and moral dilemmas. This type of discussion can be easily integrated into Social Studies and Language Arts classes, as well as in Science, with examinations of

149

Table 7.2 Students' Loevinger Scores Using 10 Point Scale

	N	Mean Score	Standard Deviation	T value	Significance Level
PRE	21	6.29	0.78	1.79	.05
POST	21	6.67	1.07	4.56	.001
ONE YEAR FOLLOW UP					
	21	7.38	0.97		

moral dilemmas in scientific research. The gifted students wrote in their journals that they enjoyed the discussions, and that they were able to apply what they were learning in the discussions to their daily life at school and at home. The teachers of the students also indicated that the experiences had led to more effective student responses in the classroom when real moral dilemmas were presented.

Using the study of myths to build self-knowledge

Self-knowledge comes through facing life's challenges with courage and strength, but gifted students can accomplish this same self-knowledge vicariously and safely by reading stories and myths of Greek gods, Norse heroes, Polynesian tricksters, and Native American warriors, all replete with profound lessons about life. By reading and discussing myths, gifted students quickly recognise that myths are related to real life problems through shared inquiry. Myths have a mysterious capacity to contain and communicate paradoxes, and they encourage gifted students to experience complex relationships and ideas that help them formulate their own ideas. Myths also encourage gifted students to see through, around and over any dilemmas they may be experiencing. One dilemma many gifted students face is the high expectation of parents and the spoken and unspoken message 'You are to carry on our family name, to higher and higher levels of accomplishment.' To address this dilemma the theme of Parents and Children was used to explore 'truths' in myths.

Parents and Children theme

To explore the theme of Parents and Children, gifted students can read *Thetis and Achilles*, the story of how parents expect nothing less than everything from their children. The theme of this Greek myth revolves around the ambition Thetis has for her child. She wants her son to be a god, and in the myth, Thetis conveys tremendous insight into the secret hopes, longings and dreams that parents may unknowingly and knowingly ask of their gifted children. Thetis, the goddess mother, wants her child to be divine like her, rather than mortal like the father. Another myth, *Orion and Oenopion*, was used to explore the Parents and Children theme in which a father attempts to totally possess his daughter, and to make all her decisions for her.

Gifted students can keep daily journals to help them assess their level of understanding concerning the myths and the dilemmas; this helps gifted students recognise their ability to apply the concepts to their lives. After reading the two myths, a group of gifted adolescents shared sacrifices that their own parents had made for them and how when they failed in school work, in music and swimming competitions, their parents were disappointed or angry. Such discussions help gifted students build a better understanding of the world and how it works, but more importantly they help gifted students build a better understanding of themselves in relation to others. Other themes and myths that can be used to build self understanding include the following:

- Becoming an individual, including leaving home (Peredur, the son of Evrawe)
- Fighting for autonomy (Gilgamesh and the Tree of Life)
- Pursuing the quest for meaning (Perseus)
- Greed and ambition (King Midas) etc.

Gifted students with their well-developed reasoning, ability to engage in the higher levels of thinking and analysing or synthesising information can step back from the myth and make applications to themselves. One troubled gifted adolescent said, 'I like the fact that instead of just reading, we can discuss, and we can have our own feelings.' This ownership of feelings is an important step for gifted students in being able to recognise how they interact with others. Their insights are evident in comments concerning their reading such as 'Did you ever notice that in the darkness of loneliness, failure and loss, they always discover light and hope?' Listening to this student, it was obvious that she was viewing her particular problem with hope and perhaps new conviction that it could be solved. A boy who suffers from perfectionism in his school work, in his appearance and career choices (he wants to be an actor or talk show host) said, 'Looks, talent, power and wealth bring their own forms of suffering.' After his profound comment, there was a palpable silence as the group of students pondered his ability to face his dilemma of being perfect and offered him a respectful silence.

A project conducted with eighty-five gifted middle school students in Texas entitled Mythic Journey has demonstrated that this type of study can have positive results with gifted students, and that it represents a viable option to assist gifted students in becoming better prepared for adulthood (Sisk 2001).

Gifted students find themselves within an increasingly complex world and unless we adapt and modify the curriculum to ensure that it is not ill-fitting and help parents, counsellors and educators to understand the unique needs of gifted students and their vulnerability to perfectionism, stress, depression and suicide, we will continue to do them a great disservice, as well as a disservice to ourselves. The intellect and enthusiasm of gifted students for learning when properly channelled can bring added excitement to the schooling process.

Summary and conclusions

In spite of a recent book by Neihart *et al.* (2002) in which the authors state that there is no evidence that gifted children or youths as a group are inherently any more vulnerable or flawed in adjustment than any other group, there is considerable evidence that ill-fitting environments whether they be school, family, peers or culture greatly impact on the social and emotional development of gifted children and adults. Numerous researchers agree that gifted students are subject to unique stressors, and that they are vulnerable to difficulties with social and emotional adjustment.

Terrasier (1985) described how the unique characteristics of giftedness manifest in ill-fitting environments as dyssynchronicity and unavoidably complicate the social adjustment of gifted individuals. This problem of social adjustment can be traced to characteristics that can cause considerable concern for gifted students including persistence, intensity, perfectionism and sensitivity. Dabrowski's theory of the positive aspect of overexcitabilities provides a helpful way to understand and utilise the overexcitabilities that gifted students often possess as strengths in manifesting their talents.

The precursors to suicide were examined in an attempt to reconstruct the pressures that individuals who have committed suicide may have experienced and the added stress of university life on gifted students was examined. Students who commit suicide fall under the anxiety-withdrawal dimensions of disordered behaviour including guilty feelings, low self esteem or sense of worth, change of levels of energy or fatigue, and previous thoughts or attempts at suicide. Konza (1999) noted that Australia has the highest rate of youth suicide in the Western world, and she reminded us that there is no evidence to suggest that being gifted can protect a young person from selecting suicide as a solution to life's problems. A checklist for emotional stability and maturity was included for individuals to rate themselves on those factors. The interaction of vulnerability factors, resilience or protective factors and precipitating factors was examined as a precursor to the decision to commit suicide.

The importance of coping strategies that counsellors, educators and parents can use with gifted students were discussed including physical hardiness, group counselling, building self-awareness and visualisation integrated with using journals to build resilience. Applied research using the Dabrowski theory of overexcitability was discussed to chronicle the responses of gifted adolescents, followed by research on using moral dilemmas to promote social and emotional development in middle school gifted students and on its effect on ego maturity.

Finally, the study of myths to build self-knowledge was presented in which gifted students gained self-knowledge vicariously and safely by reading stories and myths of Greek gods, Norse heroes, Polynesian tricksters, and Native American warriors, all with profound lessons about life. The challenge for educators, counsellors and parents is how to guide gifted students in formulating their own ideas, to see through, around and over any dilemmas that they may be experiencing. Through reading and discussing myths, gifted students can experience catharsis and build considerable self-understanding, and understanding of others. Gifted students find themselves in an increasingly complex world, and they need to develop strong coping mechanisms to navigate successfully through the schooling and life process to contribute to society and lead meaningful satisfying lives.

References

Appleby, M. and Condonis, M. (1990) *Hearing the Cry*. Sydney: Rose Educational Training.

Baumeister, R. (1990) 'Suicide as an escape from self'. *Psychological Review*, **99**, 90–113.

Beck, A. T., Brown, G., Berchick, R., Stewart, B. and Steer, R. (1990) 'Relationship between hopelessness and ultimate suicide: A replication with psychiatric out-patients'. *American Journal of Psychiatry*, **147**, 190–3.

Blatt, S., Quinlain, D., Pilkonis, P. and Shea, M. (1995) 'Impact of perfectionism and need for approval on the brief treatment of depression: The National Institute of Mental Health Treatment of Depression Collaborative Research Program revisited'. *Journal of Consulting and Clinical Psychology*, **63**, 125–32.

Clark, B. (1983) *Growing up Gifted*. New York: Macmillan.

Dabrowski, K. (1964) *Positive Disintegration*. Boston: Little, Brown & Co.

Dabrowski, K. (1972) *Psychoneurosis is Not an Illness*. London: Little, Brown & Co.

Dixon, D., Cross, T., Cook, R. and Scheckel, J. (1995) 'Gifted adolescent suicide: Data base versus speculation'. *Research Briefs*, **10**, 45–9.

Genshaft, J., Greenbaum, S. and Borovsky, S. (1995) 'Stress and the gifted', in J. Genshaft, M. Bierley and C.L. Hollinger (eds) *Serving Gifted and Talented Students: A resource for school personnel*. Austin, TX: Pro-Ed, pp. 257–86.

Hawton, K., Simkin, S., Fagg, J. and Hawkins, M. (1995) 'Suicide in Oxford University students, 1976–1990'. *British Journal of Psychiatry*, **166**, 44–50.

Hayes, M. and Sloat, R. (1989) 'Gifted students at risk for suicide'. *Roeper Review*, **12**(2), 102–7.

Hoge, R. and Renzulli, J. (1993) 'Exploring the link between giftedness and self concept'. *Review of Educational Research*, **63**, 449–65.

Hollinger, C.L. (1995) 'Stress as a function of gender: Special needs of gifted girls and women', in J. L. Genshaft, Bierley, M. and C. L. Hollinger (eds) *Serving Gifted and Talented Students: A resource for school personnel*. Austin, TX: Pro-Ed, pp. 269–300.

Hollingworth, L. (1931) 'The child of very superior intelligence as a special problem in social adjustment'. *Mental Hygiene*, **15**(1), 1–16.

Konza, D. (1999) 'Emotional disturbance: The beguiling mask (Australian Perspective)', in Baldwin, A. and Vialle, W. (eds) *The Many Faces of Giftedness*. Belmont, Calif.: Wadsworth Publishing, pp. 261–87.

Loevinger, J. and Wessler, R. (1970) *The Measuring of Ego Development*. San Francisco: Jossey-Bass.

Marshall, S. (1994) 'Our gifted children: Are they asking too much?' *Gifted Child Quarterly*, **38**(4), 187–92.

Morrisey, M. (1994) 'Help me'. *Guideposts*, **37**(1), 10.

Neihart, M., Reis, S., Robinson, N. and Moon, S. (2002) *The Social and Emotional Development of Gifted Children*. Waco, Texas: Prufrock Press.

Piechowski, M. (1997) 'Emotional giftedness: The measure of intrapersonal intelligence', in N. Colangelo and G. A. Davis (eds) *Handbook of Gifted Education*. Boston: Allyn and Bacon, pp. 366–81.

Raths, L., Harmin, M. and Simon, S. (1978) *Values and Teaching: Working with Values in the Classroom*. Columbus: Merrill.

Schneidman, E. (1971) 'Perturbation and lethality as precursors of suicide in a gifted group'. *Life Threatening Behaviour*, **1**, 23–45.

Schneidman, E. (1985) *Definition of Suicide*. New York: Wiley.

Shallcross, D. and Sisk, D. (1982) *The Growing Person: How to Encourage Healthy Emotional Development in Children*. Englewood Cliffs, N.J.: Prentice-Hall.

Silverman, I. (1993) *Counselling the Gifted and Talented*. Denver: Love.

Sisk, D. (1982) 'Caring and sharing: Moral development of gifted students'. *The Elementary School Journal*, **82**(8), 221–30.

Sisk, D. (1987) *Creative Teaching of the Gifted*. New York: McGraw-Hill.

Sisk, D. (1999) 'Emotional disturbance: The beguiling mask', in A. Baldwin and W. Vialle (eds) *The Many Faces of Giftedness*. Belmont, Calif.: Wadsworth, pp. 245–59.

Sisk, D. (2001) 'The mythic journey'. *Understanding Our Gifted*, **13**(3), 18–19.

Sternberg, K. (2000) 'The theory of successful intelligence'. *Gifted Education International*, **15**(1), 4–21.

Terman, L. (1931) 'The gifted child', in C. Murchison (ed.) *A Handbook of Child Psychology*. Worcester, Mass: Clark University Press, pp. 568–84.

Terrasier, J. C. (1985) 'Dyssynchrony – uneven development', in J. Freedman (ed.) *The Psychology of Gifted Children*. New York: Wiley, pp. 265–74.

Thoreau, H. D. (1942) *Walden*. New York: World Publishing Company.

Torrance, E. P. and Sisk, D. (2000) *Teaching Gifted Children in the Regular Classroom*. Buffalo, New York: Creative Ed. Press.

Webb, I. (1993) 'Nurturing social-emotional development of gifted children', in K. A. Heller, F. J. Monks and A. H. Passow (eds) *International Handbook of Research and Development of Giftedness and Talent*. Oxford: Pergamon Press, pp. 525–38.

Webb, J., Meckstroth, E. and Tolan, S. (1982) *Guiding the Gifted Child: A Practical Source for Parents and Teachers*. Columbus: Ohio Psychology Press.

8 Children with Asperger's Syndrome and related disorders

Diane Montgomery

Asperger's Syndrome is a recently differentiated condition in education within the autistic spectrum of disorders, although it has been known in the clinical literature for decades. Like autism it is now considered to be a disorder of development (Wing 1995) that lasts throughout the lifespan but the more extreme manifestations can be ameliorated by appropriate kinds of intervention and training. According to Wing, autism or Kanner's syndrome occurs in four or five cases in 10,000 births, whereas Asperger's is more common; it is found in 36 cases in 10,000. The gender ratio is four boys to one girl. It is estimated that there are about 3,000 in the childhood autistic population in comparison with 30,000 with severe learning difficulties; but there could be at least 20,000 with Asperger's. Now that the characteristics are understood, it is possible that a number of well known eccentrics could have been Asperger cases.

Kanner (1943) first thought of autism (*autos* – Greek for self) as a single condition affecting the way people communicated and related to the world around them. However, the work of Wing (1986) established a condition known as 'classic autism', and the 'autistic continuum' or 'autistic spectrum disorders' (ASD) which co-occur and overlap (Jordan and Jones 2001) and include Asperger's Syndrome and Semantic Pragmatic Disorder.

While Asperger was working with more able young men with good structural language skills, Kanner was working with a group of 11 children who were mainly female with a much more severe condition. Both independently and separately observed patterns such as social withdrawal, obsession with routines and the development of peculiar interests to the exclusion of all else. Kanner's subjects also had severe language and social impairment and thus it was that Asperger's cases came to be seen as the more able end of the autistic spectrum. It was Wing's (1981) concern that Kanner's model did not fit all children diagnosed as autistic that caused her to coin the term 'Asperger's Syndrome' and there is increasing agreement over Wing's (1995) proposal that Autistic Spectrum Disorders involve a triad of impairments in:

- reciprocal social interaction
- social communication
- imagination and repetitive behaviour

Bishop (1989) positioned autism, Asperger's Syndrome (now the convention is Asperger Syndrome) and Semantic Pragmatic Disorder on continua between two axes from abnormal to normal as follows:

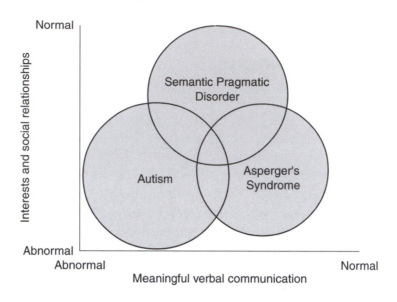

Figure 8.1 Bishop's two-dimensional approach to autistic spectrum disorders (Source: Bishop 1989, p. 117)

Social and medical models were used to explain ASD but Reichelt (2001), at Oslo University, has developed a biochemical model and suggests that the child with ASD has a genetic predisposition, an error gene. Reichelt and his colleagues screened over two million children from 1979 to 2001 in Norway and found that in children with ASD casein and gluten peptides in flour and milk cannot be properly broken down. This results in abnormally high opioid peptides being found in the urine. The opioids lead to the sensory, perceptual and behavioural disturbances reported.

Parents have to keep food journals and remove all casein and gluten products from the child's diet. At first they report that the children get worse, as frequently they have been overdosing on milk and flour products. After three days a transformation takes place. A non-communicative five-year-old began speaking in coherent sentences, others began to play constructively and in interaction with siblings, and their behaviour came back in the normal range. According to their parents, the children still remained autistic or Asperger but were able to settle in school and learn, and find suitable careers. These studies have been replicated at the University of Sunderland by Paul Shattock at the Autism Research Unit (http.//osiris.sunderland.ac.uk/autism).

Perhaps in the future a urine test in the first week of life will identify ASD and a suitable diet could prevent the opioids accumulating and doing damage as in the case of Phenylketonuria. Gene therapy could be a future scenario.

In this chapter the abilities and talents of children with Asperger's Syndrome will be the main focus but will be put in the context of autism and gifted 'savants' and children with Semantic Pragmatic Disorder.

Classic autism

According to Hermalin (1969), the following are characteristics of autism:

- aloofness
- abnormality of speech and language
- compulsive behaviours and rituals
- motor abnormalities – rocking, head banging, tiptoeing everywhere
- cognitive subnormality in most cases

At that time many autistic children were placed in secure hospitals and adults in asylums for the mentally handicapped. For example, Stan, about 40 years old, had found sanctuary in the art therapy classes. He would wait at the door for hours for the class to begin and when it did he would paint all day. His favourite subjects were detailed and beautiful copies of complex pictures of rustic scenes on jigsaw and chocolate boxes. He had been shown the technique of enlargement by covering picture and canvas with squares, which he then completed and so built up the picture. The staff were impressed. His paintings were very popular as gifts and he was paid for them. Stan was unable to speak a word or understand much of what was said to him although he had normal hearing. He made only fleeting eye contact when he was spoken to but when his painting was admired he seemed to glow with pride. Stan is characteristic of about 10 per cent of autistic people known as 'Savants'. They have isolated talents among their severe disabilities, typically these may be artistic, musical, or computational. Lorna Selfe (1977) described the case of Nadia, an autistic child with a prodigious talent for drawing at the age of three to four years. Her drawings of galloping horses were compared in their effect and depiction of movement to those of da Vinci and Michaelangelo. Strangely, as she began to learn to speak and read, her fabulous gift deteriorated to childlike proportions and stereotyped forms.

At the age of five years it is characteristic that autistic children have no speech but if they have high IQs – it is rare to find an IQ above 110, the top 30 per cent have IQs between 70 and 100 – they have the best chance of developing functional language. The language of autistic children (Hermalin 1969) has a number of distinctive features as it develops:

- echolalia
- confusion
- difficulty
- semantic and grammatical errors
- concrete speech
- phonological oddities

In addition, they show only fleeting eye contact and severe impairment in social skills, they are often very graceful and have a symmetry in facial features that is unusual. In infancy parents often recall how good the baby was and, characteristically, autism is not identified until about two years of age when no language has developed and the toddler is difficult to manage. He or she can engage in screaming bouts that last for days because a snowflake fell on them; refuse to walk round corners but only in a straight line; will walk only on tiptoe for six months; and if the furniture in a room is moved will walk across the room over the furniture in the route they have always used.

Education for autistic children in special units and schools during the 1970s featured improved facilities for them. Six year old Frances had been diagnosed as autistic and had recently joined the reception class of the special school. She had no command of speech or language. She was prone to screaming bouts, biting and head banging if she was prevented from doing something or when she wanted attention, usually when the teacher and helpers were telling a story to the other children or just talking to them. On my arrival to sit and observe and ostensibly work quietly with another pupil, Frances, from the lap of the teacher, eyed me under her lids, secretly – gaze avoiding. She left the teacher's lap to crawl over to me. The teacher warned 'Be careful, her favourite thing is to get on your lap and then wet'. She tried, I avoided. She returned to her teacher to put beads on a string. At the break the teacher warned me to guard the orange juice jug for her for a moment for Frances would suck the beads then fly across the room to lift the lid and plunge them in so nobody could drink the juice. I guarded. The teacher returned, poured out some juice and put the jug down, turning to speak to me. In an instant, Frances, whooping, had the jug, the beads were in and she was standing triumphantly watching us. She appeared greatly to enjoy the fuss the teacher made and then became upset, looked cross and wetted. More mess to clear up. I wondered whether she would have bothered to try so hard again if we had ignored her success with the beads. My role was to advise on how to help the teachers reinforce any positive behaviours, or their approximations, which these difficult pupils displayed. By school age they had indeed learned a large repertoire of anti-social activities. Frances seemed to have a cunning and manipulative way with her that suggested a considerable degree of intelligence, but not the sort that would register on an IQ test. She was highly anti-social and prone to scream for days. This was one of her better periods. However, her teacher had decided to learn Makaton and as she introduced this signing system Frances gradually became absorbed in it and calmed down considerably as she was more able to communicate her wishes.

Temple Grandin, a high functioning person with autism, explained that the condition was like watching a video of life rather than being part of it. She is now in her 40s, has a PhD and a successful international career designing livestock equipment. She has written extensively about her difficulties and frustrations and gives the following useful pointers for teachers:

- appreciate the need for structure and routine
- break instructions down into short steps and, for more than three items, write them down
- use practical demonstrations and give concrete examples for thoughts are often visual not verbal
- use artistic and computer skills and fixations to motivate and develop academic work

- use a quiet, calm voice that will not distract those who are sensitive to sound
- check for any background noise – people outside or the hum of a heater can interfere with the ability to listen
- use visual input wherever possible for they find it difficult to remember things if they cannot visualise them, for example phone numbers, instructions, lists
- reading writing in different forms is difficult and typing is easier than handwriting
- place work table near natural light as there may be sensitivity to flicker of screens and fluorescent lights; laptops are easier for there is less flicker
- remember they are 'unichannel' so do not ask them to look and listen at the same time
- in looking up to copy from the board they may lose track of ideas; put screens close to keyboards for the same reason
- coloured paper helps to reduce contrasts of black on white and coloured overlays can also help. (Grandin at http://www.autism.org/temple/inside.html)

Donna Williams (1996) in her book writes, 'I am diagnosed as having autism. ... If you ask me what the word means, I would tell you that, for me, it is about having trouble with connections ... this also causes trouble with tolerance and trouble with control' (p. vii). She then goes on to explain these problems in making connections in the following ways. Her attention is distracted from the whole and is drawn to the details, her perception is deficient in that she can only process bits or parts and does not know where she has been touched. She has difficulties with sensory integration, which is a form of unichannel operation, so she is able to listen but not see, speak but not think. Information is accumulated but without its context so she is unaware of what has been learned and needs some external trigger to recall it. Then it may be recalled in the exact voice and phrasing, which she then repeats (echolalia).

She describes the situation in which she received a serious lecture about not writing graffiti on Parliament House during an excursion. She agreed never to do that again and ten minutes later was caught outside writing different graffiti on the school wall. She was not ignoring what they said, nor trying to be funny, she had not done exactly what she had done before. For her the instruction was specific to the moment and context.

Temple and Donna might be identified as not having high functioning autism (HFA) but are certainly on the ASD continuum and more likely to be included in Asperger Syndrome (AS). However, there are researches by Klin *et al.* (1995) which distinguish HFA from AS in visuo-motor impairment (VMI), visuo-spatial impairment; non-verbal concept formation; visual memory; fine motor skills and gross motor skills. In cases where there were deficits in articulation, verbal output, auditory perception, vocabulary and verbal memory, a diagnosis of 'not Asperger Syndrome' could be given.

Asperger Syndrome (AS)

AS was originally thought to be high functioning autism but now the characteristics are more clearly defined, there are some doubts about this. In AS there is serious impairment in social skills, there are repetitive behaviours and rituals, problems in fantasy and imaginative activities and play, concrete and literal comprehension of speech and a monotonous speech pattern and motor impairment; this latter is in contrast to autism, in which there is usually good coordination, even gracefulness, but severe impairment in language, perception and social skills.

In contrast to autistic children, children with AS speak well before the age of five years and do not remain aloof. They usually speak at the normal age but walking may be delayed. Grammar is usually acquired but difficulties may arise in using pronouns correctly with substitutions of second and third person pronouns. For example, asked 'Do you want an ice cream?' they may say, 'You want an ice cream' and mimic the voice in which it is said. Their discourse is lengthy and pedantic with repetitions of words and phrases, and invented words.

Wing (1981) also found in her AS sample that there had been a lack of interest and pleasure in human company in the first year of life, which should have been there from birth, and a lack of babbling (or a limited quality in it) and a lack of interest and attention to things going on around them. As toddlers they did not bring toys to show people. There was a lack of gesture and smiles and laughter and an absence of imaginative play.

As they get older they do show an interest in people and are at least average in intelligence, with a significant number of them in the high ability range. A few are 'gifted' but the risk of psychiatric illness, especially depression, appears high. As adults they can be highly successful with important jobs, especially if they have good self care and a placid nature (Wing 1981) but they remain socially isolated, egocentric and idiosyncratic. They need to find work that fits their pattern of difficulties, which means they do not have to work with others. They cannot engage in small talk, tending to hold long monologues irrelevant to the listener, and fail to obey the interactional rules in conversation such as looking at the other person at the end of a statement to cue them to begin talking and so on; sometimes they may gaze off and stare straight through the listener. Their interests are obsessional in a limited range of topics and it is difficult to switch them off when they get started. Their speech can sometimes sound odd and monotonous. They fail to develop good social skills and will often request a set of rules to follow and advice about what to say to get a date with a peer. They appear to lack insight into their own thinking processes, they lack metacognition (Wing 1981) and have great difficulty understanding the perspective of others. In social and emotional terms they seem to remain in the egocentric stage of early childhood and lack empathy.

Neihart (2000) identified seven characteristics that children with AS have in common with gifted children, which makes it difficult in some cases to distinguish the AS. The gifted education expert may, for example, think that this is just another eccentric little gifted individual (Gallagher and Gallagher 2001). The characteristics in common are:

- verbal fluency or precocity and excellent memory
- fascination with letters or numbers and enjoys rote learning
- absorbing interest in a specific topic, memorises vast quantities of information
- annoys peers with limitless talk about the interest
- asks awkward questions and gives lengthy discourses in answers to questions
- hypersensitivity to sensory stimulation – refusal to eat this or wear that, may scream at loud noises
- extraordinary skill in a special area and average in others – an uneven pattern.

The child with AS is differentiated from the ordinary gifted according to Neihart by the following:

- pedantic seamless speech in which they run on, mixing fact and personal detail
- low tolerance to change, may ignore class and school routines completely
- does not understand humour, understanding is literal
- clumsiness in 50–90 per cent
- inappropriate affect and lack of insight – may laugh at a funeral
- frequently has stereotypic behaviours and rituals.

Early identification of the 'giftedness' may be vocabulary based; they are hyperlingual but comprehension shows deficits. There are no verbal quotient–performance quotient discrepancies unless there are also learning disabilities present (Gallagher and Gallagher 2001). In case studies they noted extended parallel play and presence of the myth of the 'goofy gifted' and found that the presence of giftedness often masked the identification of AS. They found also that identifying the giftedness alleviated some of the depression but it was the social issues that precipitated it. They are usually strong visual thinkers (Attwood 1998) and think best in concrete literal pictures. Most classrooms emphasise verbal skills and verbal learning and this can handicap the child with AS as soon as the talk moves away from the literal to the imaginative, inferential and abstract. Teachers thus need to support learning using diagrams, visualisation, pictograms, videos, concept mapping and graphic organisers. For these children rote learning is recommended and they can pass examinations that require them to recall factual information and so gain places at universities. However, rote learning is not at all recommended for ordinary gifted children! In AS learning needs to be built in a systematic way from parts to the whole, for they tend to overfocus on the detail. The lack of creativity and imagination would lead us to infer that the high functioning person with AS cannot be gifted, for Cropley (1994), in his analysis of giftedness and talent, has said that there is no true giftedness without creativity. However, this must make us think further, for Nadia and Temple and Donna are at least significant exceptions either in giftedness or in ASD.

In AS extra sensitivity to sound or touch makes them over-respond or become anxious and may even lead to panic attacks on just hearing the whistle or the school bell. They may refuse to stand in line in case they are touched or join in contact games. This can lead to confrontations with teachers who regard it as disobedience and very quickly can escalate into a major scene. For them sensory integration therapy is recommended consisting of massage, deep pressure stimulation, hand massage and rubbing and brushing.

Some children with AS pay no regard to school routines and rules at all as they see no relevance in them to themselves, which is particularly difficult to cope with in a large class.

They will, as already indicated, need social skills training and Rogers (1996), who is head of a school where many AS pupils were placed, said that he found the most problematic aspect for the school was the lack of social skills and social awareness. They had to develop social rules and step-by-step protocols for them. It is at adolescence that many do become aware of their difficulties; they may then become oversensitive to criticism and appear very vulnerable and pathetic or very childish.

Nathanson (2001), in a study of 10 young people diagnosed with AS attending college, explained that the literal interpretation of language led to difficulty for the student in interpreting the set tasks and difficulty for the lecturer in appreciating the direct 'no guile' response of some of the students to questioning and evaluation of activities. Over time staff developed strategies to cope with the comments that may be addressed very directly to the support worker or to the tutor but the initial directness has sometimes proved hard not to take personally. What others might just think, these individuals actually say.

To help with social skills training, Gray (1990) devised a set of social stories and comic strip conversations. The stories are very short and give the child a protocol of four types of sentence. These are:

- descriptive – explain where and what
- perspective – explain feelings and behaviour of others
- directive – state what the child is expected to do
- control – strategies the child can use to remember.

In using the protocol Gray advises using one directive and/or control statement to every two to five descriptive/prescriptive statements. The system works in the following way:

Sometimes my friend Toni tells me to 'chill'. (descriptive)
This means I am getting loud and bossy. (descriptive)
Toni does not want to sit with me when I am loud and bossy. (perspective)
I will lower my voice when Toni tells me to 'chill'. (directive)
When Toni says 'chill', I can imagine putting my voice on ice. (control) (p. 227)

The behaviour of children with Asperger Syndrome can be so difficult that like Kelly they finish up excluded from school and in a unit for those with social, emotional and behavioural disorders (Smith 2002) without their condition or double exceptionality ever being noticed. Their behaviour can be rigid and resistant to change, which brings the child into conflict with other children and school staff so that having been told to sit still and be quiet the child continues questioning loudly or gets up and walks around, oblivious to the instruction. Some engage in compulsive rituals such as shelf tidying or hand flapping, others are prone to sudden aggressive outbursts, temper tantrums, hyperactivity, anxiety or phobic attacks. Medication is usually only given to alleviate the more extreme psychiatric conditions such as phobic attacks, obsessional thought disorder and depression. Depression, for which the drug imipramine is given, is a high risk (Wing 1981; Attwood 2000) as they become socially isolated for they are very sensitive to teasing but continually engage in precisely the behaviours that provoke it. Ritalin is also prescribed in some cases and this helps where there are hyperactivity symptoms.

In 1996, Barber described the case of a 15 year old pupil with AS in mainstream school who had been accelerated in maths, physics, biology and modern foreign languages and supported by enrichment programmes. In Year eight he took GCSEs and obtained 'A' and 'A*' grades. With the help from a lecturer at the local university's Department of Education he pursued A levels but while he enjoyed his specialised academic programme his behavioural and social skills were of great concern. In Year nine Barber developed a special out of school programme for him. This involved bus journeys together to the city centre. On the first visit Barber paid the fare, took an agreed route through the shopping centre and discussed what to do and say if anyone stopped them and asked for directions. The next time the pupil paid the fare and 'took' the tutor on the trip. On the next occasion he went alone while she followed the bus in her car and finally he went through the whole procedure on his own. In his evaluation he wrote, 'This was useful as it helped me to gain independence and I learned how to use the bus service. I would like, if it were possible, to do this again, over a longer distance' (p. 21). As can be imagined, parents given some support could have begun this sort of training several years earlier.

Barber went on to develop a behaviour management programme for him to stop him grumbling under his breath, looking as angry as he could, and screaming when asked to do something he did not want to do. When asked why he behaved in this way he said it was because of his urge to learn and because the teachers often covered work with which he was already familiar (p. 22). The range of future behaviours that Barber had determined to target such as shopping, planning a meal and using the telephone (p. 24) illustrate the extraordinary range of high abilities and deficits – deficits in areas in which pupils at a much younger age develop competencies without specific instruction.

This structured approach is also needed in the rules of interaction in conversation, such as to look at the person when they are speaking and only get ready to speak when they signal they are coming to a close by looking away and then looking back to you. How to 'chat up' a potential girlfriend was high on the wants list of the youths in Roger's school. They required a set of rules and 'chat up' lines and sequences that they could learn and then operate on; they were unable to 'wing it' or adapt the routine if it did not go to plan. Similarly, in a shop or out on the street they could not cope with an unplanned conversational interaction and could become highly anxious and upset.

A similar project is described by Teasdale (2002) in the case of Mark, which involved taking him on a residential trip to Cambridge, where he was to apply for a university place. Completing the application forms was particularly frustrating for him. He had difficulties in writing them, acquiring the stamps, cheques, photographs, envelopes and photocopies. He had to be cajoled to produce a final neater copy than his original. As he had never travelled on his own before, the interview presented huge problems in getting him through a complex train journey and into overnight accommodation. Teasdale purchased his tickets, planned a detailed itinerary with him, drove him to the station and persuaded his mother to let him go and to remain in touch with him by mobile phone during the trip. Mark returned more eloquent, animated and confident and positive about his abilities to cope. Later he will need extra support from university tutors and the Student Welfare office to ensure he is coping with the practicalities.

Semantic Pragmatic Disorder (SPD)

Children with SPD in common with those with AS have a language impairment in a social setting but the motor, sensory and cognitive deficits are minor in contrast and also make up one of the group of specific language impairments. Bishop (1997), in studies of Specific Language Impairment (SLI), suggested that the incidence in the UK could be as high as seven per cent in children if it follows the pattern in the USA. She found there are genes that put children at risk from SLI but that environmental factors make these manifest. A phonological short term memory test was a useful indicator in both resolved and persistent cases.

According to Dehaney (2000), the characteristics of SPD are similar to those with AS in relation to speech and comprehension, imaginative play and behaviour and social interaction. Analysing SPD in relation to the teaching of English and the literacy hour, she concluded that the pace of the programme was too fast and the emphasis on oral and listening skills meant that there was a failure to comprehend before the lesson moved on. This meant that the child missed out on much learning. The child also cannot imagine or see things from another's perspective, which often even simple texts require. In the National Literacy Strategy the assumption is that what is missed can be caught up but this is not possible for these children for they need special learning support and more appropriate strategies tailored to their needs in a 'parallel class'.

Talent in SPD is seen in the non-verbal areas in visual and performance studies but as yet there is a lack of report of their dual exceptionalities.

Summary and conclusions

The autistic spectrum disorders are a complex and developing area for educationalists in mainstream settings, although they have been known about in clinical and special educational circles for many decades.

Three of the more common patterns: classic autism and Savants, Asperger Syndrome and Semantic Pragmatic Disorder have been outlined. There has been a focus on Asperger Syndrome, where a number of high achieving individuals are being discovered and their stories told. They are certainly talented and definitely gifted in ASD terms. The question of whether they can be regarded as gifted in general terms remains an interesting one.

The linkages and overlaps with non-verbal learning difficulties can be seen particularly in the AS facility with verbal skills and difficulties in coordination, but the deficits in comprehension in AS would suggest that there is deeper language difficulty, a problem in connecting labels and reflecting on mental processes in some way, a lack of theory of mind.

Promoting interest in the topic to this wider audience will bring some answers and many more examples. There are many more people with ASD than in the clinical population, who are holding down jobs or living quiet sheltered lives. For example, Maria, who was bilingual in Portuguese and English, was on her first solo trip abroad. She said her brother usually kept her locked in the house. She did not stop her monologue for hours. Her initial open friendliness deteriorated into intrusion. She needed the social skills training that schools and learning support could provide and then would not need to be locked in for her own protection and lack of guile. She could then have pursued her education and taken up a job.

There is also research needed into possible links between ASD and the occasional eccentric loner with obsessional interests and lack of empathy who suffers from depression and commits gun crimes. It might be possible with earlier identification and intervention, diet and medication to prevent such tragedies.

References

ASPEN (Asperger Syndrome Educational Network) http://www. asperger.org

Asperger, H. (1944) Die 'Autistischen Psychopathen' im Kindesalter, *Archiv für Psychiatrie und Nervenkrankheiten*, Vol. 117, pp. 76–136 (Translation and annotation in Frith (ed.) 1991).

Asperger, H. (1979) 'Problems of infantile autism', *Communication*, Vol. 13, pp. 45–52.

Attwood, T. (1998) *Asperger Syndrome: A Guide for Parents and Professionals.* Philadelphia: Taylor and Francis.

Attwood, T. (2000) *Asperger's Syndrome: A Guide for Parents and Professionals.* London: Jessica Kingsley.

Barber, C. (1996) 'The integration of a very able pupil with Asperger Syndrome into mainstream school', *British Journal of Special Education* 23(1), pp. 19–24.

Bishop, D. V. M. (1989) 'Autism, Asperger Syndrome and Semantic-pragmatic disorder': Where are the boundaries?', *British Journal of Disorders of Communication* 24, pp. 107–21.

Bishop, D. V. M. (1997) *Uncommon Understanding: Development of and Disorders of Language Comprehension in Children.* Oxford: Psychology Press.

Cropley, A. J. (1994) 'Creative intelligence: A concept of true giftedness', *European Journal of High Ability* 5, pp. 16–23.

Dehaney, R. (2000) 'Literacy hour and the literal thinker: The inclusion of children with semantic-pragmatic language difficulties in the literacy hour', *Support for Learning* **15**(1), pp. 36–40.

Ehlers, S. and Gillberg, C. (1993) 'The epidemiology of Asperger Syndrome: A total population study', *Journal of Child Psychology and Psychiatry* **34**(8), pp. 1327–50.

Frith, U. (ed.) (1991) *Autism and Asperger Syndrome.* Cambridge: Cambridge University Press.

Gallagher, S. A. and Gallagher, J. J. (2001) 'Giftedness and Asperger's Syndrome: Sorting through the issues', Presentation at the World Council for Gifted Children Conference, Barcelona, August 1–5.

Grandin, T. (2000) 'An inside view of autism' in E. Schopler and G. B. Mesibov (eds) *High Functioning Individuals with Autism.* New York: Plenum.

Gray, C. (1990) *Original Social Story Book.* New York: Future Horizons.

Harrison, J. (1998) 'Improving learning opportunities in mainstream secondary schools and colleges for students on the autistic spectrum', *British Journal of Special Education* **25**(4), pp. 179–83.

Hermalin, B. (1969) *Clinical Psychology Lecture Series on Autism Research.* London: Birkbeck College.

Jordan, R. and Jones, G. (2001) *Meeting the Needs of Children with Autistic Spectrum Disorders.* London: David Fulton.

Kanner, L. (1943) 'Autistic disturbances of affective contact', *Nervous Child*, **2**, pp. 217–50.

Klin, A., Volkmar, F., Sparrow, S., Cicchetti, D. and Rourke, B. (1995) 'Validity and neuropsychological characterisation of Asperger Syndrome: Convergence with nonverbal learning disability syndrome', *Journal of Child Psychology and Psychiatry* **36**(7), pp. 1127–40.

Nathanson, J. (2001) 'An investigation into the curriculum provision for students diagnosed with Asperger Syndrome at a Further Education College'. Unpublished MA SEN Dissertation, London: Middlesex University.

National Autistic Society (1997) *Approaches to Autism* (3rd edition). London: National Autistic Society.

Neihart, M. (2000) 'Gifted children with Asperger's Syndrome', *Gifted Child Quarterly* **44**(4), pp. 222–30.

Reichelt, C. (2001) 'Biochemical basis for autism', *The Food Programme: Radio 4*, 14th January.

Rogers, W. (1996) Presentation on 'High ability and underfunctioning' to the Conference of Swiss International Schools, Geneva.

Selfe, L. (1977) *Nadia: A Case of Extraordinary Drawing Abilities in an Autistic Child.* London: Academic Press.

Smith, L. (2002) 'An investigation of children having emotional and behavioural difficulties and dyslexic-type difficulties in three special schools and one pupil referral unit'. Unpublished MA SpLD Dissertation. London: Middlesex University.

Teasdale, R. (2000) 'A case study in double exceptionality', *Educating Able Children* **6**(2), pp. 41–2.

Williams, D. (1996) *An Inside Out Approach.* London: Jessica Kingsley.

Wing, L. (1981) 'Asperger Syndrome: A clinical account', *Journal of Psychological Medicine* **11**, pp. 115–29.

Wing, L. (1986) *The Autistic Spectrum: A Guide for Parents and Professionals.* London: Constable.

Wing, L. (1995) *Autistic Spectrum Disorders.* London: Constable.

Wing, L. and Gould, J. (1979) 'Severe impairments of social interaction and associated abnormalities in children: Epidemiology and classification', *Journal of Autism and Childhood Schizophrenia* **9**, pp. 11–29.

9 Interventions with talented at-risk populations with emotional and behavioural difficulties

Ken W. McCluskey, Philip A. Baker, Mike Bergsgaard, and Andrea L. A. McCluskey[1]

This chapter reviews several projects designed by the authors to serve at-risk populations. In these initiatives, Creative Problem Solving – in combination with mentoring, career awareness and other interventions – has been used successfully to reduce the recidivism rate of native Canadian inmates (the Second Chance programme), to reclaim talented but troubled high school dropouts (lost prizes) and other underachieving young people and to support inner city children and youths at risk of alienation, school failure, and gang involvement (MARS – Mentoring At-Risk Students).

> If education is always to be conceived along the same antiquated lines of a mere transmission of knowledge, there is little to be hoped from it in the bettering of man's future. For what is the use of transmitting knowledge if the individual's total development lags behind? (Maria Montessori (1949), *The Absorbent Mind*)

Underachievement

Underachievement is a complicated, galling phenomenon (Gallagher 1975; McCluskey and Walker 1986; Rimm 1986; Whitmore 1980). Various researchers, including Betts and Neihart (1988), have endeavoured to identify categories of young people who are most likely to fall into the trap of substance abuse, become involved in criminal activity, and/or drop out of school. Certainly, there are many high ability young people who see the educational curriculum as irrelevant (Baum, Renzulli and Hébert 1995): they often challenge authority, create disturbances and refuse to conform to the system. In their view, schools are unfeeling places with inflexible attendance and discipline policies that push nonconformists out of the door (Radwanski 1987). Students dismissed as ne'er-do-wells or underachievers by teachers may well develop confrontational behaviours to live up to the negative perceptions (Mukhopadyay and Chugh 1979). It can also be difficult to meet the diverse needs of students who have different types of talents or 'intelligences' (cf. Feldhusen 1995; Gardner 1983; Sternberg 1988) that do not fit into those typically covered by the conventional school curriculum.

There is very little doubt that schools are losing many young people who are capable of making it, but don't. A report by Statistics Canada (1991) highlighted the fact that talented students can be very much at risk – they often grow bored, discouraged and unproductive. Indeed, more than 30 per cent of the dropouts surveyed had averages of A or B, and only eight per cent identified academic problems as their reason for quitting. Most indicated that 'not belonging' was the major issue. The 'tough bright' – those who don't fit comfortably into the traditional education system – face a clear dearth of services (Peterson 1997). There are even some school administrators who, intentionally or otherwise, draw lines in the sand to force troubled and troubling students from their buildings (McCluskey 2000a). This action creates larger difficulties and costs for society as a whole.

The cost of things gone wrong

'Crime and bad lives are the measure of a State's failure, all crime in the end is the crime of the community', said H. G. Wells (1905) in *A Modern Utopia*. Educational underachievement carries with it an emotional cost. Since high school dropouts generally have a tough time obtaining and holding down jobs, quality of life is affected: many are forced to take low paying positions with little opportunity for job satisfaction or advancement. And because unemployed or under-employed people tend to be less happy than their better educated counterparts, there is considerable potential for social problems and upheaval (Levin 1989). High unemployment has been related to decreased self-esteem, a rise in suicide and mortality rates and increased need for psychiatric care (Gage 1990). Many unemployed individuals are less effective decision makers, and they tend to function well below potential (Levin 1989). Information we examined a decade or so ago (when we were beginning to develop many of our projects) indicated that there is an economic price, both personal and societal, to be paid as well.

Although it may be impossible to quantify, there is also the social cost of what might have been. 'What is the "cost" of a symphony unwritten, a cure not discovered, a breakthrough not invented? In today's complex world, and in preparing for tomorrow's certainly more complex one, we can scarcely afford to waste "talent capital" of any sort' (McCluskey and Treffinger 1998: 216).

Lack of productivity may not be the half of it. Those blocked from positive attention and legitimate paths to success are likely to turn their talents instead toward unsavoury pursuits. Troubled youth with promising interpersonal skills might, if things go awry, seek leadership positions in youth gangs. A major conclusion that arose from the First World Conference on Gifted Children in London in 1975, was that high ability individuals whose needs are not met may well become severe social problems. Lacking direction and left to make it on their own, some at-risk young people move in unfortunate directions.

Of course, large numbers of young offenders are caught by the law. In these cases in Canada, it costs approximately $46,000 each year to incarcerate one youth in a correctional facility (Manitoba Department of Justice 1995–96). More than 75 per cent of incarcerated adults had had behaviour problems and were offenders in their youth (National Crime Prevention Council 1996). Poor school performance is the best predictor of future criminal involvement – only 12 of 540 adults sentenced to prison in Manitoba in 1995 finished high school (Carson 1996).

When considering the overall state of affairs, we're reminded of the words of an old commercial: 'Pay me now, or pay me later.' Thinking it better to prevent than to lament, we decided long ago to attempt to make a difference by focusing on the at-risk domain. The literature, and our own work in a variety of settings, convinced us that there is an abundance of untapped potential out there, and far too many young people falling through the cracks, as it were. Due to lack of opportunity, it appears many 'diamonds' are destined to remain 'in the rough' unless we can begin to intervene in a productive way. Creative Problem Solving (CPS) has provided one mechanism for doing precisely that.

Planning with CPS

'One looks back with appreciation to the brilliant teachers, but with gratitude to those who touched our human feelings. The curriculum is so much necessary raw material, but warmth is the vital element for the growing plant and for the soul of the child', as Carl Jung (1943) put it in *The Gifted Child*. Actually, in the beginning, we saw Creative Problem Solving more as a planning tool to help introduce systemic change and it served that role nicely. In a volume entitled *Lost Prizes* (McCluskey, Baker *et al.* 1998), some of us, along with colleagues affiliated with a number of different programmes, offered articles that dealt with employing CPS to help plan and develop (1) a support facility for at-risk children and youth and (2) a summer institute for Sikh youngsters in our community, schools from Northern Manitoba.

It is important to give some sense of the broad impact that planning with CPS has had in our part of the world. To that end, we'll review one of the other projects discussed in the *Lost Prizes* anthology in more depth.

BEST Beginnings

BEST (an acronym for Beausejour Elementary School Team) Beginnings, a programme described in a chapter by O'Hagan, Tymko *et al.* (1995), was born at a 'breakfast club' meeting, not unlike those held by educators the world over. Between bites of toast and sips of coffee, administrators and special educators in Agassiz School Division in Manitoba voiced opinions (argued), churned out ideas, and jotted down possibilities. Basically, impromptu brainstorming – considering how best to reach some hitherto unreachable children and their parents – was underway. The players got as far as coming up with the problem statement: 'How might we creatively attract parents of at-risk children into the school?' However, seemingly overwhelming issues and challenges just kept on surfacing, until the process became bogged down in a morass of confusion.

After a variety of training sessions at home and further afield, they revisited the problem, suffice it to say that staff – recognising family dynamics and poverty as major risk factors – decided to address four main areas: (1) parent–child interactions; (2) literacy levels of parents and children; (3) development of parental skills; and (4) parent employability.

Armed with new CPS strategies, the team went on to create a do-able project designed to offer concrete support to at-risk children and their families. BEST Beginnings, in its final form, featured an integrated approach (where parents and children learned together), academic skill building for parents, and meaningful short term employment for parents in the school (Tymko and O'Hagan 1993). More specifically, parents were (1) provided with academic upgrading via computer assisted learning; (2) hired in the school to fill visible and significant roles (for example tutoring, office duties, lunch or recess supervision, library work, and making teaching materials); and (3) encouraged to read to their children at home, and to spend more time with them in community restaurants, theatres, and recreational centres. Since one of the main goals was to raise literacy levels and academic performance in general, parents also worked (on prearranged learning activities) with their own children in the classroom for several hours per day, four days per week.

The evaluative data made it clear that this CPS generated project had a tremendous impact. Parents, once suspicious and fearful of school due to aversive experiences in their own pasts, became comfortable in the educational setting. Not surprisingly, their academic skills shot up, and the children, more excited about learning once their parents had become involved, improved their grades significantly. One finding in particular was an eye-opener: for the vast majority of the 25 students (grades 1 through to 7) in the first phase of the programme, there was a substantial increase in home reading time. At the onset of BEST, parents read with their children only .36 times per week on average; 17 months later, the mean number of weekly parent–child reading sessions had risen to 4.12. Academic growth resulted. After a six-month period, educators – using pre- and post-test scores from the Johns (1988) Basic Reading Inventory – noted dramatic improvement in word knowledge for almost all students. The same instrument also showed pronounced gains in reading comprehension. Even after allowing for the maturational and educational growth that would have been expected with the passage of time, a within-subject analysis of variance performed on these data yielded a significant treatment effect ($F = 49.1$, df $= 1$, p. $< .01$). Incidentally, there also appeared to be concomitant improvement in student self concept, with mean scores on the Coopersmith (1986) Inventory rising 12.26 points during the life of the programme. Behavioural incidents – such as outbursts, fighting, and detentions – dropped off noticeably. Yet another spin-off was the organisation of intensive professional development in the at-risk realm for teachers. Training for all school staffs in CPS was part of this process, and that soon turned out to have positive ramifications for the district as a whole. With all the successes it was only natural that variations of the BEST Beginnings project eventually started up in a second Manitoba district, and in schools in our neighbouring province of Saskatchewan.

Doing with CPS

'You must train the children to their studies in a playful manner, and without any air of constraint, with the further object of discerning more readily the natural bent of their respective characters', Plato as quoted by Socrates, *The Republic, Book 7*, Section 537. About the time CPS was being used to help plan BEST Beginnings and other projects, some members of our team were asked to tackle an intervention programme with native Canadian inmates in our provincial prison system. Given the plight of our indigenous people and the state of our jails, that proposition was about as 'at-risky' as it gets. In any case, it occurred to us that those who 'make it' in today's world tend to arrive at decisions by considering the social-cultural context, selecting wisely from among possibilities, and responding in ways that meet their own needs and fit within prevailing norms. Perhaps inmates, many of whom continually re-offend, might not be as adept in terms of that sort of problem solving.

Second Chance

At the time when we were approached by Human Resources Development Canada to design and deliver what became known as the Second Chance project, it had been determined that each inmate cost Canadian taxpayers $51,047 annually (Corrections Services 1991). The situation was exacerbated by the fact that criminal acts tend to be repeated – a disproportionately large number of prisoners have had previous convictions. Gendreau, Madden *et al.* (1977) found that 65.6 per cent of inmates in our country re-offended, and Canfield and Drinnan (1991) pointed out that recidivism rates are higher for Aboriginal populations. A point of clarification here: in Canada, the term Aboriginal is used to refer to native 'First Nations' people, the Inuit, or the Métis (whose lineage is mixed – often Native and French Canadian).

Briefly, the project provided pre-release support – in the form of Creative Problem Solving training, career awareness, and work experience – to native Canadians incarcerated in Manitoba jails for drug offences, fraud, break and entry, assault, physical or sexual abuse, or even murder (as a juvenile). Many had previous convictions. The 31 inmates (27 male; 4 female) – in treatment groups of 16 and 15 – took part in an 11 week 'life skills' classroom component, followed by a four week supervised job placement. One early week of the in-class segment was devoted specifically to CPS (see Figure 9.1), and then the tools learned were interwoven and practised in later sessions dealing with anger management, conflict resolution, learning styles, peer pressure, relationship building, self-fulfilling prophecy, verbal and non-verbal communication, and career exploration (via interest inventories, resumé writing, interview simulations, and job searches).

The approach worked relatively well, but we weren't entirely satisfied. Members of our first group began to assert, as others have done in later work (Isaksen, Dorval and Treffinger 1994), that life isn't merely a 'marble drop', where problems are magically solved by applying easy-to-follow, step-by-step formulae. Fortuitously remembering the make-up of our target population and

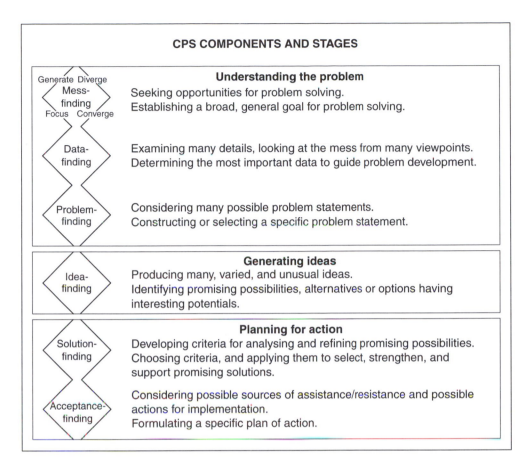

CPS COMPONENTS AND STAGES

Generate Diverge
Mess-finding
Focus Converge

Understanding the problem
Seeking opportunities for problem solving.
Establishing a broad, general goal for problem solving.

Data-finding

Examining many details, looking at the mess from many viewpoints.
Determining the most important data to guide problem development.

Problem-finding

Considering many possible problem statements.
Constructing or selecting a specific problem statement.

Idea-finding

Generating ideas
Producing many, varied, and unusual ideas.
Identifying promising possibilities, alternatives or options having interesting potentials.

Solution-finding

Planning for action
Developing criteria for analysing and refining promising possibilities.
Choosing criteria, and applying them to select, strengthen, and support promising solutions.

Acceptance-finding

Considering possible sources of assistance/resistance and possible actions for implementation.
Formulating a specific plan of action.

Figure 9.1   Linear View of CPS Components and Stages (Source: Treffinger and Isaksen 1992, p. 19)

the native emphasis on circular world views, we changed gears abruptly. Since sharing circles and models such as the Circle of Courage (Brendtro, Brokenleg and van Bockern 1990) seem to be preferred by our Aboriginal community, it only made sense to shift toward the circular representation of the CPS process shown in Figure 9.2. That simple change made a radical difference – things hummed along nicely from that point.

As in all our CPS training programmes, we strove to help the participants in question develop a creative climate, use their own problem-solving styles effectively, learn to differentiate between creative and critical thinking, and build personal 'tool boxes' of practical techniques. By training's end, the emphasis had moved toward dealing with relevant issues, generating workable ideas, and taking meaningful action. The job placement portion of the project offered all individuals a chance to practise their newfound skills in an authentic, real-life context.

To put it succinctly, our mission was successful. After individuals in our two Second Chance groups had 'done their time', completed the programme, and been released into society, they were monitored for a year to see if they would 'go straight' or run afoul of the law once more. Simultaneously, members of a matched group of native Canadian offenders – from the same home reserves as our participants – were monitored over the same period.

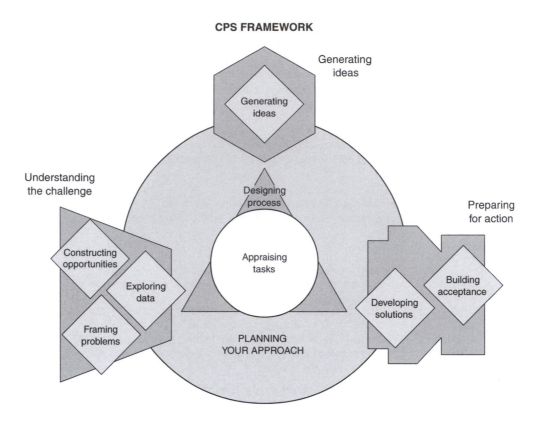

Figure 9.2 Circular View of CPS Components and Stages (Source: Treffinger, Isaksen and Dorval 2000, p. 14)

People in this control group, however, were simply warehoused through the correctional system in the traditional manner and left to fend for themselves upon release. The recidivism rates for the control group and the two Second Chance groups are compared in Figure 9.3.

This schematic makes it abundantly clear that the project had a prodigious impact. Recidivism during the follow-up year was 90.32 per cent (28 of 31) for the unsupported control group, but only 38.71 per cent (12 of 31) for our 'second chancers'. While the distressingly high rate of re-offending in the non-treated condition is an indictment of our present judicial and penal systems, the results suggest that promising alternatives – featuring a combination of CPS, career awareness, and work experience – are worthy of serious consideration.

Lost Prizes

Picking up on the successes and lessons learned in previous work, three Manitoba school districts – Agassiz, Interlake, and Lord Selkirk – began the joint Lost Prizes venture to 'recapture' at-risk, high ability school dropouts. Despite their talents, these young people had been lost to the system: they had left (or been 'asked' to leave) school and were basically 'going nowhere'. At best, they were accomplishing little; at worst, they were in serious trouble with the law. The intent was to reconnect with these troubled youths, awaken dormant creative potential, and encourage thoughtful and productive action on their part.

174

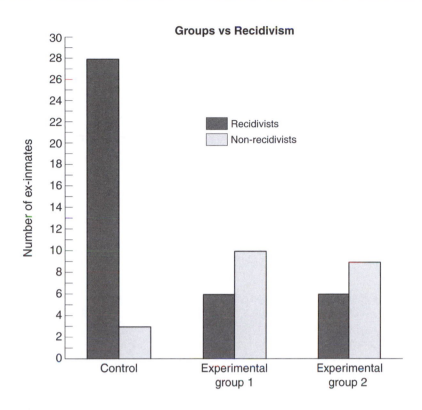

Figure 9.3 Recidivism of Native Ex-Inmates in Control and Experimental Conditions (Source: Place and McCluskey 1995, p.144)

Lost Prizes ran from September 1993 to June 1996. During that period, 88 students participated. Each year, using Feldhusen's (1995) Talent Identification and Development in Education (TIDE) model, educators in the three jurisdictions identified dropouts who had displayed talent in the domains shown in Figure 9.4.

The project ran separately, for two months per year, in each of the districts. From the outset, the majority of students let it be known that they were decidedly reluctant to return to their high schools – too many unpalatable things had happened to them there. Therefore, during the month long first phase of the programme, our facilitator – along with many invited resource people – delivered the information sessions, career exploration curriculum, and CPS training in rented premises away from the schools. This time around, using the approach outlined in Figure 9.5, we placed much more importance on the need for the re-engaged young men and women to consider how to move from their 'current reality' to a 'desired future state' (Treffinger, Isaksen and Dorval 1995).

Individual Growth Plans were mapped out to help each 'prize' identify and work toward goals (Feldhusen 1995). Gradually, the emphasis shifted to real-life problems, generating more and better alternatives, and moving good ideas into action plans. Throughout the in-class segment, there was plenty of opportunity to practise and develop the skills involved. Students completing this part of the programme earned one high school credit.

One word of caution. With our first group, we made the mistake of preparing only one Growth Plan per participant: there ended up being several

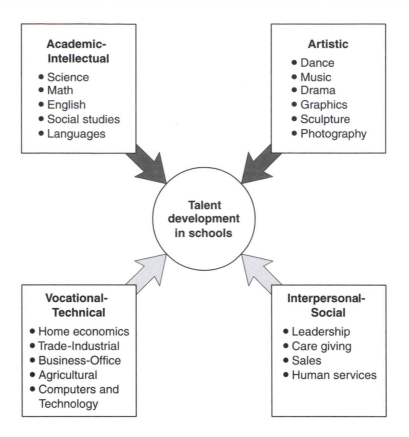

Figure 9.4 Talent Identification and Development in Education (Source: Feldhusen 1995, p. 14)

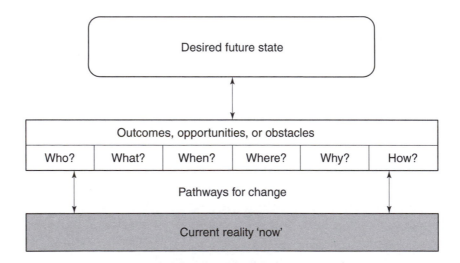

Figure 9.5 Comparing Current Realities with Desired Futures (Source: Treffinger, Isaksen and Dorval 1995, p. 33)

disappointed young people who did not achieve instant success on their chosen path; in all subsequent groups we urged the 'lost prizes' to develop multiple plans. Each student learned to ask: If my first plan doesn't work, what might I try next? And after that? Single plans usually did not do the trick, but having two or three fall-back positions worked like a charm.

Phase two of the programme, again a one month job placement (that matched student interests to the employment site), allowed the young people to gain experience in the world of work. Quite clearly, they benefited from the opportunity to encounter and address some real-life problems with the help of caring partners in the business community. Using prescribed guidelines, these workplace hosts – along with the facilitator – monitored performance. Students faring satisfactorily in the workplace received a second credit.

Entrepreneurs in the respective regions were eager to provide training grounds for the refocusing youths. In truth, the business partners were not expected to offer a traditional work placement as such, but rather to serve as 'philanthropic mentors' to guide and support the students in a concrete way. Most, working cooperatively with the school systems, bonded with, went that extra mile for, and virtually 'adopted' their students. By the way, one ingredient that helped establish a firm foundation for Lost Prizes was the in-depth training put in place for many of the business partners and educators. During this and related programmes, several of the 'names' in the fields of Creative Problem Solving, talent development and mentoring (i.e. Dorval, Feldhusen, Isaksen, Noller, Renzulli, Treffinger, and others) visited Manitoba to conduct intensive workshop sessions.

Not every one of the participants blossomed, they were, after all, chosen from a seriously at-risk population. A total of 21 young people, uninterested or overwhelmed by further troubles of one kind or another (for example run-ins with the law, family break-ups, pregnancy, illness, and so on), withdrew without completing even the first credit. And 10 others (who had earned at least one credit) moved and were impossible to track. Nonetheless, as a result of Lost Prizes, many formerly disenchanted, disillusioned, and disconnected dropouts did respond by 'getting their acts together' in dramatic fashion (once their talents were identified, appreciated, and nurtured). A 'current status' review of successful participants – summarised in Table 9.1 – showed that 24 entered the work force and obtained permanent, full-time employment (four of these graduated, and two were self-employed), 18 returned to school and were performing solidly, nine had just graduated from high school, and six more went on to university or community college after completing grade 12. Of the 88 at-risk dropouts who were enrolled in Lost Prizes, then, 57 (or 64.77 per cent) ended up returning to high school, entering post secondary programmes, or securing employment (McCluskey, Baker *et al.* 1998).

Perhaps the highlight of the project occurred in November 1995, when seven of the 'prizes' with very visible talents were invited to speak at the National Association for Gifted Children (NAGC) Conference in Tampa. Imagine the excitement of young people, most of whom had never left the province, on the plane to Florida. Imagine the trepidation of the adult supervisors, travelling with and responsible for several known drug users with chequered pasts. Happily, the former problem students – determined to make the most of the opportunity – all behaved in an exemplary manner. During the session at the conference, each spoke briefly about troubled lives and suddenly promising futures. The poets recited, the photographer showed slides of his work, and the artists displayed their wares, and the band, formed just a couple of months before the big event, belted out original and powerful songs.

The novice presenters took the proceedings seriously, rehearsed speeches and songs for hours, and bonded into a tightly knit group. It was work, but great fun as well. Five years later, the Lost Prizes travellers are all still close and supportive of one another.

Table 9.1   Number of Lost Prizes Students in Each 'Current Status' Category

Current Status	1993–94	1994–95	1995–96
Employed full-time	13	5	6
Returned to and performing well in high school	5	7	6
Just graduated from high school	5	2	2
Graduated and attending college or university	4	1	1
Withdrew	10	3	8
Unknown	4	5	1
Total	41	23	24

After the NAGC session, members of the audience began offering rather exorbitant amounts (in US dollars – gold to Canadians) for Ryan's sketches and paintings. Swamped by positive attention, compliments, and hard cash, Ryan – in the midst of signing copies of the newly released Lost Prizes book (which featured his cover art) – exclaimed excitedly: 'This is a bigger high than drugs.' That sentiment really sums up the programme.

MARS – Mentoring At-Risk Students

The question which concerned us was, 'How might we have a more enduring impact?' We've learned through experience that some elements of our programmes are 'musts', pure and simple. CPS training, for one, is an obvious 'keeper'. A project called Prism taught us that mentoring too has some exciting possibilities for reclaiming at-risk populations. However, feeling that we had fallen somewhat into the mentoring-without-thinking trap in that endeavour, we decided to backtrack and define terms and goals more carefully. The term mentoring is bandied about indiscriminately in the media and in the professional literature, to the point where many well-intentioned initiatives become loose, unfocused, and less effective than first envisioned. There is need for clarification (Treffinger 2000).

Torrance (1984: 2) has suggested that 'A mentor is a creatively productive person who teaches, counsels, and inspires a student with similar interests. The relationship is characterised by mutual caring, depth, and response.' This refreshing definition has many interesting components: it emphasises the relationship, the high expectations of the commitment, and the two-way nature of the connection. Our view that a mentor ought to become a 'talent spotter' fits nicely into this conceptualisation (McCluskey and Treffinger 1998). Daloz (1986) stated that a mentor should be a guide, rather than a tour director, who offers support through advocacy, listening, sharing, establishing structure, emphasising strengths, and making the experience positive. Kierkegaard, without using the term, captured the essence of the mentoring experience by observing that life is lived forward, but understood backward, and Grey Owl summed it up well when he noted that, 'A mentor is a person whose hindsight can become your foresight.' Like so many other terms, the word 'mentoring' has come down to us from ancient Greek literature (Nash and Treffinger 1993; Noller and Frey 1994). It originated in Homer's epic poem *The Odyssey*, wherein Odysseus (Ulysses) – setting off for the Trojan wars – left his son Telemachus in the care of his trusted friend Mentor. To complicate matters in true Homerian style, Mentor eventually turned out to be the goddess Athena in disguise. Boston (1976), linking his argument to mythology, proposed that ideal mentoring should involve three crucial elements: (1) servicing other roles while entering into the relationship (Mentor did not allow himself to be simply a full-time babysitter); (2) becoming a conduit for the wisdom of others (Mentor, as the proverbial 'guide on the side', provided direction for Telemachus by channelling information to him from many other sources); and (3) building a long-term connection (Mentor continued to provide support as the boy grew to adulthood). It is worthwhile keeping these components in mind when developing a mentoring programme.

There are other lessons to be learned from the foregoing attempts at definition: emphasise the quality of the relationship, expect creative productivity, and match mentors and mentees extremely carefully. Of course, informal, 'spontaneous' mentoring often happens naturally (Noller and Frey 1994) – unplanned connections can uncover and nurture talent in troubled individuals (cf. Brown 1983; Seita, Mitchell *et al.* 1996). In other situations, relationships are definitely planned and systematic.

At California State University, Fresno, a large-scale initiative has been developed to support young, high risk students (Meyer 1997). In that programme, pre-service teachers mentor needy elementary school children from local communities. In other words, mentoring is being used to help address issues of cultural diversity, parental neglect, poverty, transient lifestyles and low academic achievement. What better training for pre-service teachers than to establish real relationships with at-risk children? And what a potentially important support for youngsters in desperate need of attention, understanding, and direction. Through this ongoing project, collegians work with the children in the schools – typically twice a week at day's end. The amount of person power involved is considerable: by late 1997, there were 180 pre-service teachers in the programme. Undoubtedly, several lives have been touched through this work.

Following this lead, and responding to the University of Winnipeg's mandate to address urban, inner city, and Aboriginal issues, we in the B.Ed. Programme have recently introduced several mentoring projects of our own. We believe that, for a number of reasons, the University of Winnipeg's mentoring efforts move far beyond those offered by most other agencies and academic institutions. For one thing, there are several committed faculty and staff – including Mentoring Project Coordinator – who devote considerable time to the programmes. As well, although mentors opt in altruistically (i.e., we select only from among those who express an interest), there are course requirements that remove some of the uncertainties that plague many volunteer operations. Most importantly, we have the advantage of drawing mentors from a population of pre-service teachers who have received considerable preparation for the task at hand. Since careful screening took place prior to their acceptance into the B.Ed. Programme, the majority of these educators to be have solid academic ability to go along with their passionate desire to work with young people. Far from being neophytes in the university setting, our mentors – with several years of post-secondary training under their belts – already possess a broad repertoire of developing skills.

We've also upped the ante considerably by developing a third year course, Issues with At-Risk Children and Youth, to introduce our education students to topics such as resilience, gangs and gang prevention, bullying, diversity, and the 'Circle of Courage' (Brendtro, Brokenleg and van Bockern 1990). In the course, which now runs three times a year, the pre-service teachers also have an opportunity to learn about Life Space Crisis Intervention (LSCI) (Wood and Long 1991), a strength-based technique that helps caregivers: (1) reframe problems as learning opportunities (i.e., shift from 'crisis management' to 'crisis teaching'); (2) redefine the conflict cycle (i.e., understand the triggers, reconsider the phases, and explore strategies for de-escalating aggression and counter aggression); (3) decode the meaning of behaviour; and (4) recover after a crisis.

It goes without saying that Creative Problem Solving figures in the mix as well. All students in the At-Risk course are given basic information about CPS, some of its tools, and its potential role in talent development (including the use of the current realities/desired futures approach outlined in Figure 9.5. Our university now offers, on a fairly regular basis, three-credit-hour courses devoted entirely to inner city issues, LSCI, and CPS. In our CPS Summer Institutes, students – including many of our mentors – are exposed to the newest, user-friendly models and terminology, and to other recent theoretical and practical developments in the field (Isaksen 2000; Isaksen, Dorval and Treffinger 1998, 2000; McCluskey 2000b; Noller 1997; Treffinger, Isaksen and Dorval 2000; Treffinger and McCluskey 1998). The point is, of course, that our pre-service teachers are not just thrown willy-nilly into the breach: they bring relevant knowledge and talent to their mentoring relationships. Chosen from among the ranks of interested students who have completed the At-Risk course, these mentors take part in what is essentially a practicum providing the experiential link between theory and the real world. To sum up briefly, the pre-service teachers mentor for four hours or so per week for one university term. Very frequently, though, the experience gets extended: many mentors warm to their mentees, put in far more time each week than expected, and continue their involvement long after the practicum officially comes to an end. While the At-Risk course is run in fairly traditional fashion – with tests, term papers, and letter grades – the mentoring practicum itself is much more flexible.

Mentors are connected with mentees on an INSED basis, and meetings take place whenever it is most convenient for the individuals involved (including evenings and weekends). Since we didn't want to take away from the focus on the relationship, Pass/Fail grades are assigned based upon 'following through' and recording experiences in personal reaction logs. In their logs, mentors note down their objectives, action plans, strengths and needs of the mentee, supports and resources provided, successes, concerns and possible follow-up issues. Contact hours, meeting times and other observations are included as well. MARS was our first initiative. Our partner in this venture is Winnipeg Native Alliance (WNA), an agency dedicated to reclaiming Aboriginal young people who have joined youth gangs or who are at risk for gang involvement. Its founder, Troy Rupert, is a study in resilience: he has come full circle, from life in native gangs, multiple stints in the youth centre, and 'hard time' in a federal penitentiary, to tireless community worker and director of a respected social agency. WNA maintains core programmes in school outreach (geared to keeping high risk youth in the educational system), urban sports camps (to facilitate access to recreational and spiritual activities), and institutional support (to provide help, guidance, and direction to youth while in custody and upon release). As an inner city agency facing formidable challenges, WNA is always on the lookout for more human and material resources. Our mentors, matched with needy mentees by the agency personnel, have been a tremendous help in reaching at-risk children and youths who otherwise might have been lost.

With respect to data collection, it is not difficult to gather information concerning behavioural incidents, drop-out rates, and school achievement of mentees. However, although our original intent was also to obtain precise pre- and post-test measures of self-concept, creativity, and the like, in the face of feedback from mentors – who insisted that any kind of formal testing of the mentees interfered with rapport building – we abandoned the more grandiose plans in favour of relying primarily on the reaction logs, growth plans and life accomplishments. Early indications (from our Mentoring Project Coordinator, who is beginning to pull everything together for analysis) are that this type of information will end up being very rich indeed. Other 'Planet' mentoring projects followed from MARS.

Summary and conclusions

In closing, mentoring through the University of Winnipeg provides tangible, meaningful support to large numbers of at-risk children and youths. It is difficult to imagine a youngster who would not benefit from a relationship with an empathic mentor and, at present, we send out 70–80 pre-service teachers per annum. Since most of our current projects are sustainable, the waves of mentors will be available year after year. Although the emphasis is naturally upon the mentees, MARS and the other planet projects open up wonderful, authentic opportunities for pre-service teachers to experience the at-risk situation first-hand by getting into the real world trenches. As such, everyone benefits from the approach (likened, by some colleagues, to a TELESCOPE – Teaching Effective Lessons to Every Student with Capabilities Overlooked by Popular Education).

181

We have welcomed this opportunity to share some of our projects of the past decade. Because they all were designed primarily as educational support programmes, the main focus has always been on the goal of making a difference, rather than on experimental rigour. Still, although it was never our intent to attempt to quantify so many uncontrolled and overlapping treatment variables, some interesting data has emerged. Surely, it is clear that the total package approach has generally had a positive impact, and that Creative Problem Solving has been an integral part of the process.

Indeed, the CPS piece of the puzzle has become the cornerstone of much of what we do. When all is said and done, however, what really matters is that – as a result of programmes featuring a combination of interventions – many formerly at-risk individuals have succeeded in turning their lives around. 'It is the supreme art of the teacher to awaken joy in creative expression and knowledge' (Albert Einstein, Motto for the Astronomy Building of Junior College, Pasadena, California).

Note

[1] This chapter is based upon a selection of original researches by the authors initially published as Monograph 308, February 2001 by the Creativity Research Unit, The Creative Problem Solving Group, Buffalo. The Creativity Research Unit draws upon an internationally renowned network of creativity researchers with expertise in topics such as the climate for creativity, organisational leadership, change and idea management, cognition, problem solving, personality and creativity development.

References

Baum, S. M., Renzulli, J. S. and Hébert, T. (1995) *The prism metaphor: A new paradigm for reversing underachievement.* Storrs, C. T.: The National Research Center on the Gifted and Talented, The University of Connecticut.

Betts, G. and Neihart, M. (1988) 'Profiles of the gifted and talented'. *Gifted Child Quarterly,* **32**(2), pp. 248–253.

Boston, B. O. (1976) *The sorcerer's apprentice. A case study in the role of the mentor* Reston, V. A.: Council for Exceptional Children.

Brendtro, L. K., Brokenleg, M. van Bockern, S. (1990) and *Reclaiming Youth at Risk: Our Hope for the Future.* Bloomington, IN: National Educational Service.

Brown, W. (1983) *The Other Side of Delinquency.* New Brunswick, N.J.: Rutgers University Press.

Canadian Council on Social Development (1991) 'The poverty connection'. *Social Development Overview,* **1**, 9–10.

Canfield, C. and Drinnan, L. (1991) *Native and Non-native Federal Inmates: A Five Year History: Comparative Statistics.* Ottawa, ON: Correctional Service of Canada.

Carson, T. (1996) Interview with the warden of Stony Mountain Penitentiary. Stony Mountain, MB.

Children and Youth Secretariat (1996) *Most Needy Project*. Winnipeg, MB: Author.

Children and Youth Secretariat (1997) *Strategy Considerations for Developing Services for Children and Youth*. Winnipeg, MB: Author.

Coopersmith, S. (1986) *The Coopersmith Inventory*. Palo Alto, CA: Consulting Psychological Press.

Correctional Services of Canada (1991) 'Basic facts about corrections in Canada' (GovDocs JS 82–17). Ottawa, ON: Minister of Supply and Services, Government of Canada.

Daloz, L. A. (1986) *Effective Teaching and Mentoring: Realizing the Transformational Power of Adult Learning Experiences*. San Francisco, CA: Jossey-Bass.

Feldhusen, J. F. (1995) *Talent Identification and Development in Education (TIDE) (2nd edn)*. Sarasota, FL: Center for Creative Learning.

Gage, N. (1990) 'Dealing with the dropout problem'. *Phi Delta Kappan*, **72**(4), 280–85.

Gallagher, J. J. (1975) *Teaching the Gifted Child (2nd edn)*. Boston, MA: Allyn and Bacon.

Gardner, H. (1983) *Frames of Mind: The Theory of Multiple Intelligences*. New York: Basic Books.

Gendreau, P., Madden, P. and Leipciger, M. (1977) *Norms and Recidivism for First Incarcerates: Implications for Programming*. Toronto, ON: Planning and Research Branch, Ministry of Correctional Services.

Isaksen, S. G. (ed.) (2000) *Facilitative Leadership: Making a Difference with Creative Problem Solving*. Dubuque, I. A.: Kendall/Hunt.

Isaksen, S. G., Dorval, K. B. and Treffinger, D. J. (1994) *Creative Approaches to Problem Solving*. Dubuque, I. A.: Kendall/Hunt.

Isaksen, S. G., Dorval, K. B. and Treffinger, D. J. (1998) *Toolbox for Creative Problem Solving: Basic Tools and Resources*. Buffalo, NY: Creative Problem Solving Group – Buffalo.

Isaksen, S. G., Dorval, K. B. and Treffinger, D. J. (2000) *Creative Approaches to Problem Solving: A Framework for Change (2nd ed.)* Dubuque, I. A.: Kendall/Hunt.

Johns, J. L. (1988) *Basic Reading Inventory: Pre-primer Through Grade Eight (5th edn)*. Dubuque, I. A.: Kendall/Hunt.

Levin, B. (1989) 'Financing the education of at-risk students'. *Educational Evaluation and Analysis*, **11**(1), 47–60.

Manitoba Department of Finance (1995–96) *Public Accounts*. Winnipeg, MB: Author.

Manitoba Department of Justice (1995–96) *Annual Report*. Winnipeg, MB: Author.

McCluskey, K. W. (2000a) 'Lines in the sand: Are students with difficulties being forced from our schools?' *Reaching Today's Youth*, **4**(4), 28–33.

McCluskey, K. W. (2000b) 'Setting the stage for productive problem solving' in S. G. Isaksen (ed.), *Facilitative Leadership: Making a Difference with Creative Problem Solving*. Dubuque, I. A.: Kendall/Hunt, pp. 71–101.

McCluskey, K. W., Baker, P. A., O'Hagan, S. C. and Treffinger, D. J. (1998) 'Recapturing at-risk, talented high school dropouts: A summary of the three-year Lost Prizes Project'. *Gifted and Talented International*, **13**(2), 73–8.

McCluskey, K. W. and McCluskey, A. L. A. (2000) 'Made-in-Manitoba mentoring'. *Creative Learning Today*, **9**(1), 2–5.

McCluskey, K. W. and Treffinger, D. J. (1998) 'Nurturing talented but troubled children and youth. Reclaiming Children and Youth'. *Journal of Emotional and Behavioural Problems*, **6**(4), 215–19, 226.

McCluskey, K. W. and Walker, K. D. (1986) *The Doubtful Gift: Strategies for Educating Gifted Children in the Regular Classroom*. Kingston, ON: Ronald P. Frye.

Meyer, W. (1997) 'A turn down the harbour with at-risk children'. *Phi Delta Kappan* **79**(4), 312–16.

Mishel, L. and Frankel, D. (1991) *The State of Working America: 1990–1991 edition*. Armonk, New York: M. E. Sharp.

Montessori, M. (1949) *The Absorbent Mind*.

Mukhopadyay, S. and Chugh, A. (1979) *Developing a strategy for minimising under-achievement through teacher classroom behaviour*. Bhopal, India: Regional College of Education. (ERIC Document Reproduction Service, No. ED 207 725)

Nash, D. and Treffinger, D. J. (1993) *The Mentor: A Step-by-step Guide to Creating an Effective Mentor Program in Your School*. Waco, TX: Prufrock Press.

National Crime Prevention Council (1996) *The Determinants of Health and Children*. Ottawa, ON: NCPC.

Noller, R. B. (1997) *Mentoring: A Voiced Scarf (2nd edn)*. Mt. Holly: Snedley Group.

Noller, R. B. and Frey, B. R. (1994) *Mentoring: An Annotated Bibliography (1982–1992)*. Sarasota, FL: Center for Creative Learning.

O'Hagan, S. C., Tymko, A., Timgren, M., McCluskey, K. W. and Baker, P. A. (1995) 'The BEST Beginnings project', in K. W. McCluskey, P. A. Baker, S. C. O'Hagan and D. J. Treffinger (eds), *Lost Prizes: Talent Development and Problem Solving with At-risk Students*. Sarasota, FL: Center for Creative Learning, pp. 93–105.

Peterson, J. C. (1997) 'Bright, tough, and resilient – and not in a gifted program'. *Journal for Secondary Gifted Education*, **8**(3), 121–36.

Place, D. J. and McCluskey, A. L. A. (1995) 'Second Chance: A program to support native inmates at risk', in K. W. McCluskey, P. A. Baker, S. C. O'Hagan and D. J. Treffinger (eds), *Lost Prizes: Talent Development and Problem Solving with At-risk Students*. Sarasota, FL: Center for Creative Learning, pp. 137–46.

Radwanski, G. (1987) *Ontario Study of the Relevance of Education and the Issue of Dropouts*. Toronto, ON: Ministry of Education.

Renzulli, J. S. (1977) *The Enrichment Triad Model: A Guide for Developing Defensible Programs for the Gifted*. Mansfield Center, C. T.: Creative Learning Press.

Rimm, S. B. (1986) *Underachievement Syndrome: Causes and Cures*. Watertown, WI: Apple Publishing.

Seita, J., Mitchell, M. and Tobin, C. L. (1996) *In Whose Best Interest? One Child's Odyssey, a Nation's Responsibility*. Elizabethtown, PA: Continental Press.

Statistics Canada (1991) *School Leavers Survey*. Ottawa, ON: Employment and Immigration Canada.

Sternberg, R. J. (1988) *The Triarchic Mind: A New Theory of Human Intelligence*. New York: Penguin.

Torrance, E. P. (1984) *Mentor Relationships: How They Aid Creative Achievement, Endure, Change, and Die*. Buffalo, NY: Bearly Limited.

Treffinger, D. J. (2000) 'Mentoring and tutoring – In search of clarity'. *Creative Learning Today*, **9**(3), 1–3.

Treffinger, D. J. and Isaksen, S.G. (1992) *Creative Learning. An Introduction*. Sarasota, FL: Center for Creative Learning.

Treffinger, D. J., Isaksen, S.G. and Dorval, K. B. (2000) *Creative Problem Solving: An Introduction (3rd edn)*. Waco, TX: Prufrock Press.

Treffinger, D. J. and McCluskey, K. W. (eds) (1998) *Teaching for Talent Development: Current and Expanding Perspectives*. Sarasota, FL: Center for Creative Learning.

Tymko, A. and O'Hagan, S. C. (1993) 'Intergenerational literacy project: BEST'. *Reading Council of Greater Winnipeg*, March, pp. 4–6.

Whitmore, J. R. (1980) *Giftedness, Conflict and Underachievement*. Boston, MA: Allyn and Bacon.

Wood, M. M. and Long, N. J. (1991) *Life Space Intervention: Talking with Children and Youth in Crisis*. Austin, TX: Pro-Ed.

PART FOUR:
COGNITIVE DISABILITIES

It may seem surprising that in a book on the gifted and talented a chapter on Down's syndrome, or Down syndrome as now used in international literature, should appear. It is possible to consider the large number of Down's children as a separate group in the population whose abilities are on a normal distribution for their cohort, with their own high fliers and, at the other end of the distribution, some severely disabled learners.

However, it is only relatively recently that inclusion in mainstream schools has applied to these children, and parents have fought hard – with the support of the UK Down's Syndrome Association – to enable their children to take up places in nursery schools and then in ordinary or regular classrooms. Because we are beginning to understand these children's learning needs better, through authors such as Sandy Alton, we are beginning to see how much more they can achieve.

I was brought up next door to Tricia, a much-loved girl with Down's syndrome. She was a little younger than me but in those days there was no opportunity for her to go to school, although she wanted to. She always seemed to be much more aware and acute than her speech and motor difficulties implied. The opening later of an Adult Training Centre was a great boon for her and she developed in skills and sophistication very rapidly, but she should have been permitted to go to school.

I became even more convinced of this and interested in the subject after reading of the story of Abigail in 'Abigail defies the odds' (1990, *Times Educational Supplement*, 18.5.90, p. A5).

Abigail was a pupil in Oxfordshire, due to take GCSEs in Rural Science and Childcare along with the rest of the pupils in her year. She was the first child with Down's to achieve this it was thought. Others had taken GCSEs but were older than 16-year-old Abigail. Her parents had struggled to keep her in the mainstream, even moving house to Oxfordshire where there were units for children with special needs attached to mainstream schools. Abigail could read when she was five, helped by her mother who was a teacher. She coped in a primary school class of 30, with no special support at first. At 11 she transferred to a comprehensive school and spent 60 per cent of her time in the unit and the rest with her tutor group. As well as taking her GCSEs, she also followed GCSE courses in drama and keyboarding. She was then due to go to FE college to do an agricultural course and she hoped to work with animals.

187

News such as this was quickly followed by the ground-breaking research of Sue Buckley, who described the success of Down syndrome children in learning to read through using her visual training methods. This was later followed by Wishart's studies on the attitude to success and failure, and on the different learning needs of Down's children because of their 'avoidant' learning styles. These studies all offered fascinating insights.

Even so, I think we are only at the beginning of understanding how much these children can be enabled to achieve, as Alton's chapter shows.

In this chapter, Sandy Alton prefers to use the Down's Society convention 'Down's syndrome', but the references reflect the other authors' choices.

10 Gifted children with Down's Syndrome: a contradiction in terms?

Sandy Alton

It is easy to be misled by the concept of giftedness. In particular, wherever another label is available, it is important to look both within and beyond that label to ensure that all children are enabled to fulfil their potential. This has especial implications where the education of children with Down's syndrome is concerned.

Many more children with Down's syndrome are now entering mainstream schools in the UK and many other countries. This is the result of several factors. There has been a general push to include pupils with special needs in mainstream schools if the parents so wish. In addition, increasing amounts of research have been published enhancing knowledge about the capabilities and potential of children with Down's syndrome, opening new opportunities for learning. Parental awareness of the value and the benefits of inclusion has grown and more parents now wish their child to attend their local mainstream school with their siblings and friends.

This change has implications for schools in understanding the learning profile typical to children with Down's syndrome, both in terms of paving the way to successful inclusion and in recognising the potential of this new cohort of children whose range of ability varies enormously. When dealing with any pupils with complex special needs, the approach to differentiation must be child-centred, taking into account the particular nature of those needs. In this context, looking at *how* content is delivered is as important as the content itself. For pupils with Down's syndrome, therefore, it is essential to have a knowledge of the syndrome and any characteristic attributes and disabilities that are likely to impact upon learning.

Characteristics

Pupils with Down's syndrome develop more slowly than their peers, arriving at each stage of development at a later age and staying there for longer. The gap between pupils with Down's syndrome and their peers thus widens with age. Moreover, research has shown that many children with Down's syndrome have a particularly inefficient learning style, which can inhibit their learning and delay the acquisition and consolidation of new skills (Wishart 1993). However, it is not just a matter of general delay in development, resulting in the need for a diluted curriculum. These children have a specific learning profile with characteristic strengths and weaknesses, which can inhibit – or aid – their ability to learn new skills, information and knowledge. This learning profile is then the key to the ability to learn and acquire new skills: it is particularly important that the teaching of children with Down's syndrome is designed both to develop their learning experiences most effectively and to increase their motivation and self esteem. This learning profile, and the approaches to teaching and learning that address it, form the main body of this chapter. However, two relatively recent major developments in the approach to the education of children with Down's syndrome neatly illustrate the issues that arise when the needs of special learners are not recognised.

First, infants with Down's syndrome often have delayed speech and language and poor hearing. They are, moreover, better visual learners than auditory ones. As a result, the natural interplay between mother and baby is not sufficient to meet the needs of the child in terms of the development of speech and language skills. This can lead to a spiral of poor learning and performance, which in turn can lead to lowered motivation, poor attitude and opting out. However, an early intervention programme pioneered in Oxfordshire, which made consistent use of signing (Makaton) along with the spoken word, built on the children's strong visual skills and encouraged communication during that crucial early phase. As the child became better able to communicate through the spoken word, the signs were naturally dropped.

Similarly, an understandable assumption about children with significant language delay is that the focus must be on the oral/aural: there is no point in considering the written word. For a child with Down's syndrome, this assumption would be very wide of the mark, as a programme teaching children to read run by DownsEd in Portsmouth showed. The programme achieved considerable success, with reading ages well ahead of those implied by the children's speech. Once again, progress resulted from a recognition that, for children with this learning profile, the visual patterns of the printed word might be easier to recognise than the aural ones of speech.

Educational provision

Effective teaching and learning, then, must use the pupils' strengths and learning styles, while taking into account their areas of weakness and developmental stage. Pupils with learning difficulties are often the ones who are the most vulnerable to ill-chosen learning, making them more susceptible to avoidance behaviours and failure. This is particularly the case for pupils with Down's syndrome, who often do not cope well with many common classroom practices – whole class teaching, learning through listening, and follow up work based on the completion of text activities or worksheets.

Teachers will therefore need to review schemes of work to identify learning objectives within the subject or topic that the pupil can access and achieve with success. This may require a wide range of material. In some cases, moreover, pupils' levels of understanding and attainment may mean that programmes of study – and performance descriptions – from earlier key stages should be used. This calls for creative thinking, imagination, common sense, flexibility and additional resources. It may involve tasks being reinterpreted to enable the pupil to demonstrate achievement in age appropriate contexts.

This all requires good planning and liaison between staff to help prepare differentiated materials. With such planning and liaison, this breadth of differentiation can normally be achieved successfully and children with Down's syndrome can make effective use of their talents.

The key to effective differentiation for pupils with Down's syndrome is to **think VISUAL, think BASIC, think REINFORCE**. It also requires consideration of the *content*, the *approach and context*, *presentation* and the *assessment of the response*.

Content

- Decide upon the main focus you wish the pupil to learn i.e. appropriate learning objectives.
- Look at level descriptors below the standard key stage and at programmes of study from earlier key stages for guidance and ideas.
- Check content relates to previously acquired knowledge and skills.
- Try to reflect points from the pupil's IEP.
- Ensure pupils' personal skills such as independence and cooperation with peers can be developed.

Approach and context

- Ensure learning objectives are broken down into small steps.
- Ensure they are clearly focused and short.
- Use familiar and meaningful material.
- Build in additional repetition and reinforcement.
- Choose appropriate context – whole class, small group, partner, one to one.
- Choose appropriate level of support – LSA, peer support, class teacher.
- Consider learning outcomes at the same time as planning activities and tasks.

Presentation

- Remember: pupils learn best through a multisensory approach – seeing, copying, doing, feeling.
- Remember: many pupils benefit from more repetition and a wider range of explanation within a variety of contexts than their typically developing peers.
- Present all work visually – print, adapted worksheets, flash cards, sentence/sequencing cards, diagrams, pictures, icons, symbols.

- Ensure oral instructions are reinforced visually to serve as a reminder to stay on task.
- Use concrete and practical materials whenever possible.
- Demonstrate activities wherever possible.
- Use simple and familiar language.
- Keep instructions short and concise.
- Reinforce instructions with diagrams/signs.
- Focus on Key words – teach them carefully and ensure meanings are understood.
- Reinforce key words and subject specific vocabulary, visually with symbol, icon, and diagram.
- Be prepared to use specific/additional resources.
- Decide who will find and prepare additional resources.

Assessment of the response

- Ensure that pupils' methods of response are realistic and appropriate.
- Provide alternative means of recording – pictures, symbols, flash cards, etc.
- Look at level descriptors below the standard range for the key stage.
- To enable writing, provide the words within pupils' sight vocabulary, including key words (see section on Writing).
- Decide how progress will be monitored and recorded so that small advances are not missed.
- Review, evaluate, and amend.

When differentiating to meet the needs of pupils with Down's syndrome, one must begin with the syndrome and its characteristic learning profile. The following factors are typical of many children with Down's syndrome. Each has implications for their education. Of course, not all children will have all these characteristics and it is important to consider each individual child when developing a teaching programme.

Learning needs

Factors that facilitate learning

- Strong visual awareness and visual processing skills.
- Ability to learn and use sign, gesture and visual support.
- Ability to learn and use the written word.
- Ability and desire to learn from their peers, to imitate and take their cue from them.

Factors that inhibit learning

- Delayed motor skills, fine and gross.
- Auditory and visual impairment.

- Speech and language delay.
- Poor short-term auditory memory.
- Poor auditory processing ability.
- Shorter concentration span.
- Difficulties with consolidation and retention.
- Difficulties with generalisation, thinking and reasoning.
- Sequencing difficulties.

Some of these factors have physical implications whilst others have cognitive ones. Many will overlap and have a mixture of both. The next section attempts to deal with each factor individually, identifying its implications in the classroom, and then suggesting a range of differentiation strategies. However, many of the factors mentioned can also be found in other pupils with learning difficulties. The differentiation strategies suggested should be equally useful for all. In addition, some strategies often appear at several points because they will help to remedy several different factors.

Hearing impairment

Many children with Down's syndrome experience some hearing loss, especially in the early years. Some will have a permanent loss; others a fluctuating one. Up to 20 per cent may have a sensorineural loss, caused by developmental defects in the ear and auditory nerves. Over 70 per cent are likely to suffer from a conductive hearing loss due to glue ear and frequent upper respiratory tract infections. (These often occur as a result of small sinuses and ear canals.) Hearing levels can also fluctuate daily and it is important to ascertain whether inconsistencies in response are due to hearing loss rather than lack of understanding or poor attitude. In addition, many children have more difficulty listening in situations where there is constant background noise – for example busy classrooms – or amplification, such as school halls. Any problem with hearing will, of course, also affect a child's speech and language development.
Differentiation strategies:

- Place pupil near front of class.
- Speak clearly and directly to the pupil.
- Reinforce speech with facial expression, sign or gesture.
- Reinforce speech with visual backup – print, pictures, concrete materials.
- Write new vocabulary on the board.
- When other pupils answer, repeat these answers aloud.
- Rephrase or repeat words and phrases that may have been misheard.

Motor skills

Generally speaking, development of motor skills in many children with Down's syndrome is slower, lagging behind that of their typically developing peers. This is especially noticeable in the early years and primary age range although, given additional and appropriate practice and encouragement, many children can make good progress. The main reason for the slower development is poor muscle tone (Hypotonia) and loose joints. Both gross and fine motor skills can be affected.

Gross motor skills

Problems with gross motor skills in children with Down's syndrome often improve by the time the child has reached some ten years of age. However, many may continue to find it difficult to keep pace with peers during PE, games and sports activities and some children dislike participating in large team games, often finding them confusing and overwhelming. In many cases, this may be due to the fact that the child cannot keep up with the pace of the game, tires more quickly, is overly sensitive to the noise level, but also may not understand the rules and strategies.

Differentiation strategies:

- Provide additional visual cues – gesture, markings on hands, feet, floor to indicate correct positions etc.
- Ensure pupil understands the rules of games and activities.
- Offer pupil short breaks.
- Pair up to 'shadow' a suitable partner.
- Offer lots of encouragement and praise.
- Offer alternative opportunity to participate in small group or partner activity with set objectives if pupil is very wary of joining in large team games.

Fine motor skills

Many children have particular difficulties with their fine motor skills. In addition to Hypotonia, the fingers are often short and the thumb set lower down. This inevitably affects a pupil's level of dexterity, manipulation and hand–eye coordination skills. It is important therefore to provide a range of activities that aim to increase general dexterity and coordination, strengthen wrists and fingers and practise pincer grasp and thumb control. Children will acquire these skills better if they are learnt through meaningful and interesting activities and are fun and varied rather than learnt solely through rote learning and repetition. In addition, to achieve good fine motor control, it is important to be seated in a stable and upright position with both fleet flat on the floor and forearm comfortably on the desktop. Finally, all motor skills improve with practice!

Differentiation strategies

- Use a wide range of multisensory activities and materials – spring-loaded scissors for cutting skills, sand, finger paint, play dough, chalk, magnadoodle etc. – sensory awareness plays an important part in developing fine motor skills.

- Encourage independence in self-help skills e.g. using buttons, changing for PE etc. Give plenty of regular but short practice sessions. (See also section on Writing.)

CASE HISTORY 1

George was an able little boy who had just started in Reception. He had a sight vocabulary of over 150 words and was speaking in short phrases but he had particular difficulties with his fine motor skills. His hand–eye coordination and pencil control were very poor and he tired very quickly when practising writing or other fine motor skills. His Teaching Assistant put together an attractive box of colourful and interesting materials and activities that would develop the muscles in his wrists and fingers and practise general hand–eye coordination. Items included colourful and tactile stress balls, pop together toys, fishing games, pegs games, colourful bulldog clips in a range of sizes, mazes, and dot-to-dot activities. When George finished a class activity earlier than his peers he would choose some of the activities from his 'Hands Box'. This enabled him to strengthen his muscles and gave him added practice in coordination skills in an enjoyable but effective way.

Speech and language in the classroom

Children with Down's syndrome typically have some level of speech and language impairment, although this varies greatly. It is caused by a combination of factors, some of which are physical and some due more to perceptual and cognitive problems. First impressions of a child with Down's syndrome are often wrong as assessment is mistakenly based upon their level of speech. However, receptive skills are greater than expressive skills and so children with Down's syndrome understand language better than they are able to speak it. It is important, therefore, to be aware that this mis-match can mask other abilities. Any delay in learning to understand and use language is likely to impact upon a child's level of knowledge and understanding and thus ability to access the curriculum. It is important therefore that particular attention is given to the type of language and vocabulary used and to developing appropriate differentiation strategies when teaching pupils with Down's syndrome.

Common features of delay in language acquisition:

- Slower language development.
- Smaller vocabulary leading to less general knowledge.
- Difficulty learning the rules of grammar, leaving out connecting words, prepositions etc. This results in a telegraphic style of speech.
- Ability to learn new vocabulary more easily than grammar.
- Greater problems in understanding abstract words and curriculum specific language.
- Greater difficulty in understanding complex sentences, text and instructions.
- More difficulty articulating words due to the combination of having a smaller mouth cavity and weaker mouth and tongue muscles.
- More difficulty producing longer sentences.

Differentiation strategies:

- Give time to process language and respond.
- Listen carefully – your ear will adjust.
- Ensure face-to-face and direct eye contact.
- Use simple and familiar language and short concise sentences.
- Ensure texts are written as far as possible in familiar language containing new vocabulary only where it is essential.
- Check understanding – ask pupil to repeat back instructions.
- Reinforce speech with facial expression, gesture and sign.
- Reinforce spoken instructions with print, pictures, diagrams and symbols.
- Emphasise key words, reinforcing visually.
- Teach meanings of new vocabulary explicitly and reinforce visually – diagrams, symbol and print.
- Avoid closed questions and encourage pupil to speak in more than one word utterances.
- Encourage pupil to speak aloud in class by providing visual prompts. Reading information may be easier than speaking spontaneously.
- The use of a Home–School Diary can help pupils in telling their 'news' as well as form a basis to develop writing and language skills further.

CASE HISTORY 2

Holly attended her local mainstream secondary school and was in Year 7. In Science, the pupils were asked to conduct an experiment to find out if a cup of hot water with a lid retained heat better than one without a lid. Pupils had to record the temperature of the water in the two cups every three minutes over a 15-minute period. Although a good reader, much of the wording and vocabulary on the investigation report sheet was too complex, scientific and unfamiliar to Holly. She was therefore provided with a differentiated report sheet, which used simpler language and asked fewer questions. Holly was able to read and understand this report sheet independently but as she worked and wrote at a slower pace than her peers, she was asked to test the water every five minutes rather than three. Holly participated well in the lesson with some adult support and finished at the same time as her peers. On questioning, Holly understood the aim and conclusions of the experiment well.

CASE HISTORY 3

Joe was in a Year 7 class at his local mainstream secondary school. In English, the class were reading *The Hobbit*. This is quite a complicated text for many Year 7 pupils let alone a child with speech and language impairment. Although Joe was a good reader, both the level of the vocabulary and the pace at which the text was read aloud were too high and he had great difficulties in understanding and following the story. Joe was given an illustrated cartoon based version of *The Hobbit*, which he read alongside the class text. As a strong visual learner, Joe was thus enabled to understand the more unfamiliar vocabulary, which was being continually reinforced visually. His support assistant would provide further reinforcement and consolidation for the section he had read at other stages during the lesson, much of which involved testing his understanding of the text through cloze procedure. Joe was quite happy to be given a differentiated text and developed a basic understanding of the key characters and story.

Writing skills

Producing any form of written work is a highly complex task. Difficulties in short-term auditory memory, speech and language, fine motor skills and the organising and sequencing of information make a considerable impact on the acquisition and development of writing skills for many pupils with Down's syndrome.

Particular areas of difficulty:

- Sequencing words into grammatically correct sentences.
- Sequencing events/information into the correct order.
- Taking notes and dictation.
- Organising thoughts and relevant information on to paper.
- Lengthy written tasks.
- Copying text from blackboard.
- Creative writing.

Differentiation strategies:

- Allow pupils in first stages of emergent writing to trace over words and then copy underneath until ready to form letters independently.
- Provide additional resources to aid writing as a physical process: chunky pens and pencils, slanted writing board, pencil grips.
- Provide squared paper to encourage consistency in size of letters: reduce the size of the squares over time.
- Some pupils may need to write on lined paper for longer than their peers and/or will need lines spaced further apart.
- To encourage more independence in early stages of emergent writing, provide child with an emergent writing folder.
- Provide additional visual cues and support to lessen cognitive demands on pupil: e.g. flash cards, key words, picture cues and sequences, sentence cues.
- To increase learning experiences and keep pupil motivated, use a wide range of multisensory activities and materials as alternatives to paper and pencil when practising letter formation and print: sand, finger paint, play dough, chalk.
- Ensure that pupils are only asked to write about topics that build upon their experience and understanding.
- If copying from board, select and highlight a shorter version for the pupil to copy, focusing on what is essential for that pupil, or use cloze method on previously made worksheet.
- Pace any dictation appropriately, include repetition and ensure vocabulary is chosen to suit the ability of the pupil.

- Encourage the use of cursive script to aid fluency.
- Teach upper and lower case letters simultaneously to help with generalisation.
- Use conversation diary to reinforce link between reading and writing.
- Enable pupils who have difficulties in copying from the board to copy from text placed next to them instead.
- Provide alternative methods of recording: e.g.: scribe;
    worksheets where pupil underlines or rings correct answer;
    worksheets using cloze procedure;
    pupil sequences sentence cards or picture cards;
    pupil pastes pictures, symbols or flashcards onto page;
    provide lists of key words, word banks or flashcards, word and picture dictionaries;
    use of computer with specialist software, e.g. whole word computer programmes, such as Clicker;
    writing frames, which provide a supported and structured framework.

CASE HISTORY 4

Sally attended her local mainstream primary school in a Year 3 class. The class had been concentrating on fairy stories during the National Literacy Hour and had been asked to write their own. Sally had been making good progress with her speech and language and was beginning to speak in sentences. However, much of her speech was limited at this time to vocabulary which was thoroughly familiar to her and she therefore had more difficulties in writing from imagination rather than from familiar experiences. At the time, Sally was a keen fan of the Spice Girls and loved nothing more than to talk about them and their likes, dislikes and lives. It was therefore suggested that Sally would write about the Spice Girls. She brought in from home her magazines and pictures of the group and using these as visual aids and prompts and with key words supplied by her assistant, Sally wrote about them for the week, producing her own personal Spice Girls booklet.

Spelling

Spelling is a particular issue that may need to be addressed. The use of phonics as an aid to developing reading and spelling can be problematic, as it requires problem-solving skills, accurate hearing and discrimination of sounds, which are all areas of difficulty for many pupils with Down's syndrome. Many such pupils learn to spell words purely from relying upon their visual memory, though some do acquire a basic knowledge of phonics and are able to apply the rules they have learnt. However, development may be slower than that of their peers, and a variety of techniques to aid spelling should be used.

Differentiation strategies:

- Teach words that are within their understanding.
- Teach words aimed to promote their speech and language development.

- Teach words required for specific subjects within the context of those subjects.
- Provide small quantities of spellings to learn at one time.
- Teach simple word families.
- Teach letter sounds early on, graduating to CVC words and simple blends.
- Teach spellings as visually as possible, e.g. look-say-cover-write-check, flash cards.
- Colour code similar letter groups/patterns within words.
- In addition to visual reinforcement, use multisensory methods, e.g. finger tracing.

The above make use of the strong visual skills rather than the weaker auditory skills required in phonic methods.

CASE HISTORY 5

Georgia was a Year 9 pupil at her local secondary school. She had quite severe fine motor difficulties causing her writing to be slow and arduous and had particular problems with spellings. She therefore found it very difficult to record her work appropriately and often asked her teaching assistant to scribe for her. However, as with many pupils with Down's syndrome, Georgia was a fairly competent reader and so giving her access to a laptop computer with Clicker enabled her to record her work far more quickly, accurately and easily. This involved her assistant having to make grids for particular subjects, with spellings of key words in the grids. As a result, Georgia was able to type in connecting words independently and created far more work than if she had had to write her work out manually. In addition, she took pride in the presentation of her work; something she had not been able to do beforehand.

Reading

Children with Down's syndrome are strong visual learners and many learn to read though a whole word approach at an early age and develop their reading skills to a useful and practical level. The written word, which makes language visual, overcomes the difficulties that many children with Down's syndrome have with learning through listening and there are strong links between learning to read, improving working memory, and developing speech and language skills in children with Down's syndrome.

Reading also improves articulation by providing more language practice, while seeing sentences in print helps the children learn about correct sentence structure for use in spontaneous speech. Furthermore, reading is an area of the curriculum where many of the children can excel and is an excellent differentiation tool through which children with Down's syndrome can access the curriculum. The written word, therefore, should be used to reinforce all verbal input and compensate for poor auditory processing skills. This means that all instructions, new vocabulary and key words should be written down and reinforced visually with diagrams to enforce meaning. (Also see section below on short-term auditory memory.) Reading is therefore an important tool to help children with Down's syndrome:

- Improve speech and language skills.
- Develop understanding.
- Access the curriculum.
- Increase self-esteem.

The key method for teaching a child with Down's syndrome to read is through building up a whole word sight vocabulary: from the age of three or four, many children are able to build up a sight vocabulary of familiar and meaningful words in this way. Using phonics to decode words can be more difficult for young children with Down's syndrome because it involves accurate hearing and good auditory discrimination of sounds as well as problem-solving skills – all common areas of difficulty in children with Down's syndrome. However, many children with Down's syndrome can gain a basic knowledge of phonics, which should be gradually introduced once the child has a sight vocabulary of approximately 50 words. Generally speaking, once they have attained a reading age of over seven, children can start to apply this knowledge to aid their reading.

Assessing comprehension is complicated by short-term auditory memory problems. Break text into smaller parts and, where possible, assess using visual techniques. Comprehension worksheets should include written questions, multiple choice, and cloze procedure.

Short-term auditory memory

Short-term auditory memory (also called working or verbal memory) helps us to make sense of language. We use this memory to hold, process, understand and assimilate spoken language long enough to respond to it. It relates directly to the speed with which children can articulate words, and influences the speed at which they learn new words and learn to read. Many children with Down's syndrome have difficulties with short-term memory. In addition, their memory spans may not increase at the same rate as their typically developing peers. This means there is an increasing difference between mental age and memory performance in children with Down's syndrome. In addition, research (Broadley *et al.* 1994) shows that children with Down's syndrome do not appear to develop normal strategies, such as rehearsal and organisation or chunking skills, to help them remember information. Long-term memory is not usually impaired; neither is the visual memory, which is often far stronger.

Difficulty with working memory means that they may have more difficulties with:

- Processing and retaining words and information.
- Understanding and responding to spoken language.
- Following verbal instructions, especially longer ones.
- Learning and remembering new, abstract or unfamiliar vocabulary.

- Learning routines.
- Developing organisational skills.
- Remembering sequences or lists.
- Coping with instructions directed to whole class.
- Learning to read and write.

Critically, words disappear too quickly from memory. A child struggling to process and remember what was said can quickly become overloaded if given unfamiliar vocabulary or long, complicated sentences. The child will either switch off completely or retain only parts, often from either the beginning or end of a sentence. This poses real problems for children in school situations with a high auditory content, such as:

- Listening to a new story.
- Whole class discussions.
- Hearing unfamiliar subject-specific vocabulary.
- Circle time or 'carpet time'.
- Assembly.
- Being given instructions.
- Mental maths.

Any deficit in short-term auditory memory will, therefore, greatly affect pupils' ability to respond to the spoken word or learn from any situation heavily reliant on auditory skills. In addition, it is important not to confuse the effects of poor short-term auditory memory with behavioural problems. When differentiating work for pupils with Down's syndrome, it is important, therefore, to adopt appropriate teaching strategies, which do not rely on this memory alone. A variety of approaches and media are needed in order to tap into other memories and store information in different ways. Teaching primarily through the auditory route fails to maximise learning, particularly when teaching physical or practical skills.

Children with Down's syndrome are strong visual but poor auditory learners. Wherever possible, they need visual support and concrete and practical materials to reinforce auditory input.

Differentiation strategies:

- Help the children to be aware when they have to listen, e.g. pointing to your ears.
- Limit amount of verbal instruction at any one time – chunk into smaller, simple phrases.
- Repeat individually to pupil any information/instructions given to class as a whole.
- Pause, Repeat, Check – ask child to repeat back or clarify.
- Provide regular repetition and rehearsal.
- Allow time for child to process and respond to verbal input.
- Ensure all auditory/oral instructions are reinforced visually to serve as a permanent reminder to stay on task. Use dry-wipe board for on-the-spot drawings, diagrams and writing down of key words.

- Plan for visual translation and reinforcement during whole class instruction/discussion, e.g. quick sketches, diagrams, writing of key words on dry-wipe board by LSA to help pupil keep pace and stay focused.
- Accompany key words and subject-specific words with pictures, icons and symbols; develop your own if necessary.
- Use key words, icons and diagrams rather than full text.
- Underline and highlight key words.
- Make use of word trees, maps or webs.
- Association – help child link information with a more familiar word, picture, idea or image.
- Provide regular over-learning opportunities to recall information, even after you think the child has learned it.
- Make use of the procedural memory by role-play, drama, and physical movement.
- Provide plenty of practice when teaching routines, key procedures and sequences.
- Make use of routines to help learning and organisational skills.
- Rehearsal – help child achieve silent rehearsal by whispering information to themselves more and more softly until they can do it silently.
- Encourage child to take daily messages.
- Assess comprehension on short pieces of text (e.g. page by page) and through visual means, e.g. written worksheets with cloze procedure for answers.
- Make use of songs, rhymes and rhythm to aid learning sequences, e.g. the alphabet, times tables, days of the week, as well as for teaching phonological awareness/skills and sound patterns. The tune alone can trigger the speech sequence for the child.
- Play games to develop memory, e.g. memory games like Kim's game or Pairs/Pelmanism; listening games like Sound Lotto, Simon Says, Guess Who, Twenty Questions.

Number skills

Many children with Down's syndrome have more difficulty in this area, since it involves abstract concepts and problem solving skills. In addition, they are less likely to develop concepts from exploratory play and loosely structured sessions. However, development seems to follow the same stages as with their peers, but teachers must ensure that pupils have learnt the pre-skills necessary as building blocks. Many pupils have not consolidated these key skills and are moved on too quickly. Where the pre-skills are sound, pupils do learn number skills and progress.

Differentiation strategies:

- Use concrete and practical materials.
- Reinforce all number work visually.
- Offer repetition, reinforcement and variety in small steps.
- Explain specific maths vocabulary, use it consistently and teach rules.

- Encourage generalising skills to new situations.
- Teach maths for life skills.

Shorter concentration span

Many children with Down's syndrome have shorter concentration and attention spans than their typically developing peers. They tend to be more easily distracted and have more difficulty focusing on multiple tasks. Some pupils with Down's syndrome may find it difficult coping with longer sessions or double lessons and situations where there is a high distractibility element. In addition, the intensity of supported learning, especially in a one-to-one situation, is much higher and the child tires much more easily than an unsupported child.

Differentiation strategies:

- Shorter work sessions: two short sessions are more valuable than one long one. Intersperse with different activities for younger children.
- Recognise that children need breaks in their learning to process and internalise. In an ordinary classroom environment, this often occurs naturally, but special care must be taken when a pupil receives additional support.
- Focus on one aim at a time.
- Build a range of short, focused and clearly defined tasks into the lesson.
- Vary level of demand from task to task.
- Vary type of support.
- Use peers to keep pupil on task.
- At carpet times, place the child at the front near the class teacher.
- Provide a carpet square to encourage the child to sit in one place.
- In secondary double lessons, it may be more suitable for pupils to attend the first lesson only, using the second for individual reinforcement or work on basic skills.

CASE HISTORY 6

Jenny attended her mainstream secondary school as a Year 7 pupil. I first heard that there was trouble at school when they reported that Jenny was developing a habit of disappearing just before the start of afternoon school. She was always found – either in the toilets or in the playground – but she refused to say why she was doing this. It soon became apparent that, in fact, this was happening every other Thursday afternoon before double Humanities. Jenny admitted that she didn't like double Humanities and this was why she had refused to come into class. Although Jenny had no behaviour problems, was generally cooperative and willing to work, she found the amount of new and strange vocabulary and pace of this lesson quite daunting and tiring. In addition, the teaching assistant found that a double lesson was too long for Jenny to stay focused and motivated and that the amount of content was too great for Jenny to absorb in one go. Jenny's behaviour would often deteriorate throughout the lesson and would result more often than not in Jenny being taken out of the class. It was therefore decided that Jenny would participate with the class for the first lesson. She would then walk leisurely to the library with her teaching assistant, who after allowing Jenny a short break would then reinforce and consolidate the work they had covered in the first session. On discussion with Jenny, she was happy with this idea or compromise and there were no further problems.

CASE HISTORY 7

Simon was in Year 7 at his local mainstream secondary school. He was generally well behaved in lessons but had particular difficulties with his concentration and ability to stay focused. He would tend to try chatting to his teaching assistant or fiddling with his books and pens. Class teachers would often become irritated with the background noise caused by Simon talking to his assistants or by his assistants constantly reminding him to look, listen and be quiet. However, one of his assistants made three laminated cards, each with a different symbol drawn on it. One symbol was of an ear, another of an eye and the third card had a mouth with a cross drawn over it. Whenever Simon lost concentration in lessons, the assistant showed Simon the appropriate card and laid it on his desk. These cards helped Simon to a remarkable extent and greatly reduced the amount of distracting behaviour originating from him in lessons. Moreover, Simon was very proud of these cards and received praise from his teachers for the improvement in his behaviour within the lessons.

Consolidation, retention and learning style

Pupils with Down's syndrome generally take longer to learn and to consolidate new skills and the ability to learn and retain can fluctuate from day to day. In addition, many pupils are passive learners and the consolidation of new skills on more difficult tasks may be compromised by poor self motivation, resulting in avoidance strategies or inconsistency with completing the task. Wishart's research (1996, 1993) on aspects of early cognitive development also highlights sensitivity to failure, which can lead to an unwillingness to tackle new tasks. Even if the task was only slightly above their level of development and with a little more persistence they could actually have achieved it, children were still reluctant to try. In addition, it was found that avoidance was not only a result of experiencing failure or thinking failure would be a possibility; children would also avoid a task even if they had previously been successful at it. They simply 'chose' to opt out. Skills they had achieved were therefore not consolidated and thus children were not giving themselves vital opportunities for reinforcement and consolidation. Moreover, Buckley and Bird (1993) found that it seemed to be more difficult for children with Down's syndrome to correct wrong responses once they were made.

Weaknesses such as these in the learning style of children with Down's syndrome need to be taken into account by teaching staff in order to help them learn and achieve. It is important to realise that many children are not achieving their full cognitive potential and have higher levels of ability than teachers may assume at first hand. It is vital, therefore, that as teachers we get to know children with DS to establish and build upon the way they achieve and respond positively and to support them in these ways.

Errorless Learning strategies can be used to some extent to help encourage children with Down's syndrome to achieve success, by preventing the child having to unlearn any wrong responses and by building up feelings of success and self-confidence. Teach pupils to complete a new task by guiding them through each step correctly, not allowing them to fail. As the pupil becomes more capable, the prompt can be reduced until it is not needed. However, these strategies must be used sensitively in order to create a balance – children also learn from failure.

Differentiation strategies:

- Provide extra time and opportunities for additional repetition and reinforcement.
- Move forward but continually check back to ensure that previously learned skills have not been overwhelmed by the new input.
- Present new concepts and skills in a variety of ways, using concrete, practical and visual materials.
- Offer extra explanation and help, to compensate for any difficulties in their ability to transfer knowledge, generalise and make choices.
- Provide shorter tasks that are within their capabilities so that they can achieve success.
- Promote errorless learning. (Do not overuse this: as with all pupils, it is also important that pupils with Down's syndrome learn from their mistakes.)
- Give encouragement, praise and positive messages often.
- Use peers as models and to motivate learning.

Conclusion

All this progress stems from an inclusive approach and a recognition of the increased possibilities that come from tailoring the curriculum to the learning profile typical of Down's syndrome. But the progress so far clearly shows that the journey towards fulfilment of the potential for children with Down's syndrome has only just begun.

References and Bibliography

Alton, S. (2000) *Including Pupils with Down's Syndrome*. London: Down's Syndrome Association.

Bird, G., Alton, S. and Mackinnon, C. (2000) 'Accessing the curriculum – strategies for differentiation for pupils with Down Syndrome'. *Down Syndrome Issues and Information*. London: The Down's Syndrome Educational Trust.

Broadley, I., MacDonald, J. and Buckley, S. (1994) 'Are children with Down syndrome able to maintain skills learned from a short-term memory training programme?' *Down Syndrome Research and Practice* **2**(3), pp. 116–22.

Buckley, S. (2000) 'Living with Down Syndrome'. *Down Syndrome Issues and Information*. The Down's Syndrome Educational Trust.

Buckley, S. and Bird, G. (1993) 'Teaching children with Down's Syndrome to read'. *Down Syndrome Research and Practice* **1**(1), pp. 34–9.

Buckley, S. and Bird, G. (1994) *Meeting Special Educational Needs of Children with Down's Syndrome: A Handbook for Teachers*. Portsmouth: University of Portsmouth.

Carpenter, B., Ashdown, R. and Bovair, K. (1996) *Enabling Access*. London: David Fulton.

Cunningham, C., Glenn, S., Lorenz, S., Cuckle, P. and Shepperdson, B. (1998) 'Trends and outcomes in educational placements for children with Down syndrome'. *European Journal of Special Needs Education* **13**(3).

Gross, J. (1995) *Special Educational Needs in the Primary School – A Practical Guide*. Oxford: Oxford University Press.

Laws, G., MacDonald, J., Buckley, S. and Broadley, I. (1995) 'Long term maintenance of memory skills taught to children with Down's syndrome'. *Down Syndrome Research and Practice* **3**(3), pp. 103–9.

Lewis, A. (1995) *Primary Special Needs and the National Curriculum*. (2nd edn) London: Routledge.

Lorenz, S. (1998) *Children with Down's Syndrome. A Guide for Teachers and Learning Support Assistants in Mainstream Primary and Secondary Schools*. London: David Fulton.

McNamara, S. and Moreton, G. (1997) *Understanding Differentiation*. London: David Fulton.

Petley, K. (1994) 'An investigation into the experiences of parents and head teachers involved in the integration of primary aged children with Down's syndrome into mainstream schools'. *Down Syndrome: Research and Practice* **2**(3), pp. 91–7.

Slivovitz, M. (1997) *Down Syndrome The Facts*. Oxford: Oxford University Press.

Stratford, B. and Gunn, P. (1996) *New Approaches to Down Syndrome*. London: Cassell.

Tilstone, C., Florian, L. and Rose, R. (1998) *Promoting Inclusive Practice*. London: Routledge.

Visser, J. (1993) *Differentiation: Making It Work*. Tamworth: NASEN.

Wishart, J. (1993) 'Learning the hard way: Avoidance strategies in young children with Down syndrome'. *Down Syndrome: Research and Practice* **1**(2), pp. 47–55.

Wishart, J. (1996) 'Avoidant learning styles and cognitive development in young children with Down Syndrome', in B. Stratford and P. Gunn (eds), *New Approaches to Down Syndrome*. London: Cassell.

Index